Francis Henry
Taylor

IV Form

The Hoosac School
Hoosac N. Y.

CAESAR.

WILHELM II

SCHOOL CLASSICS

EDITED UNDER THE SUPERVISION OF

JOHN TETLOW

CAESAR AND POMPEY

IN

GREECE

SELECTIONS FROM CAESAR'S CIVIL WAR
BOOK III

BY

E. H. ATHERTON

Illae autem, paribus quas fulgere cernis in armis,
Concordes animae nunc et dum nocte premuntur,
Heu! quantum inter se bellum, si lumina vitae
Attigerint, quantas acies stragemque ciebunt!

VERGIL'S AENEID VI. 826.

GINN AND COMPANY
BOSTON · NEW YORK · CHICAGO · LONDON
ATLANTA · DALLAS · COLUMBUS · SAN FRANCISCO

The Athenæum Press

GINN AND COMPANY · PRO-
PRIETORS · BOSTON · U.S.A.

PREFACE.

It has long seemed to the editor that the *Civil War* did not have its due share of attention in the programs of our preparatory schools. It is, therefore, in the hope that it, or the most interesting part of it, may become more familiar to school-boys and school-girls that this little volume makes its appearance. This is its only excuse; for it contains no new discoveries, although possibly some of the explanations may be different from all others. Be that as it may, the aim throughout has been to make the difficult points easy and to smooth the road for the beginner as far as it can be done without impairing his progress. To accomplish this purpose references to persons and places have been explained and plans of battle grounds have been prepared, that all may be as clear as possible to him. A moderate number of grammatical references have been given, partly for the clearer understanding of the text, partly that the grammar may not be too much neglected. It is earnestly hoped that the notes will also help the pupil in the study of English as well as of Latin; to that end suggestions have been made here and there, showing in each case at least one good way, if not the best, of rendering the expression into idiomatic English, and making it clear that a literal version is often not good English at all. If only some good come of the notes in this direction, this volume will not have appeared in vain.

To aid in the study of *terminations* a table is given containing some of the more common and most important. So far as I have observed, this feature is entirely new. Under each termination is placed a list of words taken from the text to illustrate its force as simply as possible. As continual repetition is necessary to fix the force of terminations, it seemed that a list, containing neither too many endings nor too many illustrations, would prove to be of use to both teacher and taught.

As the whole of the third book of the *Civil War* seemed too long for the compass of this volume, only such parts of it were selected as deal directly with the campaign between Caesar and Pompey in Greece, ending with the battle of Pharsalia. The aim has been to make the narrative continuous and smooth. In only one or two cases was it found necessary to make even a slight change or addition. The text used is mainly that of *Bernardus Dinter*, published by Teubner, though a few changes of spelling and punctuation have been made.

Other editions of the *Civil War* have been consulted continually, and information thus gained has been used freely.   Especially do I feel indebted to the excellent editions of Charles E. Moberly, M.A., of Rugby, and of B. Perrin, Ph.D., of Yale University.   For the vocabulary and numerous suggestions I am indebted to my wife, Caroline S. Atherton, whose scholarship and previous experience have made her aid of great value.   I also feel deeply grateful to Mr. John Tetlow, editor-in-chief of the series, for his many valuable criticisms and suggestions.

EDWARD H. ATHERTON.

BOSTON, Aug. 1, 1899.

CONTENTS.

---·••❦❦••·---

INTRODUCTION.

———•◦❧◦•———

THE long struggle between Caesar and Pompey for the supremacy of the Roman world, a struggle that began with intrigues and plots and culminated in the battle of Pharsalia,[1] forms one of the most interesting and instructive chapters of the history of Rome under the Republic. If this battle, which made Caesar master of the whole Roman world, had been won by Pompey, no one can tell — we can only conjecture — what the result would have been to Rome and to the world at large. It was a contest between aristocracy and all it stands for on one side and democracy and its rights on the other. A brief study of the careers and aspirations of the leaders will put us in a better position to understand how important this struggle was to the common people.

Caius Julius Caesar was born July 12, 100 B.C. He was one of the greatest men of antiquity, being gifted with a wonderful combination of powers; he was an eloquent orator and writer even among the ancients, a great general, a far-seeing statesman, an astute lawgiver, and

---

[1] So called from Pharsalia, the district of Thessaly in which the battle was fought; it is also called the battle of Pharsalus, the town in Pharsalia near which the battle took place.

a fine mathematician. His powers in every department
were marvellous. At an early age he identified himself
with the popular party, being influenced in so doing by
the fact that Marius, the people's leader, was his uncle
by marriage ; the harsh treatment he received from Sulla,
the leader of the aristocracy, also led him to favor the
people. At the age of 17 he married Cornelia, daughter
of Lucius Cinna, the most prominent leader in the Marian
party. After the defeat of Marius, Sulla ordered Caesar
to put away his wife, but he refused to do so and was
compelled to flee, with the loss of all he had. He was
finally pardoned by Sulla, who warned the aristocracy
with the remark that there were "many Mariuses in that
boy." Not being safe at home, he joined the army in
Asia Minor, but on the death of Sulla in 78 B.C. he
returned to Rome, and made it his fixed purpose to win
the favor of the people. He had no great fortune, but
was very liberal with the people, even running into debt
for the purpose of gratifying them. In 68 B.C. he held
the office of *quaestor*, and in 65 B.C. that of *aedile*. It was
customary for the *aediles* to expend immense sums of
money in celebrating the public games and festivals, in
order to win the votes of the people. Caesar took advantage of this fact and showed great prodigality. He was
Pontifex Maximus in 63 B.C., and *praetor* the year following ; and in 60 B.C. he was elected *consul*. It was at this
time that he formed with Pompey and Crassus the First
Triumvirate, a powerful combination of the three leading
men of Rome to manage the government in their own
way and for their own benefit. We shall soon see that

Caesar was the most powerful and cunning of the three; but to understand how it became possible for Pompey to join with him in this union, it is necessary to trace the course of Pompey's life, both private and public, up to this point.

Cnaeus Pompeius Magnus was born Sept. 30, 106 B.C., and was consequently about six years older than Caesar. He belonged to the aristocracy, and early devoted himself to furthering its interests. When Sulla, the partisan of the aristocracy, returned to Rome after restoring Ariobarzanes to the throne of Cappadocia, Pompey marched to help him and became one of his most distinguished generals in his quarrel with Marius. The surname *Magnus* was conferred upon him by Sulla in consequence of his victories over the Marian party in Africa. He was allowed (illegally) to enter Rome in triumph in 81 B.C. After the death of Sulla he tried to prevent the consul Lepidus from repealing Sulla's laws. For five years he was proconsul in Spain, then he returned to Rome and became consul with Marcus Crassus in 70 B.C. The aristocratic party had long feared and envied him, so at this time he broke away from it and tried to gain the favor of the people by restoring the powers of their tribunes, which Sulla had restricted. In this measure Caesar supported him, not only because he believed in it, but also because he saw that Pompey was weakening his own hold upon the aristocracy, and could all the more easily be overthrown when the proper moment should arrive.

The eastern part of the Mediterranean had long been infested with bands of pirates, who made navigation unsafe, and even carried on their depredations on the western coasts of Italy. Consequently, in 67 B.C. Aulus Gabinius, the tribune, proposed a bill to give Pompey the entire control of the war against the pirates. It was passed, and Pompey cleared the seas in three months. In 66 B.C. he received full command of the Roman army in the wars against Mithridates, king of Pontus, and easily defeated him. After bringing Tigranes, king of Armenia, to terms, making a Roman province out of Syria, and capturing Jerusalem, he returned to Rome in 62 B.C. He now had such influence that people feared he would try to seize the supreme power, but on arriving at Brundisium he disbanded his armies and thus allayed apprehension. He celebrated his third triumph 60 B.C. As the senate would not support his measures in regard to the affairs of Asia, he was quite ready to enter into the alliance with Caesar ; to make this all the more binding Caesar gave him his daughter Julia in marriage. Crassus, the third member of the Triumvirate, was the richest man in Rome, but was by no means equal in cunning to his two colleagues. In forming the alliance Caesar wished to increase his power, Pompey wished to keep the power he had, and Crassus wished to gain more wealth. Caesar was now consul (60 B.C.), and proceeded to make himself still more popular than before, although Pompey and Crassus thought he was promoting their interests. On motion of the tribune Vatinius it was voted by the people that after his consulship Caesar should receive Gallia Cisalpina and Illyricum as his province, and that he should have three legions. The senate soon added to

this Gallia Transalpina and another legion.   He was to
retain these for five years.   Caesar saw that sometime
there was to be a struggle between himself and Pompey
for the supremacy, and he wanted an army on which he
could rely implicitly.   The control of these provinces
with four legions gave him just the chance he wanted.
He could train his army and at the same time get great
booty.   While he was gaining power in Gaul, Pompey was
losing power at Rome.   In 55 B.C., by agreement of the
triumvirs, Pompey and Crassus were consuls for the second time, and Caesar was to keep his power in Gaul five
years longer, till December, 49 B.C.   Pompey received for
provinces the two Spains, but remained himself near
Rome, leaving their government to his lieutenants, as he
wished to be where he could act in case of need.   Crassus
received Syria, where he was defeated and slain by the
Parthians in 53 B.C.

In the meanwhile Caesar had conquered Gaul, entered
Britain, and won great renown and power for himself.
This made Pompey jealous, and as the death of Julia in
54 B.C. broke the only tie that still bound him to Caesar,
it now became the aim of the former to weaken and
overthrow the latter.   As the surest way to accomplish
this, Pompey again joined the aristocratic party, whose
chief desire was to deprive Caesar of his power.   Two
old laws that had long been null were reënacted : one
forbade any one to be candidate for any public office
while absent from the city, and the other made it illegal
for any one to receive a province within five years after
holding a public office.   Caesar found fault with the

former law, as he intended to stand for consul again as
soon as the legal term of ten years should have elapsed
since his previous consulship. It was already clear that
if Caesar should appear in Rome as a private individual
he would lose his life, but as consul-elect he would be safe.
It was proposed in the senate that Caesar be required to
lay down his command in Gaul more than a year before
his term of five years was ended ; but this was unreason-
able, and was consequently vetoed by the tribune Curio,
whom Caesar had already won over by immense bribes.
Still Caesar wrote a letter to the senate, in which he
declared he was ready to lay down his command if Pompey would lay down his. The senate was with difficulty
induced to listen to this letter, and almost immediately
after its reading voted that its author should lay down his
arms by a certain day or he would be considered a public
enemy. Money was voted, troops were raised, and Pompey
was made general of the forces in and near the city. The
tribunes Antonius and Cassius, who had favored Caesar,
fled to him for protection. Pompey, counting on his
great reputation as a general, had no doubts as to the
result of a war if Caesar should dare to engage in one.
Caesar, who was at this time in northern Italy, did not
hesitate, but with a small force started for Rome. Many
cities welcomed him on the way and his army increased.
Pompey found himself compelled to leave Rome and
retreat to Brundisium, and when Caesar appeared before
that place and laid siege to it, he crossed over into
Greece. Caesar had no ships and could not follow
him at once, so he returned to Rome. Thus in the

three winter months he had made himself master of all Italy.

The summer of 49 B.C. Caesar spent in subduing the Spanish provinces and Marseilles, after which he returned again to Rome. While away he had been appointed dictator, and this office he assumed on his return, to hold the consular elections and pass some laws for the relief of debtors and the restoration of exiles.

It is at this point that the following selections take up the narrative, which they carry on to the death of Pompey and Caesar's arrival in Egypt. Every school-boy knows how Caesar returned thence master of the Roman world; how he governed with moderation; how he instituted many reforms, among them that of the calendar; and how he was finally assassinated, to the loss of the whole Roman world.

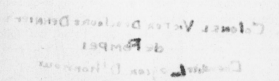

POMPEY.

Colonel Victor Des Jours Derniers
de Pompei
Chevalier Legion D'honneur

CAESAR AND POMPEY IN GREECE.

Caesar is elected consul and crosses with his army into Greece.

1. Dictatore habente comitia Caesare consules cre-
antur Iulius Caesar et P. Servilius : is enim erat annus
quo per leges ei consulem fieri liceret.   His rebus et
feriis Latinis comitiisque omnibus perficiendis xi. dies
tribuit dictaturaque se abdicat et ab urbe proficiscitur   5
Brundisiumque pervenit.   Eo legiones xii., equitatum
omnem venire iusserat.   Caesar ut Brundisium venit,
contionatus apud milites, quoniam prope ad finem
laborum ac periculorum esset perventum, aequo animo
mancipia atque impedimenta in Italia relinquerent, ipsi   10
expediti naves conscenderent, quo maior numerus militum posset imponi, omniaque ex victoria et ex sua
liberalitate sperarent, conclamantibus omnibus imperaret quod vellet, quodcumque imperavisset se aequo
animo esse facturos, ii. Non. Ian. naves solvit.   Imposi-   15
tae legiones vii.   Postridie terram attigit Germiniorum.
Saxa inter et alia loca periculosa quietam nactus statio-
nem et portus omnes timens, quod teneri ab adversariis
arbitrabantur, ad eum locum qui appellabatur Palaeste
omnibus navibus ad unam incolumibus milites exposuit.   20

I

Surrender of Oricum.

2. Pompeius erat eo tempore in Candavia iterque
ex Macedonia in hiberna Apolloniam Dyrrachiumque
habebat. Sed certior factus de adventu Caesaris, re
nova perturbatus maioribus itineribus Apolloniam
5 petere coepit, ne Caesar orae maritimae civitates
occuparet. At ille expositis militibus eodem die
Oricum proficiscitur. Quo cum venisset, L. Torquatus,
qui iussu Pompei oppido praeerat praesidiumque ibi
Parthinorum habebat, conatus portis clausis oppidum
10 defendere, cum Graecos murum ascendere atque arma
capere iuberet, illi autem se contra imperium populi
Romani pugnaturos esse negarent, oppidani autem
etiam sua sponte Caesarem recipere conarentur,
desperatis omnibus auxiliis portas aperuit et se atque
15 oppidum Caesari dedidit incolumisque ab eo con-
servatus est.

Apollonia welcomes Caesar.

3. Recepto Caesar Orico nulla interposita mora
Apolloniam proficiscitur. Cuius adventu audito L.
Staberius, qui ibi praeerat, aquam comportare in arcem
20 atque eam munire obsidesque ab Apolloniatibus ex-
igere coepit. Illi vero daturos se negare neque portas
consuli praeclusuros, neque sibi iudicium sumpturos
contra atque omnis Italia populusque Romanus iudica-
visset. Quorum cognita voluntate clam profugit Apol-
25 lonia Staberius. Illi ad Caesarem legatos mittunt
oppidoque recipiunt. Hos sequuntur Byllidenses et

Amantini et reliquae finitimae civitates totaque Epiros
et legatis ad Caesarem missis quae imperaret facturos
pollicentur.

Labienus and the army swear fidelity to Pompey. Caesar and
Pompey encamp on opposite banks of the Apsus.

4. At Pompeius cognitis his rebus quae erant
Orici atque Apolloniae gestae, Dyrrachio timens diur- 5
nis eo nocturnisque itineribus contendit. Simul Caesar
appropinquare dicebatur tantusque terror incidit eius
exercitui, quod properans noctem diei coniunxerat
neque iter intermiserat, ut paene omnes ex Epiro
finitimisque regionibus signa relinquerent, complures 10
arma proicerent, ac fugae simile iter videretur. Sed
cum prope Dyrrachium Pompeius constitisset castraque metari iussisset, perterrito etiam tum exercitu
princeps Labienus procedit iuratque se eum non
deserturum eundemque casum subiturum quemcum- 15
que ei fortuna tribuisset. Hoc idem reliqui iurant
legati ; tribuni militum centurionesque sequuntur,
atque idem omnis exercitus iurat. Caesar praeoccu-
pato itinere ad Dyrrachium finem properandi facit
castraque ad flumen Apsum ponit in finibus Apollonia- 20
tium, ut castellis vigiliisque bene meritae civitates tutae
essent, ibique reliquarum ex Italia legionum adventum
exspectare et sub pellibus hiemare constituit. Hoc
idem Pompeius fecit et trans flumen Apsum positis
castris eo copias omnes auxiliaque conduxit. 25

A conference.

5. Inter bina castra Pompei atque Caesaris unum flumen tantum intererat Apsus, crebraque inter se conloquia milites habebant, neque ullum interim telum per pactiones loquentium traiciebatur. Mittit Caesar P.
5 Vatinium legatum ad ripam ipsam fluminis, qui ea quae maxime ad pacem pertinere viderentur ageret et crebro magna voce pronuntiaret liceretne civibus ad cives de pace tuto legatos mittere, quod etiam fugitivis ab saltu Pyrenaeo praedonibusque licuisset,
10 praesertim cum id agerent, ne cives cum civibus armis decertarent? Multa suppliciter locutus est, ut de sua atque omnium salute debebat, silentioque ab utrisque militibus auditus. Responsum est ab altera parte Aulum Varronem profiteri se altero die ad conloquium
15 venturum atque eundem visurum quem ad modum tuto legati venire et quae vellent exponere possent; certumque ei rei tempus constituitur. Quo cum esset postero die ventum, magna utrimque multitudo convenit, magnaque erat exspectatio eius rei, atque om-
20 nium animi intenti esse ad pacem videbantur. Qua ex frequentia Titus Labienus prodit, submissa oratione de pace loqui atque altercari cum Vatinio incipit. Quorum mediam orationem interrumpunt subito undique tela immissa; quae ille obtectus armis militum vitavit; vol-
25 nerantur tamen complures, in his Cornelius Balbus, M. Plotius, L. Tiburtius, centuriones, militesque non nulli. Tum Labienus: *Desinite ergo de compositione loqui; nam nobis nisi Caesaris capite relato pax esse nulla potest.*

Antony crosses from Brundisium into Greece.

6. Erant eo tempore Antonius Brundisi atque Calenus, Caesaris legati ; multum ipsis militibus hortantibus neque ullum periculum pro salute Caesaris recusantibus, nacti Austrum naves solvunt atque altero die Apolloniam praetervehuntur. Qui cum essent ex 5 continenti visi, Coponius, qui Dyrrachi classi Rhodiae praeerat, naves ex portu educit, et cum iam nostris remissiore vento appropinquasset, idem Auster increbruit nostrisque praesidio fuit. Neque vero ille ob eam causam conatu desistebat, sed labore et perseve- 10 rantia nautarum se vim tempestatis superare posse sperabat praetervectosque Dyrrachium magna vi venti nihilo setius sequebatur. Nostri usi fortunae beneficio tamen impetum classis timebant, si forte ventus remisisset. Nacti portum, qui appellatur Nymphaeum, 15 ultra Lissum milia passuum III., eo naves introduxerunt (qui portus ab Africo tegebatur, ab Austro non erat tutus) leviusque tempestatis quam classis periculum aestimaverunt. Quo simul atque intro est itum, incredibili felicitate Auster, qui per biduum flaverat, 20 in Africum se vertit.

Caesar joins Antony. Pompey encamps near Asparagium.

7. Haec eodem fere tempore Caesar atque Pompeius cognoscunt. Nam praetervectas Apolloniam Dyrrachiumque naves viderant, ipsi iter secundum eas terra derexerant, sed quo essent eae delatae primis diebus 25 ignorabant. Cognitaque re diversa sibi ambo consilia

capiunt : Caesar, ut quam primum se cum Antonio
coniungeret, Pompeius, ut venientibus in itinere se
opponeret, si imprudentes ex insidiis adoriri posset ;
eodemque die uterque eorum ex castris stativis a
5 flumine Apso exercitum educunt, Pompeius clam et
noctu, Caesar palam atque interdiu.   Sed Caesari circuitu maiore iter erat longius adverso flumine, ut vado
transire posset ; Pompeius, quia expedito itinere flumen ei transeundum non erat, magnis itineribus ad
10 Antonium contendit, atque eum ubi appropinquare
cognovit, idoneum locum nactus, ibi copias conlocavit
suosque omnes in castris continuit ignesque fieri pro-
hibuit, quo occultior esset eius adventus.   Haec ad Antonium statim per Graecos deferuntur.   Ille missis ad
15 Caesarem nuntiis unum diem sese castris tenuit ; altero
die ad eum pervenit Caesar.   Cuius adventu cognito
Pompeius, ne duobus circumcluderetur exercitibus, ex
eo loco discedit omnibusque copiis ad Asparagium
Dyrrachinorum pervenit atque ibi idoneo loco castra
20 ponit.

**Caesar follows Pompey and offers battle. By a circuitous march
he cuts Pompey off from Dyrrachium.**

8. Caesar postquam Pompeium ad Asparagium esse
cognovit, eodem cum exercitu profectus expugnato in
itinere oppido Parthinorum, in quo Pompeius praesidium habebat, tertio die ad Pompeium pervenit iuxtaque
25 eum castra posuit et postridie eductis omnibus copiis
acie instructa decernendi potestatem Pompeio fecit.
Ubi illum suis locis se tenere animadvertit, reducto in

castra exercitu aliud sibi consilium capiendum existimavit. Itaque postero die omnibus copiis magno
circuitu difficili angustoque itinere Dyrrachium profectus est, sperans Pompeium aut Dyrrachium compelli
aut ab eo intercludi posse, quod omnem commeatum 5
totiusque belli apparatum eo contulisset ; ut accidit.
Pompeius enim primo ignorans eius consilium, quod
diverso ab ea regione itinere profectum videbat, angustiis rei frumentariae compulsum discessisse existimabat ; postea per exploratores certior factus postero die 10
castra movit, breviore itinere se occurrere ei posse
sperans. Quod fore suspicatus Caesar militesque
adhortatus ut aequo animo laborem ferrent, parva
parte noctis itinere intermisso mane Dyrrachium venit,
cum primum agmen Pompei procul cerneretur, atque 15
ibi castra posuit.

**Pompey encamps in a favorable position. Caesar takes measures
to secure a supply of grain.**

9. Pompeius interclusus Dyrrachio, ubi propositum
tenere non potuit, secundo usus consilio edito loco qui
appellatur Petra aditumque habet navibus mediocrem
atque eas a quibusdam protegit ventis castra commu- 20
nit. Eo partem navium longarum convenire, frumentum commeatumque ab Asia atque omnibus regionibus
quas tenebat comportari imperat. Caesar longius
bellum ductum iri existimans et de Italicis commeati-
bus desperans, quod tanta diligentia omnia litora a 25
Pompeianis tenebantur classesque ipsius quas hieme
in Sicilia, Gallia, Italia fecerat morabantur, in Epirum

rei frumentariae causa Q. Tillium et L. Canuleium
legatum misit, quodque hae regiones aberant longius,
locis certis horrea constituit vecturasque frumenti fini-
timis civitatibus descripsit.   Item Lisso Parthinisque
5 et omnibus castellis quod esset frumenti conquiri iussit.
Id erat perexiguum cum ipsius agri natura, quod sunt
loca aspera et montuosa ac plerumque frumento utun-
tur importato, tum quod Pompeius haec providerat et
superioribus diebus praedae loco Parthinos habuerat
10 frumentumque omne conquisitum spoliatis effossisque
eorum domibus per equites comportarat.

**Caesar invests Pompey's camp with a line of forts. His purpose
in so doing.**

10. Quibus rebus cognitis Caesar consilium capit
ex loci natura.   Erant enim circum castra Pompei
permulti editi atque asperi colles.   Hos primum prae-
15 sidiis tenuit castellaque ibi communit.   Inde, ut loci
cuiusque natura ferebat, ex castello in castellum perducta munitione circumvallare Pompeium instituit,
haec spectans, quod angusta re frumentaria utebatur
quodque Pompeius multitudine equitum valebat, quo
20 minore periculo undique frumentum commeatumque
exercitui supportare posset, simul, uti pabulatione
Pompeium prohiberet equitatumque eius ad rem gerendam inutilem efficeret, tertio, ut auctoritatem, qua ille
maxime apud exteras nationes niti videbatur, minueret,
25 cum fama per orbem terrarum percrebruisset illum a
Caesare obsideri neque audere proelio dimicare.

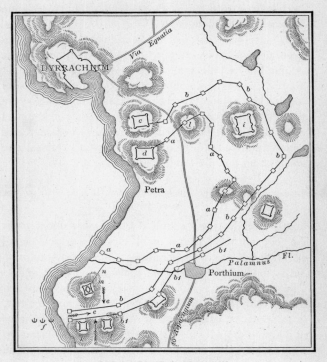

THE LINES AT DYRRACHIUM.

a. Pompey's lines.	*g*. Marcellinus' camp.
b. Caesar's lines.	*h*. Mark Antony's camp.
b¹. Caesar's second line turned outward.	*i*. Pompey's second camp.
c. Caesar's first camp.	*k*. Pompey's camp beyond the lines.
d. Pompey's first camp.	*l*. Caesar's camp beyond the lines.
e. Directions of Pompey's great attack.	*m*. Old camp of ninth legion.
f. Pompey's fleet.	*n*. Wall connecting it with river,

Pompey's counter-fortifications.

11. Pompeius neque a mari Dyrrachioque discedere volebat, quod omnem apparatum belli, tela, arma, tormenta, ibi conlocaverat frumentumque exercitui navibus supportabat, neque munitiones Caesaris prohibere poterat, nisi proelio decertare vellet ; quod eo tempore 5 statuerat non esse faciendum. Relinquebatur ut extremam rationem belli sequens quam plurimos colles occuparet et quam latissimas regiones praesidiis teneret Caesarisque copias quam maxime posset distineret; idque accidit. Castellis enim xxiv. effectis xv. milia 10 passuum circuitu amplexus hoc spatio pabulabatur ; multaque erant intra eum locum manu sata quibus interim iumenta pasceret. Atque ut nostri perpetuas munitiones habebant perductas ex castellis in proxima castella, ne quo loco erumperent Pompeiani ac nostros 15 post tergum adorirentur, ita illi interiore spatio perpetuas munitiones efficiebant, ne quem locum nostri intrare atque ipsos a tergo circumvenire possent. Sed illi operibus vincebant quod et numero militum praestabant et interiore spatio minorem circuitum habe- 20 bant. Atque cum erant loca Caesari capienda, etsi prohibere Pompeius totis copiis et dimicare non constituerat, tamen suis locis sagittarios funditoresque mittebat, quorum magnum habebat numerum, multique ex nostris volnerabantur, magnusque incesserat 25 timor sagittarum, atque omnes fere milites aut ex coactis aut ex centonibus aut ex coriis tunicas aut tegimenta fecerant quibus tela vitarent.

Predicament of Caesar's ninth legion.

12. In occupandis praesidiis magna vi uterque nite-
batur : Caesar, ut quam angustissime Pompeium contineret, Pompeius, ut quam plurimos colles quam
maximo circuitu occuparet ; crebraque ob eam causam
5 proelia fiebant.   In his cum legio Caesaris nona praesidium quoddam occupavisset et munire coepisset, huic
loco propinquum et contrarium collem Pompeius occupavit nostrosque opere prohibere coepit ; et cum una
ex parte prope aequum aditum haberet, primum sagit-
10 tariis funditoribusque circumiectis, postea levis armaturae magna multitudine missa tormentisque prolatis
munitiones impediebat ; neque erat facile nostris uno
tempore propugnare et munire.   Caesar cum suos ex
omnibus partibus volnerari videret, recipere se iussit
15 et loco excedere.   Erat per declive receptus.   Illi
autem hoc acrius instabant neque regredi nostros patie-
bantur quod timore adducti locum relinquere videbantur.   Dicitur eo tempore glorians apud suos Pompeius
dixisse : non recusare se quin nullius usus imperator
20 existimaretur, si sine maximo detrimento legiones
Caesaris sese recepissent inde quo temere essent
progressae.

Caesar succeeds in extricating it with slight loss.

13. Caesar receptui suorum timens crates ad extremum tumulum contra hostem proferri et adversas
25 locari, intra has mediocri latitudine fossam tectis
militibus obduci iussit locumque in omnes partes

quam maxime impediri. Ipse idoneis locis funditores instruxit, ut praesidio nostris se recipientibus
essent. His rebus comparatis legionem reduci iussit.
Pompeiani hoc insolentius atque audacius nostros
premere et instare coeperunt cratesque pro munitione 5
obiectas propulerunt, ut fossas transcenderent. Quod
cum animadvertisset Caesar, veritus ne non reducti
sed reiecti viderentur maiusque detrimentum capere-
tur, a medio fere spatio suos per Antonium, qui ei
legioni praeerat, cohortatus tuba signum dari atque 10
in hostes impetum fieri iussit. Milites legionis ix.
subito conspirati pila coniecerunt et ex inferiore loco
adversus clivum incitati cursu praecipites Pompeianos
egerunt et terga vertere coëgerunt ; quibus ad recipiendum crates disiectae longuriique obiecti et institutae 15
fossae magno impedimento fuerunt. Nostri vero, qui
satis habebant sine detrimento discedere, compluribus
interfectis, v. omnino suorum amissis, quietissime se
receperunt pauloque citra eum locum morati aliis com-
prehensis collibus munitiones perfecerunt. 20

Corn abundant in Pompey's camp, scarce in Caesar's.

14. Erat nova et inusitata belli ratio cum tot castel-
lorum numero tantoque spatio et tantis munitionibus
et toto obsidionis genere, tum etiam reliquis rebus.
Nam quicumque alterum obsidere conati sunt, percul-
sos atque infirmos hostes adorti aut proelio superatos 25
aut aliqua offensione permotos continuerunt, cum ipsi
numero equitum militumque praestarent ; causa autem
obsidionis haec fere esse consuevit, ut frumento hostes

prohiberent.   At tum integras atque incolumes copias
Caesar inferiore militum numero continebat, cum illi
omnium rerum copia abundarent ; cotidie enim magnus undique navium numerus conveniebat quae com-
5 meatum supportarent, neque ullus flare ventus poterat,
quin aliqua ex parte secundum cursum haberent.   Ipse
autem consumptis omnibus longe lateque frumentis
summis erat in angustiis.   Sed tamen haec singulari
patientia milites ferebant.   Recordabantur enim ea-
10 dem se superiore anno in Hispania perpessos labore
et patientia maximum bellum confecisse ; meminerant
ad Alesiam magnam se inopiam perpessos, multo etiam
maiorem ad Avaricum, maximarum gentium victores
discessisse.   Non, illis hordeum cum daretur, non
15 legumina recusabant ; pecus vero, cuius rei summa
erat ex Epiro copia, magno in honore habebant.

A substitute.

15. Est etiam genus radicis inventum ab iis qui
vacabant ab operibus, quod appellatur chara, quod
admixtum lacte multum inopiam levabat.   Id ad simi-
20 litudinem panis efficiebant.   Eius erat magna copia.
Ex hoc effectos panes, cum in conloquiis Pompeiani
famem nostris obiectarent, volgo in eos iaciebant, ut
spem eorum minuerent.   Iamque frumenta maturescere incipiebant, atque ipsa spes inopiam sustentabat
25 quod celeriter se habituros copiam confidebant ; cre-
braeque voces militum in vigiliis conloquiisque audie-
bantur prius se cortice ex arboribus victuros quam
Pompeium e manibus dimissuros.

Hardships of Pompey's men from lack of water and fodder.

16. Libenter etiam ex perfugis cognoscebant equos eorum tolerari, reliqua vero iumenta interisse ; uti autem ipsos valetudine non bona cum angustiis loci et odore taetro ex multitudine cadaverum et cotidianis laboribus, insuetos operum, tum aquae summa inopia 5 adfectos. Omnia enim flumina atque omnes rivos qui ad mare pertinebant Caesar aut averterat aut magnis operibus obstruxerat, atque ut erant loca montuosa et aditus perangusti vallium, has sublicis in terram de-missis praesaepserat terramque adiecerat, ut aquam 10 contineret. Itaque illi necessario loca sequi demissa ac palustria et puteos fodere cogebantur atque hunc laborem ad cotidiana opera addebant ; qui tamen fontes a quibusdam praesidiis aberant longius et cele-riter aestibus exarescebant. At Caesaris exercitus op- 15 tima valetudine summaque aquae copia utebatur, tum commeatus omni genere praeter frumentum abunda-bat, cuius cotidie melius succedere tempus maiorem-que spem maturitate frumentorum proponi videbant. In novo genere belli novae ab utrisque bellandi ra- 20 tiones reperiebantur. Illi cum animadvertissent ex ignibus, nocte cohortes nostras ad munitiones excu-bare, silentio aggressi universi intra multitudinem sagittas coniciebant et se confestim ad suos recipie-bant. Quibus rebus nostri usu docti haec reperiebant 25 remedia, ut alio loco ignes facerent . . . . . .

. . . .

. . . .

Caesar's lieutenant, Sulla, comes to the rescue. Pompey averts a disaster.

17. Interim certior factus P. Sulla, quem discedens castris praefecerat Caesar, auxilio cohorti venit cum legionibus duabus ; cuius adventu facile sunt repulsi Pompeiani. Neque vero conspectum aut impetum
5 nostrorum tulerunt primisque deiectis reliqui se verterunt et loco cesserunt. Sed insequentes nostros, ne longius prosequerentur, Sulla revocavit. At plerique existimant, si acrius insequi voluisset, bellum eo die potuisse finire. Cuius consilium reprehendendum non
10 videtur. Aliae enim sunt legati partes atque imperatoris : alter omnia agere ad praescriptum, alter libere ad summam rerum consulere debet. Sulla a Caesare praesidio castris relictus liberatis suis hoc fuit contentus neque proelio decertare voluit (quae res tamen
15 fortasse aliquem reciperet casum), ne imperatoris sibi partes sumpsisse videretur. Pompeianis magnam res ad receptum difficultatem adferebat. Nam ex iniquo progressi loco in summo constiterant ; si per declive sese reciperent, nostros ex superiore insequentes loco
20 verebantur. Neque multum ad solis occasum temporis supererat ; spe enim conficiendi negoti prope in noctem rem duxerant. Ita necessario atque ex tempore capto consilio Pompeius tumulum quendam occupavit, qui tantum aberat a nostro castello ut telum tormen-
25 tumve missum adigi non posset. Hoc consedit loco atque eum communivit omnesque ibi copias continuit.

Two minor engagements.

18. Eodem tempore duobus praeterea locis pugnatum est; nam plura castella Pompeius pariter disti-
nendae manus causa temptaverat, ne ex proximis
praesidiis succurri posset. Uno loco Volcatius Tullus
impetum legionis sustinuit cohortibus tribus atque 5
eam loco depulit; altero Germani munitiones nostras
egressi compluribus interfectis sese ad suos incolumes
receperunt.

Losses on both sides. Caesar's men rewarded.

19. Ita uno die VI. proeliis factis, tribus ad Dyrrachium, tribus ad munitiones, cum horum omnium 10
ratio haberetur, ad duo milia numero ex Pompeianis
cecidisse reperiebamus, evocatos centurionesque complures (in eo fuit numero Valerius Flaccus, L. filius,
eius qui praetor Asiam obtinuerat); signaque sunt
militaria sex relata. Nostri non amplius xx. omnibus 15
sunt proeliis desiderati. Sed in castello nemo fuit omnino militum quin volneraretur, quattuorque ex una
cohorte centuriones oculos amiserunt. Et cum laboris
sui periculique testimonium adferre vellent, milia sagittarum circiter xxx. in castellum coniecta Caesari 20
renuntiaverunt, scutoque ad eum relato Scaevae cen-
turionis inventa sunt in eo foramina cxx. Quem
Caesar, ut erat de se meritus et de re publica, donatum
milibus cc. conlaudatumque ab octavis ordinibus ad
primipilum se traducere pronuntiavit (eius enim opera 25
castellum magna ex parte conservatum esse constabat)

cohortemque postea duplici stipendio, frumento, veste,
congiariis, militaribusque donis amplissime donavit.

**Pompey strengthens his new fort, but finally abandons it. Caesar's
offers of battle refused.**

20. Pompeius noctu magnis additis munitionibus
reliquis diebus turres exstruxit et in altitudinem pe-
5 dum xv. effectis operibus vineis eam partem castrorum
obtexit, et quinque intermissis diebus alteram noctem
subnubilam nactus obstructis omnibus castrorum portis
et ad impediendum obiectis tertia inita vigilia silentio
exercitum eduxit et se in antiquas munitiones recepit.
10 Omnibus deinceps diebus Caesar exercitum in aciem
aequum in locum produxit, si Pompeius proelio decertare vellet, ut paene castris Pompei legiones subiceret;
tantumque a vallo eius prima acies aberat, uti ne telum
tormentumve adigi posset. Pompeius autem, ut famam
15 opinionemque hominum teneret, sic pro castris exercitum constituebat ut tertia acies vallum contingeret,
omnis quidem instructus exercitus telis ex vallo adactis
protegi posset.

Pompey's devices to secure a substitute for fodder.

21. Caesar quo facilius equitatum Pompeianum ad
20 Dyrrachium contineret et pabulatione prohiberet, aditus duos angustos magnis operibus praemunivit castellaque his locis posuit. Pompeius ubi nihil profici
equitatu cognovit, paucis intermissis diebus rursum
eum navibus ad se intra munitiones recipit. Erat
25 summa inopia pabuli, adeo ut foliis ex arboribus

strictis et teneris harundinum radicibus contusis equos
alerent; frumenta enim quae fuerant intra munitiones
sata consumpserant.   Cogebantur Corcyra atque Acarnania longo interiecto navigationis spatio pabulum
supportare, quodque erat eius rei minor copia, hordeo   5
adaugere atque his rationibus equitatum tolerare.   Sed
postquam non modo hordeum pabulumque omnibus
locis herbaeque desectae sed etiam frons ex arboribus
deficiebat, corruptis equis macie conandum sibi aliquid
Pompeius de eruptione existimavit.   10

Raucillus and Egus. Their arrogant conduct.

22. Erant apud Caesarem in equitum numero Allobroges ii. fratres, Raucillus et Egus, Adbucilli filii,
qui principatum in civitate multis annis obtinuerat,
singulari virtute homines, quorum opera Caesar omnibus Gallicis bellis optima fortissimaque erat usus. His 15
domi ob has causas amplissimos magistratus manda-
verat atque eos extra ordinem in senatum legendos
curaverat agrosque in Gallia ex hostibus captos prae-
miaque rei pecuniariae magna tribuerat locupletesque
ex egentibus fecerat. Hi propter virtutem non solum 20
apud Caesarem in honore erant, sed etiam apud exercitum cari habebantur; sed freti amicitia Caesaris et
stulta ac barbara adrogantia elati despiciebant suos
stipendiumque equitum fraudabant et praedam omnem
domum avertebant.   Quibus illi rebus permoti universi 25
Caesarem adierunt palamque de eorum iniuriis sunt
questi et ad cetera addiderunt falsum ab his equitum
numerum deferri, quorum stipendium averterent.

Rebuked by Caesar, they desert to Pompey.

23. Caesar neque tempus illud animadversionis esse existimans et multa virtuti eorum concedens rem totam distulit ; illos secreto castigavit quod quaestui equites haberent, monuitque ut ex sua amicitia omnia ex-
5 spectarent et ex praeteritis suis officiis reliqua spera-
rent. Magnam tamen haec res illis offensionem et contemptionem ad omnes attulit, idque ita esse cum ex aliorum obiectationibus tum etiam ex domestico iudicio atque animi conscientia intellegebant. Quo
10 pudore adducti et fortasse non se liberari sed in aliud tempus reservari arbitrati, discedere a nobis et novam temptare fortunam novasque amicitias experiri consti-
tuerunt. Et cum paucis conlocuti clientibus suis qui-
bus tantum facinus committere audebant, primum conati
15 sunt praefectum equitum C. Volusenum interficere, ut postea bello confecto cognitum est, ut cum munere aliquo perfugisse ad Pompeium viderentur ; postquam id difficilius visum est neque facultas perficiendi daba-
tur, quam maximas potuerunt pecunias mutuati, pro-
20 inde ac suis satisfacere et fraudata restituere vellent, multis coëmptis equis ad Pompeium transierunt cum iis quos sui consili participes habebant.

They are welcomed by Pompey and tell him all about Caesar's
army and camp.

24. Quos Pompeius, quod erant honesto loco nati et instructi liberaliter magnoque comitatu et multis
25 iumentis venerant virique fortes habebantur et in

honore apud Caesarem fuerant, quodque novum et
praeter consuetudinem acciderat, omnia sua praesidia
circumduxit atque ostentavit. Nam ante id tempus
nemo aut miles aut eques a Caesare ad Pompeium
transierat, cum paene cotidie a Pompeio ad Caesarem 5
perfugerent, volgo vero universi in Epiro atque Aetolia
conscripti milites earumque regionum omnium quae a
Caesare tenebantur. Sed hi cognitis omnibus rebus,
seu quid in munitionibus perfectum non erat, seu quid
a peritioribus rei militaris desiderari videbatur, tem- 10
poribusque rerum et spatiis locorum et custodiarum
varia diligentia animadversa, prout cuiusque eorum
qui negotiis praeerant aut natura aut studium ferebat,
haec ad Pompeium omnia detulerunt.

Pompey prepares to assault the southern end of Caesar's lines.

25. Quibus ille cognitis eruptionisque iam ante 15
capto consilio, ut demonstratum est, tegimenta galeis
milites ex viminibus facere atque aggerem iubet comportare. His paratis rebus magnum numerum levis
armaturae et sagittariorum aggeremque omnem noctu
in scaphas et naves actuarias imponit et de media 20
nocte cohortes LX. ex maximis castris praesidiisque
deductas ad eam partem munitionum ducit quae per-
tinebat ad mare longissimeque a maximis castris Caesaris aberat. Eodem naves quas demonstravimus
aggere et levis armaturae militibus completas quas- 25
que ad Dyrrachium naves longas habebat mittit, et
quid a quoque fieri velit praecipit. Ad eas munitiones
Caesar Lentulum Marcellinum quaestorem cum legione

IX. positum habebat. Huic, quod valetudine minus commoda utebatur, Fulvium Postumum adiutorem submiserat.

Description of the place assaulted. The assault succeeds.

26. Erat eo loco fossa pedum xv. et vallum contra
5 hostem in altitudinem pedum x. tantundemque eius
valli agger in latitudinem patebat ; ab eo intermisso
spatio pedum DC. alter conversus in contrariam partem
erat vallus humiliore paulo munitione. Hoc enim
superioribus diebus timens Caesar, ne navibus nostri
10 circumvenirentur, duplicem eo loco fecerat vallum, ut,
si ancipiti proelio dimicaretur, posset resisti. Sed
operum magnitudo et continens omnium dierum labor,
quod milium passuum in circuitu munitiones xvii. erat
complexus, perficiendi spatium non dabat. Itaque
15 contra mare transversum vallum qui has duas munitiones coniungeret nondum perfecerat. Quae res nota
erat Pompeio, delata per Allobrogas perfugas, magnum-
que nostris attulerat incommodum. Nam ut ad mare
II. cohortes nonae legionis excubuerant, accessere
20 subito prima luce Pompeiani ; simul navibus circum-
vecti milites in exteriorem vallum tela iaciebant, fos-
saeque aggere complebantur, et legionarii interioris
munitionis defensores scalis admotis tormentis cuiusque generis telisque terrebant, magnaque multitudo
25 sagittariorum ab utraque parte circumfundebatur.
Multum autem ab ictu lapidum, quod unum nostris
erat telum, viminea tegimenta galeis imposita defende-
bant. Itaque cum omnibus rebus nostri premerentur

atque aegre resisterent, animadversum est vitium munitionis quod supra demonstratum est, atque inter duos
vallos, qua perfectum opus non erat, navibus expositi
in aversos nostros impetum fecerunt atque ex utraque
munitione deiectos terga vertere coëgerunt.   5

Reinforcements cannot stay the rout. The eagle-bearer.

27. Hoc tumultu nuntiato Marcellinus . . . cohortes subsidio nostris laborantibus submittit ex castris ;
quae fugientes conspicatae neque illos suo adventu
confirmare potuerunt neque ipsae hostium impetum
tulerunt.   Itaque quodcumque addebatur subsidio id 10
corruptum timore fugientium terrorem et periculum
augebat ; hominum enim multitudine receptus impe-
diebatur.   In eo proelio cum gravi volnere esset adfectus aquilifer et iam viribus deficeretur, conspicatus
equites nostros, *Hanc ego*, inquit, *et vivus multos per* 15
annos magna diligentia defendi et nunc moriens eadem fide
Caesari restituo.   Nolite, obsecro, committere, quod ante
in exercitu Caesaris non accidit, ut rei militaris dedecus
admittatur, incolumemque ad eum deferte.   Hoc casu
aquila conservatur omnibus primae cohortis centurioni- 20
bus interfectis praeter principem priorem.

Antony checks the enemy's advance.   Caesar changes his plans.

28. Iamque Pompeiani magna caede nostrorum
castris Marcellini appropinquabant non mediocri terrore inlato reliquis cohortibus, et M. Antonius, qui
proximum locum praesidiorum tenebat, ea re nuntiata 25
cum cohortibus XII. descendens ex loco superiore cer-

nebatur.   Cuius adventus Pompeianos compressit
nostrosque firmavit, ut se ex maximo timore conligerent.   Neque multo post Caesar significatione per
castella fumo facta, ut erat superioris temporis consue-
5 tudo, deductis quibusdam cohortibus ex praesidiis
eodem venit. Qui cognito detrimento cum animadvertisset Pompeium extra munitiones egressum, ut
libere pabulari posset nec minus aditum navibus haberet, commutata ratione belli, quoniam propositum
10 non tenuerat, castra secundum mare iuxta Pompeium
munire iussit.

An abandoned camp.

29. Qua perfecta munitione animadversum est a
speculatoribus Caesaris cohortes quasdam, quod instar legionis videretur, esse post silvam et in vetera
15 castra duci.   Castrorum hic situs erat.   Superioribus
diebus nona Caesaris legio, cum se obiecisset Pompeianis copiis atque opere, ut demonstravimus, circummuniret, castra eo loco posuit.   Haec silvam quandam
contingebant neque longius a mari passibus CCC.
20 aberant.   Post mutato consilio quibusdam de causis
Caesar paulo ultra eum locum castra transtulit, paucis-
que intermissis diebus eadem Pompeius occupaverat
et quod eo loco plures erat legiones habiturus, relicto
interiore vallo maiorem adiecerat munitionem.   Ita
25 minora castra inclusa maioribus castelli atque arcis
locum obtinebant.   Item ab angulo castrorum sinistro
munitionem ad flumen perduxerat circiter passuum
CCCC., quo liberius a periculo milites aquarentur.   Sed

is quoque mutato consilio quibusdam de causis, quas
commemorari necesse non est, eo loco excesserat. Ita
complures dies manserant castra; munitiones quidem
omnes integrae erant.

Pompey occupies it, but is attacked by Caesar.

30. Eo signo legionis inlato speculatores Caesari 5
renuntiarunt. Hoc idem visum ex superioribus quibusdam castellis confirmaverunt. Is locus aberat a
novis Pompei castris circiter passus quingentos. Hanc
legionem sperans Caesar se opprimere posse et cupiens
eius diei detrimentum sarcire reliquit in opere cohortes 10
duas quae speciem munitionis praeberent; ipse diverso
itinere quam potuit occultissime reliquas cohortes
numero xxxiii., in quibus erat legio nona multis amissis centurionibus deminutoque militum numero, ad
legionem Pompei castraque minora duplici acie eduxit. 15
Neque eum prima opinio fefellit. Nam et pervenit
priusquam Pompeius sentire posset, et tametsi erant
munitiones castrorum magnae, tamen sinistro cornu,
ubi erat ipse, celeriter aggressus Pompeianos ex vallo
deturbavit. Erat obiectus portis ericius. Hic paulis- 20
per est pugnatum, cum inrumpere nostri conarentur,
illi castra defenderent, fortissime Tito Pulione e loco
propugnante. Sed tamen nostri virtute vicerunt exci-
soque ericio primo in maiora castra, post etiam in
castellum quod erat inclusum maioribus castris inru- 25
perunt, et quod eo pulsa legio sese receperat, non
nullos ibi repugnantes interfecerunt.

Caesar's men climb over the side-rampart.

31. Sed fortuna, quae plurimum potest cum in reliquis rebus tum praecipue in bello, parvis momentis
magnas rerum commutationes efficit; ut tum accidit.
Munitionem, quam pertinere a castris ad flumen supra
5 demonstravimus, dextri Caesaris cornus cohortes igno-
rantia loci sunt secutae, cum portam quaererent castro-
rumque eam munitionem esse arbitrarentur. Quod
cum esset animadversum, coniunctam esse flumini,
prorutis munitionibus defendente nullo transcende-
10 runt, omnisque noster equitatus eas cohortes est
secutus.

**Pompey arrives with reinforcements. The attacking force flees in
confusion.**

32. Interim Pompeius hac satis longa interiecta
mora et re nuntiata v. legiones ab opere deductas
subsidio suis duxit; eodemque tempore equitatus eius
15 nostris equitibus appropinquabat, et acies instructa a
nostris qui castra occupaverant cernebatur, omniaque
sunt subito mutata. Legio Pompeiana celeris spe sub-
sidi confirmata ab decumana porta resistere conabatur
atque ultro in nostros impetum faciebat. Equitatus
20 Caesaris, quod angusto itinere per aggeres ascendebat,
receptui suo timens initium fugae faciebat. Dextrum
cornu, quod erat a sinistro seclusum, terrore equitum
animadverso, ne intra munitionem opprimeretur, ea
parte quam proruerat sese recipiebat, ac plerique ex
25 his, ne in angustias inciderent, ex x. pedum munitione

se in fossas praecipitabant, primisque oppressis reliqui
per horum corpora salutem sibi atque exitum parie-
bant. Sinistro cornu milites, cum ex vallo Pompeium
adesse et suos fugere cernerent, veriti ne angustiis
intercluderentur, cum extra et intus hostem haberent, 5
eodem quo venerant receptu sibi consulebant, omniaque erant tumultus, timoris, fugae plena, adeo ut, cum
Caesar signa fugientium manu prenderet et consistere
iuberet, alii eodem cursu fugerent, alii ex metu etiam
signa dimitterent neque quisquam omnino consisteret. 10

A cause of disaster becomes a means of safety.

33. His tantis malis haec subsidia succurrebant,
quo minus omnis deleretur exercitus, quod Pompeius
insidias timens, credo, quod haec praeter spem acci-
derant eius qui paulo ante ex castris fugientes suos
conspexerat, munitionibus appropinquare aliquamdiu 15
non audebat, equitesque eius angustiis atque his a
Caesaris militibus occupatis ad insequendum tarda-
bantur. Ita parvae res magnum in utramque partem
momentum habuerunt. Munitiones enim a castris ad
flumen perductae expugnatis iam castris Pompei pro- 20
priam expeditamque Caesaris victoriam interpellave-
runt, eadem res celeritate insequentium tardata nostris
salutem attulit.

Caesar's losses. Pompey saluted as Imperator. Murder of the prisoners.

34. Duobus his unius diei proeliis Caesar deside-
ravit milites DCCCCLX. et equites . . . Tuticanum 25

Gallum, senatoris filium, notos equites Romanos C.
Fleginatem Placentia, A. Granium Puteolis, M. Sacra-
tivirum Capua, tribunos militum et centuriones XXXII.;
sed horum omnium pars magna in fossis munitionibus-
5 que et fluminis ripis oppressa suorum in terrore ac
fuga sine ullo volnere interiit; signaque sunt militaria
amissa XXXII.   Pompeius eo proelio imperator est
appellatus.   Hoc nomen obtinuit, atque ita se postea
salutari passus neque in litteris quas scribere est soli-
10 tus neque in fascibus insignia laureae praetulit.   At
Labienus cum ab eo impetravisset ut sibi captivos
tradi iuberet, omnes productos ostentationis, ut videbatur, causa, quo maior perfugae fides haberetur, commilitones appellans et magna verborum contumelia
15 interrogans solerentne veterani milites fugere, in omnium conspectu interfecit.

Pompey's followers unduly elated.

35. His rebus tantum fiduciae ac spiritus Pompeianis accessit, ut non de ratione belli cogitarent, sed
vicisse iam viderentur.   Non illi paucitatem nostro-
20 rum militum, non iniquitatem loci atque angustias
praeoccupatis castris et ancipitem terrorem intra ex-
traque munitiones, non abscisum in duas partes exercitum, cum altera alteri auxilium ferre non posset,
causae fuisse cogitabant.   Non ad haec addebant non
25 concursu acri facto, non proelio dimicatum, sibique
ipsos multitudine atque angustiis maius attulisse detrimentum quam ab hoste accepissent.   Non denique
communis belli casus recordabantur, quam parvulae

saepe causae vel falsae suspicionis vel terroris repen-
tini vel obiectae religionis magna detrimenta intulis-
sent, quotiens vel ducis vitio vel culpa tribuni in
exercitu esset offensum; sed, proinde ac si virtute
vicissent neque ulla commutatio rerum posset acci- 5
dere, per orbem terrarum fama ac litteris victoriam
eius diei concelebrabant.

Caesar reassures his men.

36. Caesar a superioribus consiliis depulsus omnem
sibi commutandam belli rationem existimavit. Itaque
uno tempore praesidiis omnibus deductis et oppugna- 10
tione dimissa coactoque in unum locum exercitu con-
tionem apud milites habuit hortatusque est ne ea quae
accidissent graviter ferrent neve his rebus terrerentur
multisque secundis proeliis unum adversum et id medi-
ocre opponerent. Habendam fortunae gratiam, quod 15
Italiam sine aliquo volnere cepissent, quod duas Hi-
spanias bellicosissimorum hominum peritissimis atque
exercitatissimis ducibus pacavissent, quod finitimas
frumentariasque provincias in potestatem redegissent;
denique recordari debere qua felicitate inter medias 20
hostium classes oppletis non solum portibus sed etiam
litoribus omnes incolumes essent transportati. Si non
omnia caderent secunda, fortunam esse industria sublevandam. Quod esset acceptum detrimenti, cuiusvis
potius quam suae culpae debere tribui. Locum se 25
aequum ad dimicandum dedisse, potitum esse hostium
castris, expulisse ac superasse pugnantes. Sed sive
ipsorum perturbatio sive error aliquis sive etiam

fortuna partam iam praesentemque victoriam inter-
pellavisset, dandam omnibus operam, ut acceptum incommodum virtute sarciretur. Quod si esset factum,
futurum ut detrimentum in bonum verteret, uti ad
5 Gergoviam accidisset, atque ei qui ante dimicare
timuissent ultro se proelio offerrent.

They are eager to wipe out their disgrace.

37. Hac habita contione non nullos signiferos igno-
minia notavit ac loco movit. Exercitui quidem omni
tantus incessit ex incommodo dolor tantumque studium
10 infamiae sarciendae, ut nemo aut tribuni aut centu-
rionis imperium desideraret et sibi quisque etiam poenae loco graviores imponeret labores, simulque omnes
arderent cupiditate pugnandi, cum superioris etiam
ordinis non nulli ratione permoti manendum eo loco
15 et rem proelio committendam existimarent. Contra
ea Caesar neque satis militibus perterritis confidebat
spatiumque interponendum ad recreandos animos puta-
bat, et relictis munitionibus magno opere rei frumentariae timebat.

Caesar breaks camp. Pompey harasses his rear.

20 **38.** Itaque nulla interposita mora sauciorum modo
et aegrorum habita ratione impedimenta omnia silentio
prima nocte ex castris Apolloniam praemisit; haec
conquiescere ante iter confectum vetuit. His una
legio missa praesidio est. His explicitis rebus duas
25 in castris legiones retinuit, reliquas de quarta vigilia
compluribus portis eductas eodem itinere praemisit

parvoque spatio intermisso, ut et militare institutum
servaretur et quam serissime eius profectio cognoscere-
tur, conclamari iussit statimque egressus et novissimum
agmen consecutus celeriter ex conspectu castrorum
discessit. Neque vero Pompeius cognito consilio eius 5
moram ullam ad insequendum intulit, sed id spectans,
si in itinere impeditos perterritos deprehendere posset,
exercitum e castris eduxit equitatumque praemisit ad
novissimum agmen demorandum, neque consequi potuit quod multum expedito itinere antecesserat Caesar. 10
Sed·cum ventum esset ad flumen Genusum, quod ripis
erat impeditis, consecutus equitatus novissimos proelio
detinebat. Huic suos Caesar equites opposuit expe-
ditosque antesignanos admiscuit cccc., qui tantum
profecerunt ut equestri proelio commisso pellerent 15
omnes compluresque interficerent ipsique incolumes se
ad agmen reciperent.

By a ruse Caesar gains a day's march on Pompey.

39. Confecto iusto itinere eius diei quod proposu-
erat Caesar, traductoque exercitu flumen Genusum in
veteribus suis castris contra Asparagium consedit mili- 20
tesque omnes intra vallum castrorum continuit equitatumque per causam pabulandi emissum confestim
decumana porta in castra se recipere iussit. Simili
ratione Pompeius confecto eius diei itinere in suis
veteribus castris ad Asparagium consedit. Eius mili- 25
tes, quod ab opere integris munitionibus vacabant, alii
lignandi pabulandique causa longius progrediebantur,
alii, quod subito consilium profectionis ceperant magna

parte impedimentorum et sarcinarum relicta, ad haec
repetenda invitati propinquitate superiorum castrorum
depositis in contubernio armis vallum relinquebant.
Quibus ad sequendum impeditis, quod fore provi-
5 derat, Caesar meridiano fere tempore signo profectionis
dato exercitum educit duplicatoque eius diei itinere
VIII. milia passuum ex eo loco procedit; quod facere
Pompeius discessu militum non potuit.

Caesar retains his advantage.

40. Postero die Caesar similiter praemissis prima
10 nocte impedimentis de quarta vigilia ipse egreditur, ut,
si qua esset imposita dimicandi necessitas, subitum
casum expedito exercitu subiret. Hoc idem reliquis
fecit diebus. Quibus rebus perfectum est ut altissimis
fluminibus atque impeditissimis itineribus nullum acci-
15 peret incommodum. Pompeius primi diei mora inlata
et reliquorum dierum frustra labore suscepto, cum se
magnis itineribus extenderet et praegressos consequi
cuperet, quarto die finem sequendi fecit atque aliud
sibi consilium capiendum existimavit.

Caesar's new plan of action. He sets out to join Domitius.
Pompey hastens to Scipio.

20   **41.** Caesari ad saucios deponendos, stipendium exercitui dandum, socios confirmandos, praesidium urbi-
bus relinquendum necesse erat adire Apolloniam. Sed
his rebus tantum temporis tribuit quantum erat properanti necesse; timens Domitio, ne adventu Pompei
25 praeoccuparetur, ad eum omni celeritate et studio

incitatus ferebatur. Totius autem rei consilium his
rationibus explicabat, ut, si Pompeius eodem conten-
deret, abductum illum a mari atque ab iis copiis quas
Dyrrachi comparaverat, frumento ac commeatu abs-
tractum pari condicione belli secum decertare cogeret; 5
si in Italiam transiret, coniuncto exercitu cum Domitio
per Illyricum Italiae subsidio proficisceretur ; si Apolloniam Oricumque oppugnare et se omni maritima ora
excludere conaretur, obsesso Scipione, necessario illum
suis auxilium ferre cogeret. Itaque praemissis nuntiis 10
ad Cn. Domitium Caesar scripsit et quid fieri vellet
ostendit praesidioque Apolloniae cohortibus IV., Lissi
I., III. Orici relictis, quique erant ex volneribus aegri
depositis, per Epirum atque Athamaniam iter facere
coepit. Pompeius quoque de Caesaris consilio con- 15
iectura iudicans ad Scipionem properandum sibi existimabat : si Caesar iter illo haberet, ut subsidium
Scipioni ferret ; si ab ora maritima Oricoque discedere
nollet, quod legiones equitatumque ex Italia exspec-
taret, ipse ut omnibus copiis Domitium aggrederetur. 20

Domitius barely escapes falling into Pompey's power.

42. His de causis uterque eorum celeritati studebat,
et suis ut esset auxilio et ad opprimendos adversarios
ne occasioni temporis deesset. Sed Caesarem Apollonia a derecto itinere averterat, Pompeius per Candaviam iter in Macedoniam expeditum habebat. Accessit 25
etiam ex improviso aliud incommodum, quod Domitius,
qui dies complures castris Scipionis castra conlata
habuisset, rei frumentariae causa ab eo discesserat

et Heracliam, quae est subiecta Candaviae, iter fecerat,
ut ipsa fortuna illum obicere Pompeio videretur.   Haec
ad id tempus Caesar ignorabat.   Simul a Pompeio litteris per omnes provincias civitatesque dimissis proelio
5 ad Dyrrachium facto, latius inflatiusque multo quam
res erat gesta fama percrebruerat, pulsum fugere Caesarem paene omnibus copiis amissis.   Haec itinera
infesta reddiderat, haec civitates non nullas ab eius
amicitia avertebat.   Quibus accidit rebus ut pluribus
10 dimissi itineribus a Caesare ad Domitium et a Domitio
ad Caesarem nulla ratione iter conficere possent.   Sed
Allobroges, Raucilli atque Egi familiares, quos perfugisse ad Pompeium demonstravimus, conspicati in
itinere exploratores Domiti, seu pristina sua consuetu-
15 dine, quod una in Gallia bella gesserant, seu gloria
elati, cuncta ut erant acta exposuerunt et Caesaris
profectionem, adventum Pompei docuerunt.   A quibus
Domitius certior factus vix IV. horarum spatio ante-
cedens hostium beneficio periculum vitavit et ad Aegi-
20 nium, quod est oppidum oppositum Thessaliae, Caesari
venienti occurrit.

Gomphi captured and plundered by Caesar.

43. Coniuncto exercitu Caesar Gomphos pervenit,
quod est oppidum primum Thessaliae venientibus ab
Epiro ; quae gens paucis ante mensibus ultro ad Cae-
25 sarem legatos miserat, ut suis omnibus facultatibus
uteretur, praesidiumque ab eo militum petierat.   Sed
eo fama iam praecurrerat quam supra docuimus de
proelio Dyrrachino, quod multis auxerat partibus.

Itaque Androsthenes, praetor Thessaliae, cum se victoriae Pompei comitem esse mallet quam socium Caesaris in rebus adversis, omnem ex agris multitudinem
servorum ac liberorum in oppidum cogit portasque
praecludit et ad Scipionem Pompeiumque nuntios 5
mittit, ut sibi subsidio veniant : se confidere munitionibus oppidi, si celeriter succurratur ; longinquam
oppugnationem sustinere non posse. Scipio discessu
exercituum ab Dyrrachio cognito Larisam legiones
adduxerat ; Pompeius nondum Thessaliae appropin- 10
quabat. Caesar castris munitis scalas musculosque
ad repentinam oppugnationem fieri et crates parari
iussit. Quibus rebus effectis cohortatus milites docuit
quantum usum haberet ad sublevandam omnium rerum
inopiam potiri oppido pleno atque opulento, simul 15
reliquis civitatibus huius urbis exemplo inferre terrorem et id fieri celeriter, priusquam auxilia concurrerent. Itaque usus singulari militum studio, eodem
quo venerat die post horam nonam oppidum altissimis
moenibus oppugnare aggressus ante solis occasum 20
expugnavit et ad diripiendum militibus concessit, statimque ab oppido castra movit et Metropolim venit,
sic ut nuntios expugnati oppidi famamque antecederet.

**Metropolis, alarmed at the fate of Gomphi, surrenders. Other towns
do the same.**

44. Metropolitae primum eodem usi consilio isdem
permoti rumoribus portas clauserunt murosque armatis 25
compleverunt, sed postea casu civitatis Gomphensis
cognito ex captivis quos Caesar ad murum producen-

dos curaverat, portas aperuerunt. Quibus diligentis-
sime conservatis, conlata fortuna Metropolitum cum
casu Gomphensium nulla Thessaliae fuit civitas praeter Larisaeos, qui magnis exercitibus Scipionis tene-
5 bantur, quin Caesari pareret atque imperata faceret.
Ille idoneum locum in agris nactus quo prope iam
matura erant frumenta, ibi adventum exspectare Pompei eoque omnem belli rationem conferre constituit.

**Pompey and Scipio join forces. Quarrels over the disposal of the
expected booty.**

45. Pompeius paucis post diebus in Thessaliam
10 pervenit contionatusque apud cunctum exercitum suis
agit gratias, Scipionis milites cohortatur ut parta iam
victoria praedae ac praemiorum velint esse participes,
receptisque omnibus in una castra legionibus suum
cum Scipione honorem partitur classicumque apud
15 eum cani et alterum illi iubet praetorium tendi. Auc-
tis copiis Pompei duobusque magnis exercitibus con-
iunctis pristina omnium confirmatur opinio et spes
victoriae augetur, adeo ut, quicquid intercederet temporis, id morari reditum in Italiam videretur, et, si
20 quando quid Pompeius tardius aut consideratius faceret,
unius esse negotium diei, sed illum delectari imperio
et consulares praetoriosque servorum habere numero
dicerent. Iamque inter se palam de praemiis ac sacerdotiis contendebant in annosque consulatum definie-
25 bant, alii domos bonaque eorum qui in castris erant
Caesaris petebant ; magnaque inter eos in consilio
fuit controversia, oporteretne Lucili Hirri, quod is a

Pompeio ad Parthos missus esset, proximis comitiis
praetoriis absentis rationem haberi, cum eius necessarii fidem implorarent Pompei, praestaret quod proficiscenti recepisset, ne per eius auctoritatem deceptus
videretur, reliqui in labore pari ac periculo ne unus 5
omnes antecederet recusarent.

**Caesar again offers battle. He forms and trains a mixed force of
light-armed men and cavalry.**

46. Re frumentaria praeparata confirmatisque militibus et satis longo spatio temporis a Dyrrachinis
proeliis intermisso, quo satis perspectum habere militum animum videretur, temptandum Caesar existi- 10
mavit quidnam Pompeius propositi aut voluntatis ad
dimicandum haberet. Itaque ex castris exercitum
eduxit aciemque instruxit, primo suis locis pauloque
a castris Pompei longius, continentibus vero diebus,
ut progrederetur a castris suis collibusque Pompeianis 15
aciem subiceret. Quae res in dies confirmatiorem eius
exercitum efficiebat. Superius tamen institutum in
equitibus quod demonstravimus servabat, ut, quoniam
numero multis partibus esset inferior, adulescentes
atque expeditos ex antesignanis electos mutatis ad 20
pernicitatem armis inter equites proeliari iuberet,
qui cotidiana consuetudine usum quoque eius generis
proeliorum perciperent. His erat rebus effectum ut
equitum mille etiam apertioribus locis VII. milium
Pompeianorum impetum, cum adesset usus, sustinere 25
auderent neque magno opere eorum multitudine terrerentur. Namque etiam per eos dies proelium secun-

dum equestre fecit atque unum Allobrogem ex duobus
quos perfugisse ad Pompeium supra docuimus cum
quibusdam interfecit.

Caesar decides to break camp, but Pompey offers battle on fair terms.

47. Pompeius, qui castra in colle habebat, ad infi-
5 mas radices montis aciem instruebat, semper, ut videbatur, exspectans si iniquis locis Caesar se subiceret.
Caesar nulla ratione ad pugnam elici posse Pompeium
existimans hanc sibi commodissimam belli rationem
iudicavit, ut castra ex eo loco moveret semperque
10 esset in itineribus, haec spectans, ut movendis castris
pluribusque adeundis locis commodiore re frumentaria
uteretur, simulque in itinere ut aliquam occasionem
dimicandi nancisceretur et insolitum ad laborem Pompei exercitum cotidianis itineribus defatigaret. His
15 constitutis rebus, signo iam profectionis dato taberna-
culisque detensis, animadversum est paulo ante extra
cotidianam consuetudinem longius a vallo esse aciem
Pompei progressam, ut non iniquo loco posse dimicari
videretur. Tunc Caesar apud suos, cum iam esset
20 agmen in portis, *Differendum est*, inquit, *iter in prae-*
sentia nobis et de proelio cogitandum, sicut semper depo-
poscimus. Animo simus ad dimicandum parati; non
facile occasionem postea reperiemus, confestimque expe-
ditas copias educit.

Pompey, relying on his cavalry, is confident of success.

25 **48.** Pompeius quoque, ut postea cognitum est,
suorum omnium hortatu statuerat proelio decertare.

Namque etiam in consilio superioribus diebus dixerat, priusquam concurrerent acies, fore uti exercitus Caesaris pelleretur. Id cum essent plerique admirati, *Scio me,* inquit, *paene incredibilem rem polliceri; sed rationem consili mei accipite, quo firmiore animo in proe-* 5 *lium prodeatis. Persuasi equitibus nostris, idque mihi facturos confirmaverunt, ut, cum propius sit accessum, dextrum Caesaris cornu ab latere aperto aggrederentur et circumventa ab tergo acie prius perturbatum exercitum pellerent quam a nobis telum in hostem iaceretur. Ita* 10 *sine periculo legionum et paene sine volnere bellum conficiemus. Id autem difficile non est, cum tantum equitatu valeamus.* Simul denuntiavit ut essent animo parati in posterum et, quoniam fieret dimicandi potestas, ut saepe cogitavissent, ne usu manuque reliquorum opi-* 15 nionem fallerent.

Labienus, after speaking contemptuously of Caesar's army, swears never to return to camp unless victorious.

49. Hunc Labienus excepit et, cum Caesaris copias despiceret, Pompei consilium summis laudibus efferret, *Noli,* inquit, *existimare, Pompei, hunc esse exercitum qui Galliam Germaniamque devicerit. Omnibus interfui* 20 *proeliis, neque temere incognitam rem pronuntio. Perexigua pars illius exercitus superest; magna pars deperiit, quod accidere tot proeliis fuit necesse, multos autumni pestilentia in Italia consumpsit, multi domum discesserunt, multi sunt relicti in continenti. An non audistis* 25 *ex iis qui per causam valetudinis remanserunt cohortes esse Brundisi factas? Hae copiae quas videtis ex delec-*

tibus horum annorum in citeriore Gallia sunt refectae, et
plerique sunt ex coloniis Transpadanis. Ac tamen quod
fuit roboris duobus proeliis Dyrrachinis interiit. Haec
cum dixisset, iuravit se nisi victorem in castra non
5 reversurum, reliquosque ut idem facerent hortatus est.
Hoc laudans Pompeius idem iuravit ; nec vero ex reliquis fuit quisquam qui iurare dubitaret. Haec cum
facta sunt in consilio, magna spe et laetitia omnium
discessum est ; ac iam animo victoriam praecipiebant,
10 quod de re tanta et a tam perito imperatore nihil frustra confirmari videbatur.

Formation of Pompey's line of battle.

50. Caesar cum Pompei castris appropinquasset,
ad hunc modum aciem eius instructam animadvertit.
Erant in sinistro cornu legiones duae traditae a Cae-
15 sare initio dissensionis ex senatus consulto, quarum
una prima, altera tertia appellabatur ; in eo loco ipse
erat Pompeius. Mediam aciem Scipio cum legionibus Syriacis tenebat. Ciliciensis legio coniuncta cum
cohortibus Hispanis, quas traductas ab Afranio docui-
20 mus, in dextro cornu erant conlocatae. Has firmissi-
mas se habere Pompeius existimabat. Reliquas inter
aciem mediam cornuaque interiecerat numeroque cohortes cx. expleverat. Haec erant milia xlv., evocatorum circiter duo, quae ex beneficiariis superiorum
25 exercituum ad eum convenerant ; quae tota acie di-
sperserat. Reliquas cohortis vii. in castris propinquis-
que castellis praesidio disposuerat. Dextrum cornu
eius rivus quidam impeditis ripis muniebat ; quam ob

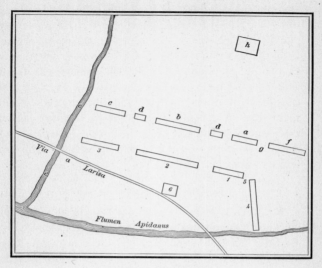

BATTLE OF PHARSALIA.

Acies Pompei.

- *a.* Duae legiones a Caesare traditae.
- *b.* Scipio ad mediam aciem.
- *c.* Legio Ciliciensis cum cohortibus Hispanis in dextro cornu.
- *d.* Reliquae cohortes.
- *e.* Rivus quidam.
- *f.* Equitatus (Labieno legato), sagittarii, funditoresque in sinistro cornu
- *g.* Pompeius.
- *h.* Castra Pompei.

Acies Caesaris.

1. Decima legio (Sulla legato) in dextro cornu.
2. Cn. Domitius ad mediam aciem.
3. Legiones nona octavaque (Antonio legato) in sinistro cornu.
4. Acies quarta.
5. Caesar.
6. Castra Caesaris.

causam cunctum equitatum, sagittarios funditoresque
omnes sinistro cornu obiecerat.

Formation of Caesar's line of battle.

51. Caesar superius institutum servans decimam
legionem in dextro cornu, nonam in sinistro conlocaverat, tametsi erat Dyrrachinis proeliis vehementer   5
attenuata, et huic sic adiunxit octavam ut paene unam
ex duabus efficeret, atque alteram alteri praesidio esse
iusserat.   Cohortes in acie LXXX. constitutas habebat,
quae summa erat milium XXII.; cohortes duas castris
praesidio reliquerat.   Sinistro cornu Antonium, dextro 10
P. Sullam, media acie Cn. Domitium praeposuerat.
Ipse contra Pompeium constitit.   Simul his rebus
animadversis quas demonstravimus, timens ne a multitudine equitum dextrum cornu circumveniretur, celeriter ex tertia acie singulas cohortes detraxit atque ex 15
his quartam instituit equitatuique opposuit, et quid fieri
vellet ostendit, monuitque eius diei victoriam in earum
cohortium virtute constare.   Simul tertiae aciei totique
exercitui imperavit ne iniussu suo concurreret: se, cum
id fieri vellet, vexillo signum daturum.   20

Caesar reminds his men of his desire for peace, then gives the signal for battle.

52. Exercitum cum militari more ad pugnam cohor-
taretur suaque in eum perpetui temporis officia prae-
dicaret, imprimis commemoravit testibus se militibus
uti posse, quanto studio pacem petisset, quae per
Vatinium in conloquiis, quae per Aulum Clodium cum 25

Scipione egisset, quibus modis ad Oricum cum Libone
de mittendis legatis contendisset.   Neque se umquam
abuti militum sanguine neque rem publicam alterutro
exercitu privare voluisse.   Hac habita oratione expo-
5 scentibus militibus et studio pugnae ardentibus tuba
signum dedit.

Valiant conduct of Crastinus, a volunteer veteran.

53. Erat Crastinus evocatus in exercitu Caesaris, qui
superiore anno apud eum primum pilum in legione x.
duxerat, vir singulari virtute.   Hic signo dato, *Sequi-*
10 *mini me,* inquit, *manipulares mei qui fuistis, et vestro*
imperatori quam constituistis operam date.   Unum hoc
proelium superest; quo confecto et ille suam dignitatem
et nos nostram libertatem recuperabimus.   Simul respi-
ciens Caesarem, *Faciam,* inquit, *hodie, imperator, ut*
15 *aut vivo mihi aut mortuo gratias agas.*   Haec cum
dixisset, primus ex dextro cornu procucurrit, atque
eum electi milites circiter cxx. voluntarii eiusdem
centuriae sunt prosecuti.

Pompey leaves Caesar to make the attack. He is criticised for so doing.

54. Inter duas acies tantum erat relictum spati ut
20 satis esset ad concursum utriusque exercitus.   Sed
Pompeius suis praedixerat ut Caesaris impetum exci-
perent neve se loco moverent aciemque eius distrahi
paterentur ; idque admonitu C. Triari fecisse dicebatur, ut primus excursus visque militum infringeretur
25 aciesque distenderetur atque in suis ordinibus dispo-

síti dispersos adorirentur ; leviusque casura pila sperabat in loco retentis militibus quam si ipsi immissis
telis occucurrissent, simul fore ut duplicato cursu Caesaris milites exanimarentur et lassitudine conficerentur.
Quod nobis quidem nulla ratione factum a Pompeio 5
videtur, propterea quod est quaedam animi incitatio
atque alacritas naturaliter innata omnibus quae studio
pugnae incenditur.   Hanc non reprimere sed augere
imperatores debent ; neque frustra antiquitus institutum est ut signa undique concinerent clamoremque 10
universi tollerent ; quibus rebus et hostes terreri et
suos incitari existimaverunt.

**Caesar's men advance, halt to get breath, then charge. Defeat of
Pompey's cavalry.**

55. Sed nostri milites dato signo cum infestis pilis
procucurrissent atque animadvertissent non concurri
a Pompeianis, usu periti ac superioribus pugnis exer- 15
citati sua sponte cursum represserunt et ad medium
fere spatium constiterunt, ne consumptis viribus appro-
pinquarent, parvoque intermisso temporis spatio ac
rursus renovato cursu pila miserunt celeriterque, ut
erat praeceptum a Caesare, gladios strinxerunt. Ne- 20
que vero Pompeiani huic rei defuerunt. Nam et tela
missa exceperunt et impetum legionum tulerunt et
ordines conservarunt pilisque missis ad gladios redie-
runt.   Eodem tempore equites ab sinistro Pompei
cornu, ut erat imperatum, universi procucurrerunt 25
omnisque multitudo sagittariorum se profudit. Quorum impetum noster equitatus non tulit, sed paulatim

loco motus cessit, equitesque Pompei hoc acrius instare et se turmatim explicare aciemque nostram a latere aperto circumire coeperunt. Quod ubi Caesar animadvertit, quartae aciei quam instituerat sex co-
5 hortium dedit signum. Illi celeriter procucurrerunt infestisque signis tanta vi in Pompei equites impetum fecerunt ut eorum nemo consisteret omnesque conversi non solum loco excederent, sed protinus incitati fuga montes altissimos peterent. Quibus submotis omnes
10 sagittarii funditoresque destituti inermes sine praesidio interfecti sunt. Eodem impetu cohortes sinistrum cornu pugnantibus etiam tum ac resistentibus in acie Pompeianis circumierunt eosque a tergo sunt adortae.

Pompey's infantry gives way. His own cowardly conduct.

56. Eodem tempore tertiam aciem Caesar, quae
15 quieta fuerat et se ad id tempus loco tenuerat, procurrere iussit. Ita cum recentes atque integri defessis successissent, alii autem a tergo adorirentur, sustinere Pompeiani non potuerunt atque universi terga verterunt. Neque vero Caesarem fefellit quin ab iis cohor-
20 tibus quae contra equitatum in quarta acie conlocatae essent initium victoriae oriretur, ut ipse in cohortandis militibus pronuntiaverat. Ab his enim primum equitatus est pulsus, ab isdem factae caedes sagittariorum ac funditorum, ab isdem acies Pompeiana a sinistra
25 parte circumita atque initium fugae factum. Sed Pompeius, ut equitatum suum pulsum vidit atque eam partem cui maxime confidebat perterritam animadvertit, aliis quoque diffisus acie excessit protinusque se

in castra equo contulit et iis centurionibus quos in
statione ad praetoriam portam posuerat clare, ut milites exaudirent, *Tuemini*, inquit, *castra et defendite dili-*
genter, si quid durius acciderit. Ego reliquas portas
circumeo et castrorum praesidia confirmo. Haec cum 5
dixisset, se in praetorium contulit, summae rei diffi-
dens et tamen eventum exspectans.

Caesar follows up his advantage and captures the enemy's camp.

57. Caesar Pompeianis ex fuga intra vallum com-
pulsis nullum spatium perterritis dare oportere existimans milites cohortatus est ut beneficio fortunae 10
uterentur castraque oppugnarent. Qui, etsi magno
aestu (nam ad meridiem res erat perducta), tamen ad
omnem laborem animo parati imperio paruerunt. Castra a cohortibus quae ibi praesidio erant relictae in-
dustrie defendebantur, multo etiam acrius a Thracibus 15
barbarisque auxiliis. Nam qui ex acie refugerant
milites et animo perterriti et lassitudine confecti missis plerique armis signisque militaribus magis de reliqua fuga quam de castrorum defensione cogitabant.
Neque vero diutius qui in vallo constiterant multitu- 20
dinem telorum sustinere potuerunt, sed confecti volneribus locum reliquerunt, protinusque omnes ducibus
usi centurionibus tribunisque militum in altissimos
montes qui ad castra pertinebant confugerunt.

The luxurious appointments of the camp. Pompey escapes.

58. In castris Pompei videre licuit trichilas structas, 25
magnum argenti pondus expositum, recentibus caespi-

tibus tabernacula constrata, Luci etiam Lentuli et non
nullorum tabernacula protecta hedera, multaque praeterea quae nimiam luxuriam et victoriae fiduciam de-
signarent, ut facile existimari posset nihil eos de
5 eventu eius diei timuisse qui non necessarias conquirerent voluptates.   At hi miserrimo ac patientis-
simo exercitu Caesaris luxuriem obiciebant, cui semper
omnia ad necessarium usum defuissent.   Pompeius,
iam cum intra vallum nostri versarentur, equum nac-
10 tus detractis insignibus imperatoriis decumana porta
se ex castris eiecit protiṇusque equo citato Larisam
contendit.   Neque ibi constitit, sed eadem celeritate
paucos suos ex fuga nactus, nocturno itinere non intermisso, comitatu equitum xxx. ad mare pervenit navem-
15 que frumentariam conscendit, saepe, ut dicebatur,
querens tantum se opinionem fefellisse ut, a quo
genere hominum victoriam sperasset, ab eo initio fugae
facto paene proditus videretur.

Remnant of Pompey's army besieged on a hill.

59. Caesar castris potitus a militibus contendit ne
20 in praeda occupati reliqui negoti gerendi facultatem
dimitterent.   Qua re impetrata montem opere circum-
munire instituit.   Pompeiani, quod is mons erat sine
aqua, diffisi ei loco relicto monte universi iugis eius
Larisam versus se recipere coeperunt.   Qua re anim-
25 adversa Caesar copias suas divisit partemque legionum in castris Pompei remanere iussit, partem in sua
castra remisit, iv. secum legiones duxit commodioreque
itinere Pompeianis occurrere coepit et progressus milia

passuum VI. aciem instruxit. Qua re animadversa
Pompeiani in quodam monte constiterunt. Hunc
montem flumen subluebat. Caesar milites cohortatus,
etsi totius diei continenti labore erant confecti noxque
iam suberat, tamen munitione flumen a monte seclusit, 5
ne noctu aquari Pompeiani possent. Quo perfecto
opere illi de deditione missis legatis agere coeperunt.
Pauci ordinis senatorii qui se cum iis coniunxerant
nocte fuga salutem petiverunt.

They surrender and are pardoned.

60. Caesar prima luce omnes eos qui in monte con- 10
sederant ex superioribus locis in planitiem descendere
atque arma proicere iussit. Quod ubi sine recusatione
fecerunt passisque palmis proiecti ad terram flentes ab
eo salutem petiverunt, consolatus consurgere iussit et
pauca apud eos de lenitate sua locutus quo minore 15
essent timore, omnes conservavit militibusque suis
commendavit, ne qui eorum violaretur neu quid sui
desiderarent. Hac adhibita diligentia ex castris sibi
legiones alias occurrere et eas quas secum duxerat in
vicem requiescere atque in castra reverti iussit eodem- 20
que die Larisam pervenit.

The losses on both sides.

61. In eo proelio non amplius CC. milites desidera-
vit, sed centuriones, fortes viros, circiter XXX. amisit.
Interfectus est etiam fortissime pugnans Crastinus,
cuius mentionem supra fecimus, gladio in os adver- 25
sum coniecto. Neque id fuit falsum quod ille in

pugnam proficiscens dixerat. Sic enim Caesar existimabat, eo proelio excellentissimam virtutem Crastini
fuisse, optimeque eum de se meritum iudicabat. Ex
Pompeiano exercitu circiter milia xv. cecidisse vide-
5 bantur ; sed in deditionem venerunt amplius milia
xxiv. (namque etiam cohortes quae praesidio in castellis fuerant sese Sullae dediderunt), multi praeterea
refugerunt, signaque militaria ex proelio ad Caesarem
sunt relata clxxx. et aquilae ix. L. Domitius ex castris
10 in montem refugiens, cum vires eum lassitudine defecissent, ab equitibus est interfectus.

Caesar pursues Pompey. Pompey's flight.

62. Caesar omnibus rebus relictis persequendum
sibi Pompeium existimavit quascumque in partes se
ex fuga recepisset, ne rursus copias comparare alias
15 et bellum renovare posset, et quantumcumque itineris
equitatu efficere poterat cotidie progrediebatur legio-
nemque unam minoribus itineribus subsequi iussit.
Erat edictum Pompei nomine Amphipoli propositum,
uti omnes eius provinciae iuniores, Graeci civesque
20 Romani, iurandi causa convenirent. Sed utrum aver-
tendae suspicionis causa Pompeius proposuisset, ut
quam diutissime longioris fugae consilium occultaret,
an novis delectibus, si nemo premeret, Macedoniam
tenere conaretur, existimari non poterat. Ipse ad an-
25 coram una nocte constitit, et vocatis ad se Amphipoli
hospitibus et pecunia ad necessarios sumptus corrogata,
cognito Caesaris adventu ex eo loco discessit et Mytilenas paucis diebus venit. Biduum tempestate reten-

tus navibusque aliis additis actuariis in Ciliciam atque
inde Cyprum pervenit. Ibi cognoscit consensu omnium
Antiochensium civiumque Romanorum qui illic ne-
gotiarentur arcem captam esse excludendi sui causa
nuntiosque dimissos ad eos qui se ex fuga in finitimas 5
civitates recepisse dicerentur, ne Antiochiam adirent:
id si fecissent, magno eorum capitis periculo futurum.

Pompey seeks an asylum with Ptolemy, king of Egypt.

63. Quibus cognitis rebus Pompeius, deposito ad-
eundae Syriae consilio pecunia societatis sublata et a
quibusdam privatis sumpta et aeris magno pondere ad 10
militarem usum in naves imposito duobusque milibus
hominum armatis, partim quos ex familiis societatum
delegerat, partim a negotiatoribus coëgerat, quos ex suis
quisque ad hanc rem idoneos existimabat, Pelusium
pervenit. Ibi casu rex erat Ptolemaeus, puer aetate, 15
magnis copiis cum sorore Cleopatra bellum gerens,
quam paucis ante mensibus per suos propinquos atque
amicos regno expulerat; castraque Cleopatrae non longo
spatio ab eius castris distabant. Ad eum Pompeius
misit ut pro hospitio atque amicitia patris Alexandria 20
reciperetur atque illius opibus in calamitate tegeretur.
Sed qui ab eo missi erant, confecto legationis officio,
liberius cum militibus regis conloqui coeperunt eosque
hortari ut suum officium Pompeio praestarent neve eius
fortunam despicerent. In hoc erant numero complures 25
Pompei milites, quos ex eius exercitu acceptos in Syria
Gabinius Alexandriam traduxerat belloque confecto
apud Ptolemaeum, patrem pueri, reliquerat.

He is treacherously murdered.

64. His tunc cognitis rebus, amici regis qui propter
aetatem eius in curatione erant regni, sive timore
adducti, ut postea praedicabant, sollicitato exercitu
regio, ne Pompeius Alexandriam Aegyptumque occu-
5 paret, sive despecta eius fortuna, ut plerumque in calamitate ex amicis inimici exsistunt, his qui erant ab
eo missi palam liberaliter responderunt eumque ad
regem venire iusserunt ; ipsi clam consilio inito Achil-
lam, praefectum regium, singulari hominem audacia, et
10 L. Septimium, tribunum militum, ad interficiendum
Pompeium miserunt. Ab his liberaliter ipse appellatus et quadam notitia Septimi productus, quod bello
praedonum apud eum ordinem duxerat, naviculam parvulam conscendit cum paucis suis ; ibi ab Achilla et
15 Septimio interficitur. Item L. Lentulus comprehendi-
tur ab rege et in custodia necatur.

Strange happenings on the day of Caesar's victory.

65. Caesar cum in Asiam venisset, reperiebat T.
Ampium conatum esse pecunias tollere Epheso ex
fano Dianae eiusque rei causa senatores omnes ex pro-
20 vincia evocasse, ut his testibus in summa pecuniae
uteretur, sed interpellatum adventu Caesaris profu-
gisse. Ita duobus temporibus Ephesiae pecuniae
Caesar auxilium tulit. . . . Item constabat, Elide in
templo Minervae repetitis atque enumeratis diebus,
25 quo die proelium secundum Caesar fecisset, simulacrum Victoriae, quod ante ipsam Minervam conloca-

tum esset et ante ad simulacrum Minervae spectavisset,
ad valvas se templi limenque convertisse. Eodemque
die Antiochiae in Syria bis tantus exercitus clamor et
signorum sonus exauditus est ut in muris armata civitas discurreret. Hoc idem Ptolemaide accidit. Per- 5
gami in occultis ac reconditis templi, quo praeter
sacerdotes adire fas non est, quae Graeci ἄδυτα appel-
lant, tympana sonuerunt. Item Trallibus in templo
Victoriae, ubi Caesaris statuam consecraverant, palma
per eos dies inter coagmenta lapidum ex pavimento 10
exstitisse ostendebatur.

**Caesar follows Pompey, and on arriving at Alexandria learns of his
death.**

66. Caesar paucos dies in Asia moratus cum audis-
set Pompeium Cypri visum, coniectans eum Aegyptum
iter habere propter necessitudines regni reliquasque
eius loci opportunitates, cum legione una quam se ex 15
Thessalia sequi iusserat, et altera quam ex Achaia a
Q. Fufio legato evocaverat, equitibusque DCCC. et navibus longis Rhodiis x. et Asiaticis paucis Alexandriam
pervenit. In his erant legionibus hominum milia tria
cc. ; reliqui volneribus ex proeliis et labore ac magni- 20
tudine itineris confecti consequi non potuerant. Sed
Caesar confisus fama rerum gestarum infirmis auxiliis
proficisci non dubitaverat, aeque omnem sibi locum
tutum fore existimans. Alexandriae de Pompei morte
cognoscit. 25

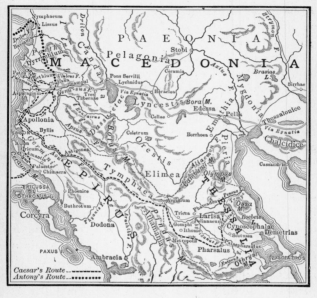

MAP SHOWING THE ROUTES OF CAESAR AND ANTONY IN
THESSALY AND MACEDONIA.

NOTES.

———◦◦⁂◦◦———

N. B. The references are to page and line of the text. When no letter precedes the grammatical references, they refer to Allen and Greenough's New Latin Grammar; when H. precedes, to Harkness' Complete Latin Grammar.

The following abbreviations occur:

abl.	ablative.	i.e. (*id est*)	that is.
abl. abs.	ablative absolute.	indecl.	indeclinable.
acc.	accusative.	indef.	indefinite.
adj.	adjective.	inf.	infinitive.
adv.	adverb.	M. *or* masc.	masculine.
cf. (*confer*)	compare.	N., n.	neuter ; note.
chap.	chapter.	nom.	nominative.
comp.	comparative.	num.	numeral.
conj.	conjunction.	part.	participle.
dat.	dative.	pass.	passive.
dep.	deponent.	perf.	perfect.
e.g. (*exempli gratia*)	for example.	plu.	plural.
etc. (*et cetera*)	and so forth.	prep.	preposition.
et seq. (*et sequentia*)	and the following.	pres.	present.
		pron.	pronoun.
		sc. (*scilicet*)	understand.
F.	feminine.	superl.	superlative.
fut.	future.	v.	verb.
gen.	genitive.	voc.	vocative.

1 1 CHAP. I. **Dictatore:** *as dictator* (282 ; H. 393). In public crises the senate could call upon the consuls to appoint a *dictator*. The dictator held absolute power for a time not exceeding six months. In later times the consuls were invested by the senate with *dictatorial* powers, the usual formula beginning *Videant ne,* etc. In Chapters 21 and 22 of Book II. of the *Civil War* we find that Caesar had been, by connivance with the praetor Lepidus, appointed dictator while he was besieging Massilia, and that he at once set out for Rome. He used his power to hold the *comitia,* or election (this being one of the purposes for which the dictator was regularly appointed), and was himself chosen *consul* for the following year, 48 B.C., with Publius Servilius as his colleague. This he did that his consulship might have some show of legality. He held his dictatorship only eleven days.

1 1 comitia: i.e. *Centuriata,* one of the three public assemblies at Rome, the other two being the *Comitia Curiata* and the *Comitia Tributa.* At the *Comitia Centuriata* the entire people was divided, for the purpose of voting, into 195 *centuriae,* or centuries, the division being made chiefly according to the amount of property. It was at this assembly that all the higher magistrates were elected (as on this occasion the *consuls*), that laws were passed, and trials held. Each century had one vote, the majority of its members deciding what that vote should be. The order of voting was determined by lot, and the first vote had great influence on the following voters. It was necessary for one of the chief magistrates, such as dictator, consul, or praetor, to summon the assembly. It will thus be understood how *comitia habere* came to mean *to hold an election.*

1 1 consules: for the year 48 B.C., the consuls being elected some time before they entered upon the duties of their office, as in the case of the President with us. In the interval they were known as *consules designati.* They were the chief magistrates of the Republic, and two were chosen each year; at first each was preceded in the city by twelve lictors bearing the *fasces,* or bundles of *rods* with an axe tied up in the centre, but afterwards they enjoyed this mark of dignity and power alternately. They entered upon their office January 1 and were obliged to take the oath of office within five days of that time. Like the ἄρχων ἐπώνυμος at Athens, they gave their names to the year.

1 2 Iulius Caesar: the Latins of early mythical times had only one name, as Romulus, Latinus, Numitor, etc., to designate the individual. When the Romans had become united into one nation, they usually bore two names, one for the individual and one for the *gens*. In later times they had three: thus Caesar's full name was Caius Iulius Caesar, of which Caius was the *praenomen*, or name of the individual, Iulius the *nomen*, or name of the *gens*, Caesar the *cognomen*, or name of the family. Sometimes there was a fourth name, called *agnomen*, given as an honorary distinction, e.g. Publius Cornelius Scipio *Africanus*.

l 2   annus: the law provided that no one should hold the same office a second time until ten years had intervened. Caesar had been consul in 60 B.C., and was, therefore, now eligible again. Cf. Introduction, pages x. and xiv.

l 3   consulem: the more common construction is the dat. (455. a; H. 612. 2 and 3).

l 3   liceret: 535; H. 591. 1.

l 4   feriis Latinis: this was a sacrificial festival which Tarquinius Superbus, founder of the Latin League, established in honor of Jupiter Latiaris. It was celebrated annually on Mount Albanus by the consuls soon after they assumed office. The day was a great holiday and crowds of people flocked thither. No magistrate could take the field without holding this festival and there invoking the favor of the gods against the national enemies.

l 5   dictatura: 400; H. 462.

l 6   Brundisium: modern Brindisi, on the east coast of Italy. It has a fine harbor and was then, as it now is, the port from which travellers usually embarked for Greece.

l 6   legiones: the *legion* was the unit of the Roman army, as the regiment is of ours, but was much larger. The number of men varied at different times, but Caesar's legions contained on an average about 3600 men. The legion was divided into ten cohorts (*cohortes*); each cohort was subdivided into three maniples (*manipuli*); and each maniple contained two centuries (*centuriae*). The legion, therefore, contained ten cohorts, or thirty maniples, or sixty centuries. Originally the infantry was drawn up for battle in three lines: in front the raw recruits, called the *hastati* because they were armed with a *hasta*, or long spear; next the *principes*, men of mature age; and in the rear the veterans, called sometimes *triarii*, sometimes *pilani ;* the latter were armed with two *pila*, or heavy javelins. Under Caesar the men were all armed alike, and the ten cohorts of a legion were drawn up in three lines (*tertia acies*), four in the front line and three in each of the other two; the names *hastati*, *principes*, and *triarii* were still retained, but only to designate the centurions. Each century had a centurion (*centurio*) to

1. FUNDITOR.   2, 2. MILITES LEVIS ARMATURAE.   3, 3. LEGIONARII.

command it; consequently a legion had sixty centurions. These were men of long experience and of great courage; they fought in the thick of the fray, a thing which the commander-in-chief (*dux*) or the lieutenant (*legatus*) rarely did, and as they were looked up to by the common soldiers, they wielded a vast influence in deciding the contest. The first centurion of a legion, i.e. the centurion of the first century of *triarii*, had charge of the eagle, or standard, of the legion; he was called *primipilus* and ranked above all the other centurions. There was a body (*ala*) of cavalry connected with each legion. It consisted of 300 men and was subdivided into *turmae*, or squadrons. Caesar's cavalry was made up of auxiliaries, and was usually commanded by a *legatus*. An army was also usually accompanied by bodies of light-armed troops (*levis armaturae milites*), used for various purposes.

The legions were designated by numbers, as the *tenth* and *ninth*, but sometimes also by special names, as of the country from which they came. Cicero, in his Fourteenth Philippic against Antony,

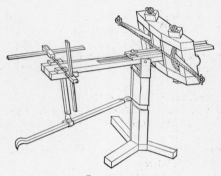

CATAPULTA.

delivers an eloquent panegyric in honor of the soldiers of the *Legio Martia*, or Martian Legion, who had fallen in the defense of their country.

From Polybius we learn that each legionary soldier received as pay (*stipendium*) three and one-half *asses* (about seven cents) a day, and a centurion twice as much. Caesar, according to Suetonius, doubled their pay before the Civil War. The common soldiers also received an allowance of corn, and the centurions twice as much.

1 9 **esset perventum:** 208. d ; H. 302. 6. For the mood, see 580 ; H. 643.

1 10 **impedimenta:** literally, *that which gets in the way of the feet, a hindrance ;* then applied in the plural to the baggage of an army, because it hindered its march so much. It consisted of tents, artillery, such as *ballistae* for hurling large stones and *catapultae* (see cut on page 55) for hurling huge darts, — in fact, all the baggage that the soldiers could not carry themselves. It was carried on pack-animals, and of course a large number of men had to accompany it in order to drive the animals and care for them when they halted. All these made a long baggage train, which would prove a great hindrance to an army on the march. Beside the *impedimenta* each legionary soldier was expected to carry a pack (*sarcina*) of articles for his own use. Cf. note on **30** 1.

1 10 **relinquerent:** 588; H. 642. 4. *Contionatus*, etc., may be translated *harangued his men, urging them to*, etc.

1 11 **quo . . . posset:** 531. a; 414. a. N.; H. 568. 7 ; 479.

1 13 **imperaret** and **esse facturos:** both depend on *conclamantibus;* for the former, see 588; H. 642. 4; for the latter, 580; H. 642.

1 15 **II. Non. Ian.:** i.e. *pridie Nonas Ianuarias*, Jan. 4, 48 B.C. See 631; H. 754. In 46 B.C. Caesar reformed the calendar by adding eighty days to that year, and by the reformed calendar this date would have been Nov. 5, 49 B.C. We thus see that Caesar actually crossed into Greece in the autumn of 49 B.C. and not, as he states, in the following midwinter.

1 15 **Impositae:** sc. *sunt.*

1 17 **inter:** 435; H. 676. 1.

2 2 CHAP. 2. **in hiberna:** to go *into winter-quarters.*

2 3 **re nova:** *this news*, i.e. the news of Caesar's arrival in Greece. Notice that the English generally requires a more definite word than *thing* to render *res.*

2 6 **At ille:** *but the latter* (Caesar); *ille* is often used at the beginning of a new sentence when there is a change of subject, and must usually be translated by some such expression as *the latter, the other*, or by the name itself.

2 8 **iussu:** 94. c; 404; H. 143; 475. 3.

2 9 **Parthinorum:** a tribe of Illyria, near Lissus ; see map opposite page 51.

2 9 **conatus portis,** etc. The English language does not favor so long sentences as the Latin ; consequently it is best to try to divide the sentence into two or more parts without losing the meaning of the original, e.g. *closed the gates and attempted to defend the town; but when,* etc.

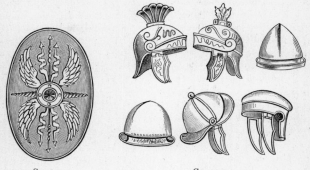

SCUTUM. GALEAE.

2 10 arma : all the legionary soldiers were armed in the same way in Caesar's time. The defensive armor consisted of shield (*scutum*), helmet (*cassis* or *galea*), and corselet (*lorica*) which was fastened by the sword-belt (*cingulum*), and sometimes greaves (*ocreae*). The offensive armor consisted of the sword (*gladius*) and the javelin (*pilum*).

The *scutum* was made of wickerwork or of wood; a common size was four feet long by two and one-half wide. It was worn on the left arm and was often curved to fit the body. The *cassis* was a metal helmet and the *galea* one of leather. Sometimes the helmet was a mere cap fitting the head closely; sometimes it was lined with felt or sponge to make it easy to wear and

LORICA.

to deaden blows. It was often adorned with bosses and crests. The *lorica* was a sort of loose coat or shirt of linen or leather covered with scales or hooks of metal. This allowed free movement of the limbs and body and yet was a great protection against a sword or even arrows and darts.

The *gladius* was a straight, two-edged sword used in close encounters with the enemy.

The *pilum* was a strong, heavy spear; the shaft was of wood and about five and one-half feet long, while the head, about nine inches long, was of iron. This made a ponderous weapon, which could be hurled a short distance or used for thrusting.

2 19 CHAP. 3. **arcem:** in ancient times nearly every town depended on its own strength and resources for protection; consequently it was necessary that there should be some place which, like the blockhouses in the early history of our own country, could be a refuge in case of attack.

GLADIUS.

Therefore, in choosing a site for a settlement it was customary to pick out some inaccessible hill or rock and fortify it. Hence arose the *arx* (cf. *arceo, shut in, ward off*), *the thing that shuts in* and so *wards off, the citadel.*

2 21 **negare:** 463; H. 610.

2 22 **praeclusuros:** *prae-, before, in the face of.*

2 22 **neque sibi,** etc.: *would not presume to come to a decision contrary to that of all Italy and the Roman people.* For *contra atque,* see 384. N. 2; H. 657. 1. N.

2 26 **oppido:** 429. 1; H. 485. 2.

3 5 CHAP. 4. **Dyrrachio:** 367. c; H. 426. 4. All Pompey's supplies were there.

3 8 **exercitui:** 370; H. 429.

3 10 **signa:** a silver or bronze eagle (*aquila*) was the standard of the whole legion, whence the legion itself was sometimes called *aquila.* The bearer of the eagle was the *aquilifer,* who was the *primipilus,* or first centurion of the first cohort of a legion, and was promoted to this position for his courage and strength. Each cohort, maniple, and century had a standard, but what the device was is

PILA.

not now clearly known, though it is probable that in some cases it was an animal. The bearers of these standards were called *signiferi*. The figures and devices were borne on a crosspiece at the end of a long pole or staff, which had a spike at the lower end with which to stand it in the ground or even to repel an attack. The standard of the cavalry was a sort of flag called *vexillum*. These standards were used as rallying points for the troops in case of a rout. They were looked upon by the soldiers

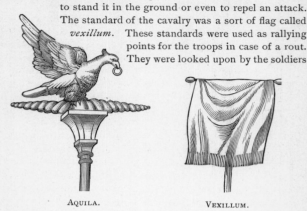

AQUILA.   VEXILLUM.

with great reverence and were guarded with great care, being kept in times of peace in the public treasury.

3 12 **castraque metari :** i.e. *castra munire*, which Caesar commonly uses. *Metari* (from *meta, a goal*) indicates the measuring off of the ground, the fixing of the *limits* of the camp. Camps among the Romans were of three kinds in the time of Caesar : first, *castra hiberna*, winter-quarters, where the armies passed the winter in tents or huts built with special care to protect them against the inclement weather ; second, *castra stativa*, permanent camps, established at different points for the settlement or occupation of a country. Many of these became towns, and the origin of the second part of such names as Dorchester, Colchester, etc., can be traced to them ; third, the ordinary camps, constructed daily by an army on the march. No Roman army passed the night without the protection of a camp more or less completely fortified according to circumstances.

If an attack of the enemy was feared, the camp was made stronger than usual. The form of the camp was always the same, being a rectangle whose length was to its width as 3 is to 2. A body of men was sent ahead of the main army to pick out a suitable spot, which, if possible, was on a slope near water, wood, and provender. There

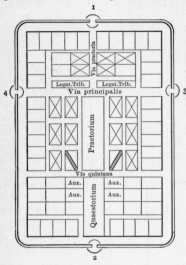

ROMAN CAMP.

1. Porta praetoria. 2. Porta decumana. 3. Porta principalis dextra. 4. Porta principalis sinistra. Legat. Trib., i.e. Legati et Tribuni militum. Aux., i.e. Auxilia.

were two main streets at right angles to each other; one ran lengthways of the camp, dividing it into halves, and ended in front (i.e. next the enemy) in the *porta praetoria*, and in the rear in the *porta decumana ;* this was called the *via praetoria.* The other street, called the *via principalis,* ended on the right in the *porta principalis dextra,* and on the left in the *porta principalis sinistra.*

The camp was surrounded by an *agger*, or rampart, and outside of this by a *fossa*, or moat. Inside the rampart a broad space was left for the free passage of the soldiers in case they were called on to defend the camp against an attack and for the storage of booty. Within this space were pitched the tents (*tabernacula*), the legions surrounding the cavalry and auxiliaries. The *contubernium* mentioned in **30** 3 is a tent which ten men and their *decanus*, or officer, occupied; sometimes the word also designates the *men* themselves, as well as the *tent.* The *praetorium* mentioned in **34** 15 was the general's tent; the word was also used to indicate the open space around this tent.

3 14 **Labienus:** *Titus Atius Labienus* had been tribune of the people in 63 B.C., and during Caesar's campaigns in Gaul was his most trusted lieutenant. At the outbreak of the Civil War, however, in 49 B.C., he had gone over to Pompey, and became very bitter against Caesar. He was slain in the Battle of Munda in Spain, 45 B.C.

3 14 **procedit:** *stepped forth.*

3 15 **eundemque:** sometimes a clause with a negative is connected with a following clause that has no negative by the conjunction *que*, which by a difference of idiom must then be translated by *but*.

3 16 **ei:** i.e. *Pompeio.*

3 16 **Hoc idem:** 390. c ; H. 409. 1.

3 17 **legati, tribuni militum, centuriones:** it has been seen in the note on *legiones*, **1** 6, that in battle the real leaders of the Roman soldiers were the *centurions*, who were promoted for their bravery from the rank and file, and rarely, if ever, rose above the position of centurions. They always came from the common people, while the *tribunes of the soldiers* and the *lieutenants* came from the patricians, or wealthy classes. Each legion had six *military tribunes*, appointed by the consul in command of the army. They commanded by turns, and it was their duty to preserve order in camp, to drill the men, to procure provisions, etc. The number of *legati* varied with the size of the army and the importance of the undertaking from three to the fifteen that Pompey had in Asia. They were men of great military experience, capable of advising and assisting their general in all measures, but they had no independent power, and their general was always responsible for their acts (see **14** 10 et seq.). In the absence of the general one of them acted in his stead. They were nominated by the general they served under, but this nomination had to receive the sanction of the senate. The general, or commander-in-chief (*dux belli*), was one of the consuls or proconsuls.

3 21 **castellis:** *fortified posts* or *redoubts* for a more or less permanent occupation.

3 21 **vigiliis:** *outposts* or *sentinels* within easy communication of one another.

3 22 reliquarum legionum: when Caesar reached Brundisium, he found there only a small number of transports — far too few to carry his whole army, which according to **1** 6 consisted of twelve legions. Seven of these had crossed with him into Greece. The remaining five are referred to here. Pompey's army at this time far outnumbered Caesar's, and his fleets ruled the sea.

3 23 sub pellibus: *under skins*, i.e. *in tents*. The Roman tents were generally covered with skins stretched on ropes and wooden props; this was for warm weather. In winter the soldiers were usually quartered in towns or, if in camps, in huts made of stone or turf. They looked upon it as very severe treatment if they had to live in tents in winter.

TABERNACULA.

3 25 auxiliaque: all the foreign allies of Rome were obliged to send a certain quota of troops to serve with the Roman armies. These were never legionary soldiers, but light-armed troops (*milites levis armaturae*) or cavalry, and were allowed to fight in the way peculiar to each nation. Thus one nation would be famous for its archers (*sagittarii*) and another for its slingers (*funditores*). The Cretans were famous archers, and the inhabitants of the Balearic Isles were famous slingers. The auxiliaries were made up largely of slingers and archers.

4 1 CHAP. 5. **bina castra:** why is *bina* used? 137. b; H. 164. 3.

4 4 P. Vatinium: an unprincipled adventurer whom Cicero calls one of the greatest villains that ever lived. He was one of Caesar's tools and when tribune of the people helped Caesar obtain the Gallic provinces and Illyricum; for this help he was made Caesar's lieutenant and supported him till his death.

4 7 liceretne: asking *if it was not allowable ;* 586 ; H. 642.

4 8 quod etiam: sc. *id* as antecedent to *quod.*

4 9 saltu Pyrenaeo: "supposed to refer to the wreck of Sertorius' army" in Spain.

4 9 praedonibusque: the *pirates* who had infested the Mediterranean, and whose power Pompey had completely overthrown.

4 .10 **cum id agerent, ne,** etc.: *when their aim was not to allow,* etc.

4 10 **cives cum civibus:** notice how different cases of the same word are often put close together for emphasis; cf. *civibus ad cives* above.

4 15 **visurum quem ad modum:** *would see how they might,* i.e. *would provide a way for them to.*

4 17 **Quo:** i.e. *ad conloquium.*

4 17 **cum esset ventum:** i.e. *when they had come.* Cf. *esset perventum,* **1** 9.

4 19 **exspectatio eius rei:** *interest in this event.*

4 21 **submissa oratione:** *in a moderate speech, speaking calmly.*

4 24 **quae ille:** i.e. *Vatinius;* cf. note on *at ille,* **2** 6.

4 28 **nisi:** 420. 4; H. 489. 2.

5 1 Chap. 6. **Antonius:** the famous Mark Antony, one of the most profligate men Rome ever produced. He won Caesar's favor in the Gallic wars, and became his most devoted partisan and an able *legatus.* In 49 B.C., through Caesar's influence, he became tribune of the people. At the Battle of Pharsalia he commanded the left wing of Caesar's army. After Caesar's death he tried to succeed to his power, but was defeated by Octavianus. When Caesar crossed from Italy to Greece, he left Antony at Brundisium with such troops as he could not, through lack of transports, take with him, but with orders to cross over as soon as possible. On its way back to Italy Caesar's fleet had been partially destroyed by Pompey's fleet commanded by Marcus Bibulus, so that lack of ships and the fear of an attack had thus far kept Antony from crossing.

5 4 **nacti Austrum:** *taking advantage of a south wind.* The Roman vessels were square-rigged, and so a south wind would be especially advantageous, as they could run before it.

5 5 **Apolloniam:** 395 and N. 2; H. 413.

5 8 **remissiore vento:** abl. abs. expressing cause; *because the wind had died down* (literally, *become more gentle*). Antony's ships were transports using the wind for a motive power; Coponius had warships which were driven by oars.

5 14 **si ... remisisset:** *if the wind should happen to die out*

Not a past condition contrary to fact, but a vivid future indirectly quoted; 592. 2; H. 649. I.

5 17 ab Africo tegebatur: by an island off the mouth of the harbor.

5 19 intro est itum: i.e. *introitum est,* as often in prose. Tmesis; 640.

6 2 CHAP. 7. **venientibus** and **imprudentes** both refer to Antony's soldiers.

6 3 si . . . posset: 576. a; H. 649. II. 3.

6 4 castris stativis: *permanent camp,* any camp occupied for more than a single night. Cf. *castra metari,* **3** 12.

6 6 Sed Caesari circuitu, etc.: *but Caesar had a longer march* (than Pompey) *to make, following a more roundabout route up the river.* The river was too deep for him to cross near his camp, especially with Pompey's army on the opposite bank. Consult the map opposite page 51 for these and the following movements.

6 9 magnis itineribus: *forced marches.*

6 13 quo esset: when is *quo* used to express purpose? See note on **quo posset, 1** 11. Cf. *'ut posset,* line 7, and *ne circumcluderetur,* line 17.

6 14 per Graecos: *by the Greeks,* i.e. through their agency, implying that the news spread among them and so reached Antony, and that they were not voluntary agents.

6 15 sese castris tenuit: *remained in camp; castris* expresses means, as well as place; 429. 1; H. 485. 2; Lodge's *Gildersleeve's Latin Grammar,* 389, last ¶. Cf. line 12, *in castris continuit.*

6 18 ad Asparagium: *to the neighborhood of Asparagium.*

6 19 idoneo loco: why no preposition? Cf. *castris,* line 15.

6 22 CHAP. 8. **eodem:** adverb; *to the same place.*

6 22 expugnato oppido: *having taken a town by assault.* Compare *ex-pugnare, to take by assault,* and *op-pugnare, to attack, assail,* without necessarily being successful.

6 26 acie instructa . . . fecit: best rendered as if it read *aciem instruxit et . . . fecit.*

6 26 decernendi: *decernere* means *to decide by combat, to fight a decisive battle.*

6 27 **Ubi . . . animadvertit** : compare with *postquam . . . cognovit*, line 21. In place of either construction we might have had *cum* with what mood and tense ?

7 2 **omnibus copiis** : ablative of accompaniment, as in **6** 18; 413. a ; H. 474. 2.

7 5 **commeatum** : *provisions*, especially grain.

7 6 **apparatum** : all sorts of military *supplies*, such as weapons, armor, artillery, etc. Caesar's army was not large enough to force Pompey into a decisive battle by attacking him behind his fortifications, and so he employs the only means in his power to draw him out : he threatens his base of supplies.

7 6 **ut accidit** : *and so* (literally, *as*) *it turned out.*

7 8 **diverso ab ea regione itinere** : *in the opposite direction from that region*, i.e. from Dyrrachium.

7 14 **Dyrrachium** : i.e. *ad Dyrrachium ;* Pompey is completely outgeneralled.

7 17 CHAP. 9. **ubi propositum**, etc. : *not being able to keep to his purpose.*

7 21 **navium longarum** : up to the beginning of the First Punic War the Romans had no fleet worthy of the name ; but then they saw clearly that they could not succeed against Carthage without a pow-

NAVIS TRIREMIS.

erful navy, and in the year 260 B.C. the senate ordered a fleet to be built. Accordingly, taking as a model a wrecked Carthaginian *quinquereme*, they built a large fleet, and, in spite of some reverses, in the course of a few years became a great naval power. For description of the different kinds of ships and their equipment, etc., consult Harper's *Dictionary of Classical Literature and Antiquities.*

7 23 **comportari imperat**: *impero* takes a passive or deponent infinitive; but what construction does it require when the dependent verb is in the active?

7 24 **ductum iri**: for the more common form of expression see **37** 2.

7 27 **fecerat**: i.e. *faciendas curaverat;* so *constituit,* **8** 3.

8 2 **hae regiones**: sc. *Epiri.*

8 4 **Lisso Parthinisque**: *from Lissus and the Parthinians;* to be taken with *conquiri.*

8 5 **quod esset**: 592. 1; H. 652. 1.

8 10 **spoliatis**, etc.: *while their homes were robbed*, etc.

8 12 CHAP. 10. **consilium**: a bold plan, as Pompey's forces greatly outnumbered his own.

8 13 **ex loci natura**: *suited to (in accordance with) the nature of the ground.*

8 16 **ferebat**: i.e. *postulabat.*

8 16 **perducta munitione**: *by drawing a line of fortifications.*

8 17 **instituit**: *began. Instituo* with the infinitive generally means *to begin*, while *constituo* with the infinitive means *to determine, to resolve;* cf. *hiemare constituit,* **3** 23.

8 18 **haec spectans**: *with this in view*, referring to the purpose clauses *quo ... posset, uti ... efficeret,* and *ut ... minueret,* which are in apposition with *haec.*

8 21 **simul**: here equivalent to *deinde, in the second place.*

8 22 **ad rem gerendam**: expresses purpose, *for carrying on the war*, or *for active operations.*

8 23 **ille**: i.e. Pompey. So *illum* just below.

8 25 **percrebruisset**: cf. *remisisset,* **5** 14.

8 26 **proelio dimicare**: *to fight a decisive battle.*

9 2 CHAP. 11. **tela, arma:** *missiles, arms. Tela* are weapons that are thrown from a distance, such as arrows (*sagittae*), javelins (*pila*), etc. ; *arma* are weapons for close combat, such as the sword (*gladius*), battle-axe (*bipennis* or *securis*), club (*clava*), etc., but *may* include defensive armor, like the shield (*clipeus*), the corselet (*lorica*), the helmet (*galea*), etc. Cf. note on *arma*, **2** 10.

9 2 **tormenta:** *engines of war*, like the *catapulta, ballista*, and *scorpio*, corresponding to modern *artillery.*

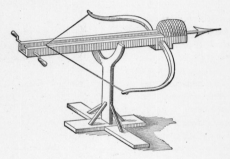

SCORPIO.

9 5 **nisi . . . vellet:** 516. f; H. 545. II. 3.

9 6 **Relinquebatur ut:** *the only course left was to ;* the verb is impersonal, its real subject being *ut . . . distineret.*

9 9 **quam maxime posset:** 593 ; H. 652. Notice that *posset* might have been expressed with *quam plurimos* or *quam latissimas.*

9 10 **idque accidit:** cf. *ut accidit*, **7** 6.

9 12 **multaque:** *and many things*, i.e. many kinds of grain.

9 14 **munitiones perductas:** *a line of fortifications which had been drawn ;* the participle is equivalent to a relative clause. Caesar tries to make the investment complete by connecting the redoubts with a wall flanked by a ditch.

9 16 **illi:** to whom does *illi* refer?

9 16 **interiore spatio :** *in the space within*, or merely *within our line ;* but in line 20 it expresses cause.

9 21 **Atque cum erant loca**: *and whenever there were points*, etc.; 519, 520; H. 601. 4. When *cum* means *whenever*, i.e. denotes repeated action, it takes the indicative.

9 23 **suis locis**: *at suitable points; suus* is often equivalent to *idoneus;* its opposite is *alienus.*

9 28 **quibus vitarent**: purpose clause; 531. 2; H. 590.

10 1 CHAP. 12. **In occupandis praesidiis**: *in occupying posts;* when is the gerundive used, and when the gerund? 503, 507; H. 623; 631. 1.

10 4 **maximo circuitu**: 409; H. 476.

10 8 **una ex parte**: *on one side;* notice that the Latin means *from one side,* as if to call attention to "the place from which the action proceeds"; 429. b; H. 485. 4. Cf. *ex omnibus partibus,* line 13.

10 12 **uno tempore**: *at one and the same time.*

10 14 **recipere se**: *se* is the object of *recipere,* the subject *eos* being omitted.

10 15 **per declive**: *down a slope.* The two hills seem to have been connected by a ridge somewhat lower than the two summits; along this ridge Pompey's men can charge without receiving the hail of missiles that must fall upon Caesar's men as soon as they abandon the hill and begin to retreat down the opposite slope.

10 15 **Illi**: i.e. Pompeiani.

10 19 **non recusare**, etc.: *he did not object to being considered;* 558; H. 595. 2.

10 20 **si . . . recepissent**: what tense would have been used in the direct discourse? 589. a. 3. example 2; H. 644. 2.

10 23 CHAP. 13. **receptui**: cf. *Dyrrachio,* **3** 5.

10 23 **ad extremum tumulum**: *the edge* or *brow of the hill next the enemy.* The fascines, or hurdles (*crates*), were of wicker-work and seem in this case to have been fastened to poles (called *longurii* below) set upright in the ground, thus forming a line of mantlets behind which the soldiers could work on the ditch in comparative safety (*tectis militibus*).

10 24 **adversas**: *facing* the enemy, i.e. so as to protect Caesar's men from the enemy's missiles, as mentioned just below.

10 25 **mediocri latitudine :** *of moderate width*, i.e. *of less than the usual width*, for which see note on *vallum contra hostem*, **20** 4.

11 9 **a medio fere spatio :** i.e. from a point about halfway up the slope down which he wished his men to retreat.

11 10 **tuba :** the *tuba* was a long, straight trumpet, the *cornu* being curved ; it produced a harsh and fear-inspiring note and was used in war for signals of every kind, as well as at games and public festivals.

11 12 **pila :** the *pilum*, or javelin, was a thick, heavy spear used sometimes to hurl and sometimes to thrust with ; the *iaculum* and *spiculum* were light *darts* of much the same shape, generally used as missiles. *Hasta* is a general word and includes all kinds of spears, large or small, heavy or light. Cf. notes on *tela*, **9** 2, and *arma*, **2** 10.

11 12 **ex inferiore loco :** *from lower ground*, and so at a disadvantage. The Roman army always tried to attack a foe from higher ground, as this gave the second and third ranks of spearmen a chance to hurl their spears over the heads of the first rank.

TUBA.

11 13 **cursu :** to be taken with *incitati ;* 418 ; H. 480.

11 13 **praecipites :** predicate adjective agreeing with *Pompeianos;* 393. N. ; H. 410. 3.

11 14 **ad recipiendum :** i.e. *ad se recipiendos.*

11 17 **compluribus :** sc. *hostium.*

11 22 CHAP. 14. **tantoque spatio,** etc.: *when we consider the length of the lines and the number of the fortifications ;* for the abls. *numero*, etc., see 404 ; H. 475.

11 24 **Nam . . . continuerunt :** a general truth, with which Caesar contrasts his own attempts at this time. Notice the perfect tense used, as is the gnomic aorist in Greek, to express a general truth by referring to one case of it in the past ; see 518 ; H. 538. 5.

11 26 **cum ipsi :** *while they themselves.*

12 1 **At tum :** *but at this time.*

12 2 **continebat :** *tried to hold in check.*

12 2   **illi :** refers to *milites* implied in *copias* just above.

12 4   **navium :** sc. *onerariarum ; transports* were much bulkier than *naves longae*, having round bottoms and being intended for carry- ing large cargoes slowly. They were mostly pro- pelled by sails, but some- times by oars.

NAVIS ONERARIA.

12 6   **quin haberent :** *without their* (i.e. the ships) *having a fair wind from some direc- tion ;* 559 ; H. 595. 4.

12 6   **Ipse :** i.e. Cae- sar ; 298. c ; H. 509.

12 10   **in Hispania :** Caesar had gone to Spain the year before to subdue it before follow- ing up Pompey.   At one time a great storm caused the rivers to rise so high that his army was cut off from provisions and suffered great hardships.

12 12   **ad Alesiam :** *near Alesia.*   Alesia and Avaricum (below) were two Gallic towns, in the siege of which Caesar's army under- went great privations.   Caesar describes the sieges in the *Gallic War*, Book VII.

12 14   **Non, illis hordeum cum daretur :** i.e. *non hordeum recu- sabant, cum illis daretur.*

12 15   **pecus vero :** the Roman soldiers usually lived on grain, a monthly supply of which was issued regularly, and they would not eat meat unless forced to by circumstances.

12 19   CHAP. 15.   **ad similitudinem panis :** *a sort of bread.*

12 21   **panes :** *loaves of bread,* while *panis* above is collective.

12 22   **famem nostris obiectarent :** *taunted our men with hunger ;* literally, *threw hunger in the faces of our men.*

12 23   **maturescere :** it was now June, and Pompey had been hemmed in nearly four months.

12 26 **in vigiliis:** the night from sunset to sunrise was divided into four *vigiliae*, or *watches*, which varied in length according to the season of the year. It was also divided into twelve *hours*. The *bucinator* blew the signals on a *bucina* (trumpet) for the four military watches of the night.

12 27 **ex arboribus:** i.e. *arborum*.

13 2 CHAP. 16. **eorum:** i.e. *Pompeianorum*.

13 3 **ipsos:** i.e. *Pompeianos*.

13 5 **insuetos operum:** gives the reason why their health was *unfavorably affected by their daily labors*. Many of Pompey's followers, belonging to the rich and aristocratic families of Rome, were *not used to hard work;* for the case of *operum*, cf. 349; H. 451. 1.

13 5 **cum . . . tum:** *not only . . . but also*. Notice that the second member, as always, is the more important.

13 9 **has:** i.e. *valles;* what Caesar did may be explained as follows : where the small streams passed through the line of hills extending parallel with the coast and back of Caesar's line of redoubts, he dammed them up, forcing them to flow, some north, some south, into streams that did not enter Pompey's lines. He tried to cut off Pompey's troops from the river Palamnus, but we shall see later that he did not succeed.

13 11 **illi:** i.e. *Pompeiani*.

13 16 **tum:** *and besides.*

13 18 **cuius melius tempus:** *the proper* (literally, *better*) *season for which*, i.e. *harvest time.*

13 20 **rationes:** *methods.*

13 26 **ut alio . . . facerent:** the next words were probably *alio excubarent*. A considerable passage must have been lost here. The following chapter shows at least that the account of an attack by Pompey upon one of Caesar's redoubts is gone.

14 1 CHAP. 17. **P. Sulla:** nephew of the great dictator. He was elected to the consulship for 65 B.C., but was convicted of bribery and so debarred from assuming the duties of that office. He was suspected of being an accomplice of Catiline. In the Civil War he chose Caesar's side, and commanded the right wing at the Battle of Pharsalia.

14 2 **castris:** i.e. Caesar's first camp, marked *c* on the plan opposite page 8. Caesar had gone to attack Dyrrachium, and it is supposed that the preceding chapter contained an account of the attack.

14 9 **potuisse finire:** supply *eum* as subject, easily understood from *voluisset.*

14 10 **atque imperatoris:** i.e. *atque aliae partes imperatoris.* Cf. note on *legati,* etc., **3** 17.

14 12 **ad summam rerum:** *for the general welfare.*

14 13 **hoc:** refers to *liberatis suis.*

14 15 **reciperet:** 446 and 447. 3. N.; H. 552 and 554. 3.

14 17 **ad receptum:** cf. *ad recipiendum,* **11** 14.

14 21 **spe conficiendi negoti:** *in hope of success.*

14 22 **necessario atque ex tempore:** *as the needs of the time required.*

14 23 **tumulum:** marked *i* on the plan.

14 25 **adigi:** *to be driven to,* i.e. *to reach* (it).

15 3 CHAP. 18. **ne succurri posset:** used impersonally, *that no aid might arrive.*

15 4 **Volcatius Tullus:** one of Caesar's officers, mentioned also in the *Gallic War.*

15 6 **Germani:** probably Caesar's German cavalry.

15 7 **incolumes:** not acc.

15 9 CHAP. 19. **tribus ad Dyrrachium:** see note on *castris,* **14** 2.

15 12 **evocatos:** men whose term of military service had expired and who had consequently been disbanded. They were sometimes *called out* by some general to serve under him and were then called *evocati,* which may be translated by *volunteer veterans.* The *veterani* differed from them in that they were not disbanded at the expiration of their term, but continued in service. Both were probably released from the common duties of fortifying a camp, and many of them were promoted to be centurions.

15 13 **L. filius:** i.e. *Luci* [*Valeri Flacci*] *filius.*

15 15 **non amplius XX.:** i.e. *non amplius quam viginti; amplius* has no effect on the following numeral; 407. c; H. 471. 4.

15 17 **quin volneraretur :** cf. *quin haberent,* **12** 6.

15 18 **cohorte :** for the divisions of the Roman army and its officers, cf. note on *legiones,* **1** 6.

15 21 **scutoque :** cf. note on *arma,* **2** 10.

15 24 **milibus CC. :** sc. *sestertium ;* i.e. 200,000 *sestertii ;* as the *sestertius* is reckoned at five cents, this must mean a gift of some $10,000. This and the following lines illustrate well how Caesar rewarded valor and fidelity both in individuals and companies.

15 24 **ab octavis ordinibus ad primipilum :** *from first centurion of the eighth cohort to first centurion of the first cohort* of his legion, i.e. the chief centurion of the legion, a great promotion. The ten cohorts of a legion were ranked in importance from the tenth up to the first, and each had six centurions. In natural sequence a centurion was promoted from the lowest of the six through the others to the first, and then to the lowest in the next higher cohort, where the same process was repeated. Cf. notes on *legati,* etc., **3** 17, and *centurionibus,* **21** 20.

16 1 **veste :** the usual garment of the common soldiers and inferior officers was the *sagum,* a thick, woolen cloak open in front and generally fastened across the shoulders by a clasp. In time of war it was customary for all citizens except those of consular rank to wear the *sagum* even in the city. The general and superior officers wore the *paludamentum,* a purple cloak shaped much like the *sagum* and worn like it ; it was ornamented according to the rank of the wearer. When a general received the *imperium,* or military command, he offered up his vows in the capitol and then marched out of the city arrayed in the *paludamentum ;* he was not allowed to reënter till he had laid it aside. The common soldiers and even centurions wore on their feet *caligae,* a sort of heavy sandals, the soles of which were studded with hob-nails. In contrast with the *sagum* and *paludamentum* was the *toga,* or garb of peace, the principal outer garment worn by the Romans over the *tunica,* or tunic.

16 2 **militaribusque donis :** Kraner says this refers to *crowns, necklaces, bracelets, spears,* etc. These were given as marks of distinction.

16 5 CHAP. 20. **eam partem :** i.e. where the towers were, perhaps joining them.

16 7 **subnubilam :** notice the force of *sub, somewhat,* a force it often has when it forms a part of a compound adjective; 291. c. N.2. It seems from *alteram* that the night on which Pompey had attacked one of Caesar's redoubts (cf. note on **13** 26) was also cloudy.

16 7 **nactus :** cf. *nacti,* **5** 4.

16 8 **ad impediendum obiectis :** *thrown down* or *left as an obstacle* (ob-) *to hinder* our attack.

16 9 **antiquas munitiones :** marked *d* on the plan.

16 11 **si . . . vellet :** cf. *si posset,* **6** 3.

16 12 **ut . . . subiceret :** result.

16 13 **uti ne :** not the same as *ut non,* although the preceding *tantum* would seem to imply this. We must understand that Caesar stationed his men so near for this very purpose; 537. a. N.; H. 570. 4. Cf. also Madvig 456. Obs. 4.

16 13 **telum tormentumve :** the former refers to any missile thrown by hand, while the latter means a missile hurled by an engine. *Tormentum* literally means the engine itself. Cf. notes on *tela* and *tormenta,* **9** 2. Compare the text with **14** 24.

16 15 **hominum :** subjective gen.; *that men entertained of him.*

16 16 **tertia acies :** we must understand that Pompey drew up his army in triple line of battle.

16 20 CHAP. 21. **aditus duos :** i.e. to the town of Dyrrachium; two gorges through which two roads ran, meeting just east of the town.

16 22 **nihil profici equitatu :** Pompey sent his cavalry out to forage, as shown in *pabulatione prohiberet* above, and at the same time to do the enemy what damage they could.

17 2 **quae . . . sata :** cf. *multa sata,* **9** 12.

17 4 **navigationis spatio :** *voyage.*

17 5 **minor :** *too small.*

17 6 **adaugere :** *to increase by adding* (ad-), i.e. *to eke out.*

17 15 CHAP. 22. **optima :** predicate adj. with *erat usus, had found most valuable;* H. 477. 2.

17 16 **domi :** i.e. *apud Allobroges.*

17 17 **in senatum :** sc. *Allobrogum.*

17 17 **legendos curaverat :** *had caused to be chosen ; to cause a thing to be done* may be expressed by *efficere* followed by *ut* and the *subjunctive*, or by *curare* followed by the *gerundive*, as here.

17 19 **rei pecuniariae :** i.e. *pecuniae.*

17 23 **despiciebant :** *began to look down on.*

17 24 **praedam omnem domum avertebant :** *steal all the plunder ;* literally, *turn all the plunder aside to their own home.*

17 25 **illi :** i.e. the cavalry of the Allobroges.

17 27 **falsum . . . deferri :** besides taking something from the pay of each horseman (cf. *stipendium fraudabant* above) they sent in false names or the names of men already dead, and drawing pay for them kept it.

18 1 CHAP. 23. **neque tempus,** etc.: *thinking that no time for the punishment.*

18 3 **quod . . . haberent :** *for having used their fellow-horsemen for private gain ;* 592. 3 ; H. 649. I.

18 5 **ex praeteritis suis officiis :** *according to his past favors.*

18 5 **reliqua :** sc. *officia* from the preceding *officiis.*

18 7 **ad omnes :** *in the eyes of all.*

18 9 **animi conscientia :** *their guilty consciences.*

18 10 **liberari :** sc. *poenā.* They probably remembered the case of Acco, who, as Caesar tells us in his *Gallic War*, stirred up a rebellion of the Senones. Caesar put off the whole affair till the end of the war, because he thought the summer was the time for war, not for an investigation. He then held an investigation and punished Acco severely. The two brothers might well fear the same treatment, if they remained with Caesar.

18 16 **cum munere aliquo :** *with,* i.e. *bringing, some gift,* referring to the death of Volusenus.

18 19 **proinde ac :** sc. *si ;* cf. 524 ; H. 584. 2.

18 22 **participes :** *as accomplices.*

18 23 CHAP. 24. **Quos :** acc. governed by *duxit* in *circumduxit,* **19** 3, *circum* governing *praesidia ; quos* is also governed by *ostentavit ;* 395 ; H. 413.

19 2 **praeter consuetudinem**: *unusual;* equivalent to an adj. in the same construction as *novum*, which is here used substantively.

19 4 **miles**: *foot-soldier, infantryman*, as contrasted with *eques, cavalryman.*

19 6 **volgo vero universi**: *in truth about all.*

19 7 **earumque regionum omnium**: gen. of characteristic, for which we might have had *in iis regionibus omnibus conscripti.*

19 8 **Sed hi**: i.e. the brothers.

19 8 **cognitis**: *since they knew.*

19 10 **temporibusque rerum**: *the times set for* different *duties*, referring to all the regular camp duties.

19 11 **spatiis locorum**: *the distances between* different *points; animadversis* is to be supplied from *animadversa* below with both *temporibus* and *spatiis.*

19 12 **cuiusque eorum**: i.e. *each one* of Caesar's men; the clause *prout . . . ferebat* explains *varia diligentia.*

19 16 CHAP. 25. **ut demonstratum est**: at the end of Chap. **21**.

19 16 **tegimenta**: the purpose of these *coverings* was, as we find from the next chapter, to deaden the blows of stones and missiles. Another aim may have been to prevent the flashing of the helmets from betraying their presence to Caesar's men.

19 17 **aggerem**: *rubbish*, material for filling in moats. Cf. note on *expugnavit*, **33** 21.

19 21 **cohortes LX.**: as Pompey's legions were full at this time, a cohort must have contained about 360 men; so *sixty cohorts* would make a force of over 20,000 men. These were led directly against the northern side of Caesar's line at *e* (cf. map opposite page 8), while the forces on the ships were landed south of his line to attack the same point from that side.

19 21 **ex maximis castris**: marked *d* on the plan.

19 22 **ad eam partem**: the southern end of Caesar's line of fortifications, where it bent westward and came to the sea. A careful study of the plan will well repay the trouble.

19 23 **a maximis castris**: marked *c* on the plan.

19 26   **naves longas:** ships of war were usually propelled by oars and moved with astonishing speed, so that they were especially useful at this time. Consult note on **7** 21.

19 28   **quaestorem:** the *quaestors* were at first only two in number, chosen from the patricians. They had charge of the public money, received the public revenues, and paid the public debts; this latter duty they performed only by direction of the senate, being simply its agents. In later times, beginning about the year 400 B.C., their number was increased, and plebeians were sometimes elected. Henceforth a quaestor accompanied each army. At first he merely received the plunder and distributed it, but later he had charge of the money and paid the soldiers.

20 1   **positum habebat:** how different from *posuerat?* Cf. 497. b and footnote; H. 431. 3.

20 4   CHAP. 26. **pedum XV.:** i.e. *in latitudinem.*

20 4   **vallum contra hostem:** it will be noticed on the plan that there were two lines of fortifications along this side of Pompey's position. The northern one, *facing the enemy*, is here meant. The material from the ditch was used in constructing the *rampart* (*agger*). The height of the latter (as here) seems usually to have been two-thirds the width of the top of the trench. In the *Gallic War* (Book II. Chap. 5) these dimensions are respectively twelve feet and eighteen feet, and these may be taken as the usual dimensions. The outside of the *rampart* was usually turfed, and the whole work strengthened by means of *hurdles* (*crates*) imbedded in the earth.

20 10   **ut . . . resisti:** *in order that, if they should become involved in a double contest* (i.e. be attacked in the rear as well as in the front), *they might be able to offer effective resistance.* Both verbs are used impersonally.

20 13   **XVII.:** to be taken with *milium.*

20 14   **perficiendi:** i.e. *operum perficiendorum.*

20 21   **milites:** i.e. *the light-armed soldiers* mentioned in **19** 18.

20 21   **in exteriorem vallum:** *against the outer* (i.e. southern) *rampart.*

20 22   **legionarii:** i.e. Pompey's *legionaries*, or *heavy infantry*, who had marched down directly against the northern wall.

20 23 **scalis admotis:** abl. abs., while *tormentis* is abl. of means. Cf. note on **33** 11.

20 25 **sagittariorum:** also from the ships. They probably landed at the ends of the two walls and, as the cross-wall (cf. *transversum vallum*, line 15) had not been finished, could easily rush up between them and around both ends.

AQUILIFER.

21 1 **vitium munitionis:** i.e. the unfinished cross-wall.

21 4 **in aversos nostros:** *upon our men from behind.* The arrows on the plan show the direction of the three attacks.

21 6 Chap. 27. **tumultu:** equivalent here to *repentino impetu.*

21 6 **cohortes:** the number is lost.

21 7 **ex castris:** marked *g* on the plan.

21 8 **fugientes:** *the fugitives;* cc. plu. masc.

21 10 **quodcumque:** sc. *militum.*

21 11 **corruptum timore:** *carried away by the panic.*

21 13 **gravi volnere adfectus:** i.e. *graviter volneratus;* H. 476. 2.

21 14 **aquilifer:** cf. note on *signa,* **3** 10.

21 14 **viribus deficeretur:** equivalent to *vires eum deficerent.* Cf. *frons deficiebat,* **17** 8.

21 15 **Hanc:** sc. *aquilam* from *aquilifer* above.

21 17 **committere ut dedecus:** (be guilty of) *permitting a disgrace to,* etc.

21 19 **incolumemque:** we should say *but* instead of *and;* cf. note on *eundemque,* **3** 15.

21 20 **centurionibus :** as each cohort had six centurions, five were slain ; those of the *first* cohort ranked highest in the legion.

21 21 **principem priorem :** in full, *primum principem priorem,* in which *priorem* indicates the *first* centurion, *principem* of the *principes* (cf. *legiones,* **1** 6), and *primum* of the *first* cohort ; i.e. the third centurion of the first cohort and consequently of the legion. The centurions were called, beginning with the highest of the first cohort : *primus pilus* (for *pilanus*) *prior ; primus pilus posterior ; primus princeps prior ; primus princeps posterior ; primus hastatus prior ;* and *primus hastatus posterior.* The first one was also called simply *primus pilus,* or *primipilus ;* this was the most important centurionship in the legion. The centurions of the second cohort were indicated in just the same way by substituting *secundus* for *primus,* and so on with all the other cohorts. Cf. notes on *signa,* **3** 10, and *legati,* **3** 17, and *ab octavis ordinibus,* **15** 24.

21 23 CHAP. 28. **non mediocri terrore inlato :** *to the no small alarm of ;* abl. abs.

21 24 **reliquis cohortibus :** i.e. those of the ninth legion ; cf. **19** 28.

21 24 **et M. Antonius :** *when Mark Antony,* as if it read *cum M. Antonius.*

21 25 **locum praesidiorum :** marked *h* on the plan.

22 2 **ut . . . conligerent :** result.

22 3 **per castella :** *from redoubt to redoubt.*

22 7 **ut . . . posset :** result.

22 8 **nec minus :** *and nevertheless.*

22 8 **aditum navibus haberet :** *had communication with his fleet.* In **7** 19 the same expression means that the ships could make a landing.

22 10 **castra secundum mare :** marked *l* on the plan, while *k* indicates the position of Pompey's new camp.

22 13 CHAP. 29. **quod instar,** etc. : *which seemed the equivalent of a legion.* How many cohorts, then ? The relative *quod,* instead of agreeing with its antecedent *cohortes* in gender and number, agrees with the predicate nom. *instar ;* 306 ; H. 396. 2.

22 15 **hic :** *as follows.*

22 17 **ut demonstravimus :** cf. Chapters 12 and 13.

22 17 **circummuniret :** notice the change of tense from *obiecisset.* The object of the verb is *eas,* referring to *copiis.*

22 22 **eadem** [*castra*]: the same that Caesar had abandoned. With the added fortifications (mentioned below) the same as *vetera castra* above, marked *m* on the plan.

22 23 **relicto :** *having left standing.*

22 25 **maioribus :** sc. *castris.*

22 26 **locum obtinebant :** *took the place of.*

22 27 **munitionem ad flumen :** sc. *Palamnum.* This fortification, or wall, is marked *n* on the plan.

23 2 **Ita :** *in this condition,* i.e. abandoned.

23 5 CHAP. 30. **Eo :** *thither,* to be taken with *inlato.* Some indefinite word, like *rem,* referring to *signo . . . inlato* must be understood as the object of *renuntiarunt.*

23 5 **legionis :** the *cohortes quasdam* of **22** 13.

23 6 **idem :** not *īdem.*

23 8 **novis Pompei castris :** i.e. the camp outside Caesar's lines, marked *k.*

23 11 **quae . . . praeberent :** his aim was to make Pompey's men think that the redoubts were protected as usual.

23 15 **castraque minora :** just called *castra vetera,* into which Pompey had thrown his legion.

23 15 **duplici acie :** the usual formation was *acies triplex, triple line of battle,* but here the *double line of battle* was used, five cohorts probably being in each line. Cf. note on *legiones,* **1** 6.

23 19 **ipse :** i.e. Caesar.

23 20 **ericius :** a sort of *chevaux de frise,* consisting of a beam set with spikes or even sword-blades and placed before the gate of a town or fortification to prevent the advance of the foe. It is named *ericius* because of its resemblance to a hedgehog (*er*).

23 25 **castellum :** cf. *castelli atque arcis locum,* **22** 25.

23 26 **eo :** *thither,* to be construed with *receperat.*

23 27 **ibi repugnantes :** best rendered by a relative clause, *who opposed them there.* The participle is acc., not nom.

24 1 CHAP. 31. **Sed fortuna :** Caesar ought not to blame *fortune* for what happened here. If he and his men had taken ordinary precautions to secure themselves a means of retreat in case of defeat, the disaster that followed would have been less serious, if not avoided entirely.

24 1 **plurimum potest :** *plays a very important part.* A general truth, so the present tense is used, as well as in *efficit*.

24 3 **ut accidit :** cf. *idque accidit,* **9** 10.

24 4 **supra :** cf. **22** 26.

24 6 **cum . . . arbitrarentur :** *in search of the gate, thinking,* etc.

24 8 **coniunctam esse :** sc. *munitionem* as its subject, and also as the object of *transcenderunt ;* this clause explains *Quod,* which is a relative, but may be translated as if it were *id.*

24 13 CHAP. 32. **ab opere :** they were building a new camp by the sea, as we learn indirectly from **22** 10 and **23** 8.

24 15 **a nostris :** to be taken with *cernebatur.* Caesar's men caught sight of this line of battle and were discouraged. Pompey's men in the camp likewise saw it and were correspondingly encouraged.

24 18 **ab decumana porta :** see description of the Roman camp under *castra metari,* **3** 12.

24 20 **angusto itinere :** probably refers to the same thing as *prorutis munitionibus* in **24** 9. The wall extending from the camp to the river Caesar's men had pulled down for a short distance ; this opening gave them a chance to pass through when no enemy opposed, but was too narrow to afford a safe retreat for them in case of defeat, when all would want to rush through at once.

24 20 **per aggeres :** the *ramparts,* or *walls,* of the camp, to which the cavalry had come after passing through the breach in the wall.

24 21 **Dextrum cornu :** cf. *dextri cornus,* **24** 5.

24 23 **ne opprimeretur :** pure purpose, therefore not an apposi-tive of *terrore,* the subject being *dextrum cornu ;* 531. 1 ; H. 568.

24 23 **ea parte :** 429. a. N. ; H. 476.

24 25 **ne inciderent :** *that they might not get into the crush.* This sentence, as well as the next, is too long for good English. Cf. note on *conatus portis,* **2** 9.

25 3   **ex vallo :** to be taken with *cernerent.*

25 4   **angustiis :** must refer to the narrow space between the inner and outer lines of fortifications mentioned in **22** 23, et seq.

25 6   **receptu :** cf. *sese recipiebat,* **24** 24.

25 9   **eodem cursu :** *with the same speed* as before.   Plutarch says that on this occasion one of the fugitives, when Caesar tried to stop him, would have killed him, had not a centurion cut off his hand just in time.

25 10   **neque quisquam omnino :** *and not a single man halted.*

25 11   Chap. 33.   **His . . . haec :** *his* refers to the above disaster, *haec* to the following *quod*-clause.

25 12   **deleretur :** depends on the idea of *hindering* or *preventing* implied in *his . . . succurrebant ;* 558. b ; H. 568. 8.

25 16   **angustiis . . . occupatis :** *by the narrow passage and by the fact that it was,* etc.   The antecedent of *his* is *angustiis,* which refers to the opening made in the wall that extended down to the river.   A part of the right wing seems to have protected the retreat of the rest.

25 17   **ad insequendum :** *in (respect to) their pursuit.*

25 20   **propriam . . . victoriam :** *a decisive and complete victory on Caesar's part.*

25 22   **eadem res :** *and the same thing.*

25 24   Chap. 34.   **unius diei proeliis :** *battles fought within one day. Diei* is a possessive gen.

25 25   **equites :** the numeral telling how many cavalry were lost and probably the first name of Tuticanus have disappeared from the manuscripts.

26 2   **Placentia :** *of Placentia,* the abl. of place from which, used here instead of the adj. *Placentinum.*   So *Puteolis* and *Capua* below.   This construction is not common, the adj. being preferred.

26 6   **signaque militaria :** cf. note on *signa,* **3** 10.

26 7   **imperator est appellatus :** a victorious general was often saluted by his soldiers as *imperator.*   Pompey suffered himself to be thus addressed, but did not assume the usual mark of this position, the *wreath of laurel.*   He refused to use the title officially, because he had won it in *civil* war.

26 10 **praetulit :** a case of *zeugma ;* 640; H. 751. 2. N. It may be translated *employ* or *use* with *in litteris.* Generals who had won many victories were in the habit of adorning with *laurel* or *bay* their writings, especially their official correspondence, as well as the fasces which the lictors *carried before* them.

26 11 **Labienus :** the same as the one mentioned in **3** 14 and **4** 21. Cf. note on **3** 14.

26 12 **omnes productos :** equal to *omnes produxit et,* and better so translated ; *omnes* is the object of *appellans, interrogans,* and *interfecit* equally.

26 13 **perfugae :** in apposition with *sui* understood and depending on *fides ; that greater confidence might be felt in him as a deserter* by his new friends.

26 13 **commilitones :** refers to his old *companions in arms* still serving under Caesar.

26 14 **magna verborum contumelia :** *with most insulting words.*

26 15 **veterani milites :** cf. note on *evocatos,* **15** 12. After this battle Pompey was advised to embark with his army for Italy, leaving a small force to oppose Caesar, who could have followed him only by marching around the head of the Adriatic. This course would have enabled Pompey to gain possession of Rome and make extensive preparations for Caesar's approach. But after having gained a victory he was unwilling to retreat as if defeated, and so remained where he was, with disastrous consequences to himself and his army.

26 17 CHAP. 35. **fiduciae ac spiritus :** partitive gen. with *tantum ;* 346. a. 3 ; H. 442.

26 17 **Pompeianis :** dat. with the intransitive verb *accessit,* which is a compound of the preposition *ad ;* 370; H. 429.

26 18 **non cogitarent :** *no longer thought.*

26 21 **praeoccupatis :** sc. *a Pompeianis.*

26 22 **abscisum . . . exercitum :** *the cutting of the army in two.*

26 23 **altera . . . alteri :** for the idiom see 315. a ; H. 516. 1.

26 24 **causae fuisse :** sc. *fugae nostris ;* 382. 1 ; H. 433. 1.

26 25 **dimicatum :** sc. *esse.* Used impersonally.

26 26 **ipsos :** i.e. *nostros.*

26 26 **multitudine:** does not contradict *paucitatem*, **26** 19; it means merely that there were too many men crowding together to get through the narrow breach in the wall.

26 27 **accepissent:** what would have been the mood and tense of the direct discourse?

26 28 **communīs casūs:** acc.; 350. d; H. 455.

27 2 **obiectae religionis:** "as when the English in France quailed before the imaginary witchcrafts of Joan of Arc."—Moberly.

27 4 **esset offensum:** impersonal.

27 5 **vicissent:** 524 (cf. N. 2); H. 584. 1 and 2.

27 8 CHAP. 36. **a . . . depulsus:** causative; *because he had been forced to abandon.*

27 9 **Itaque,** etc.: too long a sentence to be translated literally into good English.

27 10 **uno tempore:** cf. *uno tempore,* **10** 12.

27 13 **accidissent:** *had happened.* Why subjunctive? 592. 1; H. 652. 1.

27 14 **multisque . . . opponerent:** *but contrast.* Cf. note on *eundemque,* **3** 15.

27 17 **bellicosissimorum hominum:** gen. depending on *ducibus,* which is abl. abs. with *peritissimis* and *exercitatissimis,* equivalent to the subjunctive with *cum* concessive.

27 19 **provincias:** Sicily and Sardinia, the usual sources of grain supply for the Romans.

27 21 **oppletis . . . litoribus:** another concessive abl. abs. Sc. *hostibus* after *oppletis.*

27 23 **fortunam:** *ill-luck,* contrasted with *felicitate* above.

27 24 **cuiusvis:** gen. depending on *culpae,* which is in the dat. with *tribui.*

27 25 **suae:** dat. of the possessive adj. *suus,* but equivalent to the gen. of the reflexive pronoun *sui,* and so contrasted with the gen. *cuiusvis.*

27 26 **ad dimicandum:** *to fight in;* literally, *for fighting.* As commander, Caesar had naturally chosen as favorable a position as possible for battle.

27 27 **pugnantes:** sc. *hostes* (acc.).

27 28 **ipsorum**: *their*, referring to the men Caesar was address-ing; it would have been *vestra* in the direct discourse.

28 2 **ut . . . sarciretur**: substantive clause of purpose after *dare operam;* 563. e; H. 564.

28 4 **ut . . . verteret**: substantive clause of result, subject of *futurum [esse]*; 569. a; H. 571. 1 and 619. 2 and 3.

28 4 **uti**: *as*. Why is *accidisset* in the subjunctive? 580; H. 643.

28 4 **ad Gergoviam**: why not *Gergoviae?* 428. d. Gergovia was an important town in Gaul belonging to the Arverni. Caesar attacked it, as he relates in the *Gallic War* (Book VII. Chap. 41 et seq.). It was defended stubbornly, and he was finally forced to withdraw unsuccessful. It is said to have been the only Gallic town that successfully resisted his attacks; but his failure here was only preliminary to the capture of Alesia.

28 7 CHAP. 37. **signiferos**: cf. note on *signa*, **3** 10. As the usual punishment for throwing away standards was death, Caesar here showed great clemency.

28 11 **et sibi**: we should say *but* in English. Cf. also *neque . . . que*, lines 16 and 17.

28 11 **poenae loco**: is *loco* here the same abl. as *loco* in line 8? Cf. *eo loco*, line 14.

28 13 **cum . . . non nulli . . . existimarent**: *since some thought*.

28 14 **ordinis**: 345 ; H. 440. 3.

28 18 **relictis munitionibus**: abl. abs.; *now that he had left*, etc.

28 20 CHAP. 38. **sauciorum**: to be taken with *ratione;* 348; H. 440. 2.

28 21 **habita ratione**: *looking out for*.

28 22 **prima nocte**: 293; H. 497. 4.

28 23 **ante iter confectum**: compare *abscisum exercitum*, **26** 22.

28 25 **de quarta vigilia**: cf. note on *in vigiliis*, **12** 26.

29 1 **militare institutum**: when an army broke camp, it was the regular *custom* to give three signals: the first (*vasa conclamare*) was for striking the tents and packing up the personal baggage into bundles (*sarcinae*, **30** 1) ; the second was for putting the heavy bag-gage (*impedimenta*, **30** 1) on the beasts of burden; when the third was given, the soldiers fell into line and started on their march. It was, as Caesar intimates here, looked upon as a disgrace if a general left his camp without giving these signals. The chief signals were sounded before the general's tent.

29 6 **id spectans**: cf. *haec spectans*, **8** 18. *Id* is explained by the following *si . . . posset*.

29 7 **posset**: cf. *si vellet*, **16** 11.

29 9 **neque . . . potuit**: *but could not.*

29 10 **expedito itinere**: a march over good roads, where there is nothing to hinder the advance, either obstacle or foe.

29 11 **ventum esset**: impersonal, *they had come.*

29 11 **ripis**: 415; H. 473. 2. N. 2.

29 14 **antesignanos**: the soldiers of the first line of battle were so called because they fought before the standards (*signa*). They were in Caesar's army "a special corps of picked soldiers in each legion, who left the ranks for special and important services, such as seizing suddenly an important point, supporting the cavalry, manning ships."

29 18 CHAP. 39. **iusto itinere**: *a fair*, or *ordinary*, *day's march ;* this was usually a march of four or five hours, the distance traversed depending on the difficulty of the roads.

29 19 **in veteribus suis castris**: cf. *castra posuit*, **6** 25.

29 22 **per causam pabulandi**: this is a mere ruse to make the enemy think he has encamped for the afternoon and night. Its success gives Caesar an advantage over Pompey, which the latter cannot regain.

29 23 **decumana porta**: cf. note on *castra metari*, **3** 12.

29 24 **in suis veteribus castris**: cf. *castra ponit*, **6** 19.

29 25 **ad Asparagium**: cf. note on *ad Gergoviam*, **28** 4.

29 26 **ab opere vacabant**: *had nothing to do*, the reason being given in *integris munitionibus.*

29 27 **lignandi causa**: in good faith, while *per causam pabulandi* above gave a pretended reason ; *per causam* regularly has this force in Caesar's works.

30 1 **impedimentorum**: the heavy *baggage* of the army, including the tents, heavy camp implements, artillery, etc. All these things were carried by beasts of burden, each cohort having some fifty. A driver looked after each animal and also worked about the camp ; cf. note on *impedimenta*, **1** 10.

30 1 **sarcinarum :** the *packs* the soldiers carried on their shoulders. Each man had to carry unground grain for from one to fifteen or more days, a day's allowance being nearly two pounds ; he also carried cooking utensils and tools of various kinds. All this often weighed thirty or even forty pounds. The articles were, after the time of Marius, fastened to the prongs of a forked pole carried over the right shoulder. While carrying this pack and his armor, a soldier was encumbered (*impeditus*) and naturally could do little fighting. When he had deposited his pack, he was unencumbered (*expeditus*) ; cf. *expedito itinere*, **29** 10. The packs were left in camp, when there was one ; otherwise, they were placed in a pile and kept under guard. Each man had to grind his own grain and cook his own food.

30 3 **contubernio :** compounded of *con-*, for *cum*, and *taberna*, the original for a military *tent*, as it was made of boards (*tabernae*). Ten men called *contubernales* (*messmates*) occupied each tent, under the charge of a subordinate officer called *decanus ;* cf. note on *castra metari*, **3** 12.

30 4 **Quibus . . . impeditis :** i.e. *cum sequi non possent*.

30 4 **quod :** has for its antecedent the clause *Quibus . . . impeditis*.

30 5 **signo profectionis :** cf. note on *militare institutum*, **29** 1.

30 6 **duplicatoque :** does not here seem to mean that Caesar marched his men twice as far as usual in one day, but merely that he added another day's march, long or short, to the morning's march. By this means he gained about eight miles on Pompey.

30 9 CHAP. 40. **praemissis :** cf. **28** 21.

30 12 **expedito exercitu :** cf. note on *sarcinarum*, **30** 1.

30 13 **altissimis fluminibus :** abl. abs., equivalent to *cum* concessive with the subjunctive.

30 15 **primi . . . inlata :** abl. abs. ; *as he had been delayed the first day ;* but *labore suscepto* is concessive.

30 20   CHAP. 41. **ad saucios**: cf. *sauciorum*, **28** 20.

30 20   **stipendium**: cf. note on *legiones*, **1** 6.

30 23   **tantum temporis**: only *so much time*.

30 23   **properanti**: agrees with *ei* understood, depending on *necesse ; for him hurrying*, i.e. *for him in his haste*.

30 24   **Domitio**: *Cnaeus Domitius Calvinus* was one of Caesar's lieutenants. He had been tribune of the *plebs* in 59 B.C., when he opposed Caesar (then consul) and favored his colleague Bibulus ; he became praetor in 56 B.C., and consul in 53 B.C. ; he gained the latter position through the aid of Pompey. At this time he was in Macedonia, where he had been sent with an army by Caesar to intercept Scipio, Pompey's lieutenant, who was marching from the East to aid him.

31 1   **Totius rei consilium**: *the plan of the entire campaign.*

31 1   **his rationibus**: equivalent to *haec spectans*, **8** 18.

31 6   **transiret**: sc. *Pompeius*, as also with *conaretur* below.

31 7   **proficisceretur**: sc. *Caesar*, as also with *cogeret* below.

31 7   **Apolloniam Oricumque**: both towns were now in Caesar's possession.

31 9   **obsesso Scipione**: *Quintus Caecilius Metellus Pius Scipio*, father-in-law of Pompey, who, after the death of his wife Julia, Caesar's daughter, had married Cornelia, Scipio's daughter. Scipio was a senator and belonged to the aristocracy. In character he was unjust and dishonest, and he was one of Caesar's bitterest opponents. When he ran for the consulship (53 B.C.), there was so much corruption and violence that Pompey was made sole consul. After the restoration of order Pompey made Scipio his colleague and employed him in his attacks upon Caesar. At the beginning of the Civil War Scipio was Pompey's lieutenant in Asia Minor, where he tried to raise money and troops for him. After the Battle of Pharsalia he fled to Africa and commanded the Pompeian party at the Battle of Thapsus (46 B.C.). Being defeated, he tried to escape, but, not succeeding, put an end to his own life.

31 12   **Apolloniae**: locative.

31 14   **Athamaniam**: a mountainous district in the southern part of Epirus ; its chief town was *Argithĕa*.

31 19 **legiones:** Caesar still had two legions, one of veterans and one of raw recruits, in Italy under the command of Quintus Cornificius.

31 21 CHAP. 42. **celeritati:** 367 (cf. footnote); H. 426. 1.

31 23 **Apollonia:** cf. the beginning of Chap. 41 for the cause of Caesar's going to Apollonia. A glance at the map (opposite page 51) shows that he had to march southwest from Asparagium to reach Apollonia, and then southeast to go from there to Aeginium. Pompey probably followed the *Via Egnatia*, the main road from Dyrrachium to the Hellespont, as far as Heraclia.

31 24 **Candaviam:** a mountainous region lying to the east of Dyrrachium.

31 26 **quod:** *the fact that.*

31 27 **qui . . . habuisset:** concessive; 535. e; H. 593. 2.

32 1 **subiecta:** *on the borders of.*

32 2 **obicere:** *ob* in composition generally has the force of *in the way of*, as here; cf. *obiectarent,* **12** 22.

32 4 **proelio . . . facto:** fixes the time of *dimissis.*

32 5 **latius inflatiusque,** etc.: *more widely and with greater exaggeration than the facts warranted ;* to be taken with *percrebruerat.*

32 7 **Haec:** refers to *fama* for its antecedent.

32 10 **dimissi:** *the messengers sent.*

32 12 **Allobroges:** *some Allobroges.*

32 12 **Raucilli atque Egi:** cf. Chap. 22 et seq.

32 14 **pristina sua consuetudine:** *because of their former intimacy* with them.

32 17 **profectionem . . . docuerunt:** in what case should the person whom they informed be put?

32 22 CHAP. 43. **Gomphos:** a strong fortress of Thessaly, on the borders of Epirus; it commanded the chief pass between the two countries.

32 23 **quod:** why not *qui?* 306; H. 396. 2.

32 23 **venientibus:** 378. 2; H. 425. 4; Lodge's *Gildersleeve's Latin Grammar,* 353.

32 25 **ut . . . uteretur:** substantive clause of purpose, object of some word like *imperans* to be supplied from *legatos miserat.*

32 28 **quod :** acc. ; its antecedent is *proelio.*

32 28 **multis partibus :** 414 ; H. 479. 2.

33 1 **praetor :** the word the Romans used to translate the Greek στρατηγός, military governor.

33 7 **succurratur :** impersonal ; 208. d ; H. 302. 6.

33 11 **scalas :** *scaling ladders.* Some were like our common ladders. Some consisted of several parts which, when put together, formed one large ladder. Others were made entirely of ropes or leather, and had large iron hooks at the end with which to fasten them to the wall. Those mentioned in the text seem to have been constructed on the spot out of raw material.

33 11 **musculosque :** a sort of *shed,* much stronger than the *vinea.* Caesar describes one constructed to undermine the walls of Massilia. Two timbers were laid side by side on the ground, four feet apart, in which were set upright posts five feet high ; these were joined together by rafters, and the whole was roofed over with timbers two feet thick, which were held in place by metal plates and nails. The roof was then covered with bricks and mortar, kept in place by pieces of wood fastened along the edges of the roof and projecting above it. The bricks and mortar would protect the *musculus* against fire but not against water, so they were covered with skins ; but as the skins were not proof against fire, they were covered with rags, which would deaden the blows of the stones and would not readily burn.

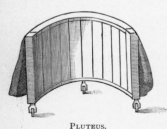

PLUTEUS.

33 12 **crates :** *hurdles, fascines,* — twigs or osiers interwoven or bound up in bundles. They were used in an assault to ward off the enemy's missiles, being placed over the soldier's head ; in **10** 23 Caesar uses them like *plutei,* as a shelter for the men to work behind, while intrenching themselves. Light ones were sometimes used to fill up moats outside the fortifications of a town, in order to facilitate the assaults of the besiegers.

33 14 **quantum usum haberet :** *how great an advantage it would be ; potiri, inferre,* and *fieri* are subjects of *haberet.*

33 15 **inopiam:** Plutarch relates that Caesar's men were worn out with hardships and were suffering with fevers. In Gomphi the soldiers found great quantities of wine, with which they soon became intoxicated, but were cured of the fevers.

33 19 **altissimis moenibus:** abl. of characteristic with *oppidum.*

33 21 **expugnavit:** a siege of unusually short duration; sometimes, if the walls of a town were especially strong and well defended, it required weeks to reduce it, if this could be accomplished at all. Many preparations were necessary, only a few of which are here mentioned. Towns were usually surrounded by a moat outside the wall, and this had to be filled in on the side chosen for the main attack. For this purpose rubbish of all sorts was used, but sometimes hurdles or fascines (*crates*), as in this case. In approaching the walls the soldiers had to be protected against the missiles hurled down upon them. This was done in different ways, according to circumstances. While they were working at some distance, the *crates* or *plutei* (a sort of large shield fastened to poles set in the ground) were enough, but as they came nearer, better protection was needed, and *vineae* and *musculi* were constructed. The *vineae* were long sheds with strong roofs and with sides of wickerwork. The ends were open, and several *vineae*, being placed end to end, made a long covered passage through which the soldiers carried material for the mound (*agger*). *Musculi* (**33** 11) and *vineae* were both constructed at a distance from the walls and then moved up, and sometimes wheels were put under them for this purpose. In some cases a mound was built on one side of the town as high as its walls and touching them, so that an assaulting party could easily make an attack. Then, again, towers were needed to overtop the walls and even the towers upon the walls. Engines of war of all sorts were brought up. Thus it can be easily seen that weeks or even months were sometimes necessary for the reduction of a town.

33 24 CHAP. 44. **primum:** seems to be used here for *primo, at first.* It is merely contrasted with *postea,* not used in a series. Cf.

322. d. N. and Lodge's *Gildersleeve's Latin Grammar*, 325. 7; but cf. also H. 657. 4. N. 2.

34 2 **Metropolitum:** for *Metropolitarum*; 43. d; H. 80. 1.

34 4 **magnis exercitibus:** *large forces*, as Scipio had only *one* army.

34 5 **pareret:** 559; H. 595. 4.

34 6 **quo:** sc. *loco.*

34 8 **eoque . . . conferre:** *to transfer thither the whole conduct of the war*, i.e. *to make that point the centre of future military operations.*

34 11 CHAP. 45. **parta iam victoria:** Pompey's success over Caesar had filled the nobles in his camp with confidence and made the whole army careless. They were already quarrelling over the fruits of a victory they had not won. The result of this overconfidence was their utter defeat.

34 14 **Scipione:** Pompey's father-in-law; cf. note on *obsesso Scipione*, **31** 9.

34 14 **classicumque cani:** *the trumpet* (literally, *trumpet-call*) *to be sounded*, as a mark of distinction. These signals were usually given before the general's headquarters. Cf. note on *militare institutum*, **29** 1.

34 15 **praetorium:** *general's tent*, or *pavilion*, which received this name because originally the name of the chief Roman magistrate was *praetor*, not *consul*. For its position, cf. note on *castraque metari*, **3** 12. For the soldier's tent, cf. note on *contubernio*, **30** 3.

34 21 **unius . . . diei:** *it was a matter of a single day;* in indirect discourse, depending on *dicerent.*

34 21 **illum:** i.e. *Pompeium.*

34 23 **sacerdotiis:** priests held their offices for life and were not responsible to any civil magistrate. So the fact that Pompey's followers were beginning to quarrel about the *priesthoods* shows that they expected to defeat Caesar's army, put to death those who held the offices, and themselves get possession of them. Caesar himself had been *pontifex maximus* since 63 B.C.

34 24 **in annosque:** *and for years* (to come).

34 27 **fuit controversia:** *there was a dispute* as to whether.

34 27 **Lucili Hirri:** objective gen. with *rationem*. Caius Lucilius Hirrus had been tribune in 53 B.C. The object of his embassy at this time was to gain allies among the Parthians, who a few years before had at an interview killed Crassus, Pompey's colleague, at that time governor of the Roman province of Syria. Nothing more is known of him except that he was made prisoner by the Parthians.

35 1 **proximis comitiis praetoriis:** *at the next election of praetors;* cf. note on *comitia,* **1** 1.

35 2 **rationem haberi:** cf. *habita ratione,* **28** 21.

35 2 **cum . . . implorarent:** translate by the present participle, *begging.*

35 3 **praestaret:** sc. *ut;* it is in an object clause of purpose after *implorarent.* Its object is *id,* the omitted antecedent of *quod.*

35 3 **proficiscenti:** agrees with *ei* understood, as indirect object of *recepisset;* cf. *properanti,* **30** 23.

35 4 **eius:** i.e. *Pompei.*

35 5 **reliqui . . . recusarent:** in the same construction as *necessarii . . . implorarent.*

35 5 **ne . . . antecederet, recusarent:** *objecting to one man's having the precedence of all the rest.* 558. b; H. 568. 8 and 596. 2; Lodge's *Gildersleeve's Latin Grammar,* 548 and N. 1.

35 9 CHAP. 46. **quo . . . videretur:** *for him to seem* (i.e. *think*); 537. 2; H. 591. 2.

35 9 **perspectum habere:** cf. note on *positum habebat,* **20** 1.

35 13 **suis locis:** cf. note on *suis locis,* **9** 23.

35 13 **pauloque . . . longius:** *and at some distance.*

35 14 **continentibus vero diebus:** *but during the succeeding days,* in contrast with *primo;* cf. note on *primum,* **33** 24.

35 15 **ut:** i.e. *sic ut, in such a way as to.*

35 15 **collibusque Pompeianis:** Pompey had encamped on the hills north of the Apidănus, about four miles from Caesar. See plan.

35 16 **Quae res:** *this manoeuvre.*

35 16 **eius:** i.e. *Caesaris.*

35 17 **Superius institutum:** cf. **29** 13. It was a favorite device

of the ancients to intermingle light-armed infantry with their cavalry for greater effectiveness. Xenophon, in his *Hellenica* (VII.
5. 24), tells us that Epaminondas employed this device at the Battle
of Mantinea.

35 20   ad pernicitatem : *for the sake of speed.*   Their heavier
armor was changed for lighter, that they might move with greater
ease and swiftness.

35 22   qui . . . perciperent : relative clause of purpose ; 531. 2 ;
H. 590.

35 24   mille : here a substantive, as the plural always is.

35 25   cum adesset usus : *when there was need.*

35 27   per eos dies : *during these days.*

36 1   unum : *Egus* or *Raucillus ;* cf. Chapters 22 and 42.

36 6   CHAP. 47.   exspectans si : *waiting to see whether.*

36 6   iniquis locis : cf. *suis locis,* **9** 23.

36 6   subiceret : cf. note on *posset,* **29** 7.

36 9   ut . . . moveret : substantive clause of purpose in apposition with *rationem.*

36 10   in itineribus : *on the march.*

36 10   haec spectans : cf. *haec spectans,* **8** 18.

36 10   movendis castris : 507. (1) ; H. 626. 1 and 630.

36 13   insolitum : Pompey's army contained many of the nobles
and aristocracy of Rome, who were unused to the hardships of
camp life and marching.   For the usual construction after *insolitum,*
cf. 349. a; H. 451. 1.

36 16   detensis : for the opposite used with *praetorium,* cf.
34 15.

36 18   non iniquo : i.e. *aequo ;* what figure of speech ? 326. c ;
H. 752. 8.

36 18   dimicari videretur : used impersonally.

36 19   apud suos : *inquam* regularly takes *apud* and the acc.,
rarely the dat.

36 20   agmen : *column of march.*

36 20   inquit : 599. c; H. 679.

36 26   CHAP. 48.   proelio decertare : *to come to a decisive engagement ;* cf. *proelio dimicare,* **8** 26.

37 6 **Persuasi** : the sarcasm of this expression is wonderful ; it was only necessary for Pompey to *persuade* his cavalry to make this manoeuvre, and Caesar's army was doomed.

37 6 **equitibus:** 367 ; H. 426. 2. *Persuasi* has for its direct object *ut . . . aggrederentur*, etc. ; 563 ; H. 564. 1.

37 8 **ab latere aperto :** Caesar's right wing, as we may infer from the statement in **38** 27 that *a stream protected Pompey's right wing* and consequently Caesar's left. Consult the plan opposite page 38.

37 9 **prius:** goes with *quam* below.

37 14 **in posterum :** sc. *diem*.

37 14 **ut :** *as.* Cf. *uti*, **28** 4.

37 15 **usu manuque :** *in the actual engagement ;* literally, *in the reality and might* (of battle) ; in contrast with *cogitavissent*.

37 15 **reliquorum :** i.e. those not present at the council.

37 17 CHAP. 49. **Labienus:** cf. **3** 14 and **26** 11.

37 17 **cum . . . despiceret :** cf. note on *cum implorarent*, **35** 2.

37 19 **Noli :** 456. (1) ; H. 561. 1.

37 20 **devicerit :** subjunctive in a subordinate clause of indirect discourse ; 580 ; H. 643. What would have been the form in the direct discourse ?

37 23 **quod . . . fuit necesse :** *which could not fail to be the result ;* the antecedent of *quod* is the clause *magna . . . deperiit.*

37 23 **autumni pestilentia :** in the siege of Brundisium the health of Caesar's veterans, who had been used to the more salubrious climate of Spain and Gaul, suffered greatly.

37 26 **ex iis :** to be construed with *esse factas ;* 403. 2 ; H. 467.

37 27 **delectibus :** *drafts*, or *levies*, of soldiers made by regular officers from lists of citizens prepared for this purpose. Certain citizens were exempt, as with us, e.g. priests and men after a fixed age, usually forty-five years.

38 1 **horum annorum :** *of these last* (two) *years.*

38 6 **Hoc :** *this step.*

38 9 **discessum est :** impersonal.

38 14 CHAP. 50. **legiones duae:** *a* on the plan. These legions had been released to Pompey at the very beginning of the Civil

War, 49 B.C. The first Pompey had lent to Caesar and now demanded back; the third (at that time called the fifteenth) the senate had demanded from Caesar to help carry on the war against the Parthians. Pompey at once used them to oppose Caesar.

38 16 in eo loco: this was the usual place for the commander-in-chief. Here he was between the infantry and cavalry and could oversee the movements of both; *g* on the plan.

38 17 Mediam aciem: *b* on the plan.

38 18 Syriacis: *that had served in Syria.*

38 18 Ciliciensis: a legion of veterans which Pompey had brought from Cilicia; it was made up of the remnants of two legions, and so he used to call it "the twin legion."

38 19 Afranio: Lucius Afranius had been Pompey's lieutenant in the Sertorian War, had gained the consulship in 60 B.C. through Pompey's influence, and with Petreius had governed Spain for Pompey. Here he had been defeated by Caesar and allowed to go free on his parole. This he violated and joined Pompey in Greece, helping him in the Battle of Pharsalia. He was present at Thapsus, and while trying to escape was taken and killed by Caesar's men. The *Spanish cohorts* were some he had taken with him from Spain.

38 20 dextro cornu: *c* on the plan.

38 20 erant conlocatae: 317. N.; H. 389. 4.

38 21 inter aciem, etc.: *d, d* on the plan.

38 23 evocatorum: cf. note on *evocatos,* **15** 12.

38 24 duo [milia]: there were *2000 volunteer veterans* besides the *45,000* men.

38 24 beneficiariis: generals conferred favors (*beneficia*) on certain soldiers, who were hence called *beneficiarii ;* the favors might be exemption from menial duties, or honors of any kind.

38 27 castellis: "Pompey had connected his camp with the hill and with water-sources by lines of forts."

38 28 rivus quidam: *e* on the plan.

39 1 equitatum, etc.: *f* on the plan. Cf. note on *auxilia,* **3** 25.

39 3 CHAP. 51. superius institutum: not the same *custom* here as in **35** 17. The *tenth legion* was his favorite and had been made his praetorian cohort (a special body-guard) in his Gallic wars (cf. *Gallic War*, Book I. Chap. 41), and it was his *custom* to give it the post of honor in battle.

39 4 **dextro cornu :** 1 on the plan.

39 4 **sinistro :** 3 on the plan.

39 6 **attenuata :** cf. **23** 13 et seq.

39 9 **milium XXII. :** about half as many as Pompey, who had 45,000 ; cf. **38** 23.

39 10 **Sinistro cornu :** 429. 2 ; H. 485. 2. 3 on the plan.

39 10 **Antonium :** cf. **5** 1.

39 11 **P. Sullam :** cf. **14** 1.

39 11 **Cn. Domitium :** cf. **30** 24 ; 2 on the plan.

39 12 **Ipse :** cf. note on *in eo loco*, **38** 16 ; 5 on the plan.

39 12 **his rebus :** *these arrangements*, referring to the disposition Pompey had made of his troops, especially of his cavalry.

39 15 **tertia acie :** cf. note on *legiones*, **1** 6.

39 15 **singulas cohortes :** probably *one cohort from each legion ;* these were six in number, as we learn from **42** 4.

39 16 **quartam :** sc. *aciem.* It will be noticed that on this occasion, in addition to the three lines of battle usually employed, Caesar formed a fourth for a special purpose, namely, to repulse the attack of the cavalry ; 4 on the plan.

39 18 **constare :** when *moneo* means *remind* it takes the acc. and inf. in indirect discourse ; when it means *advise, warn,* it takes *ut* or *ne* with the subjunctive ; 580. d ; H. 565. 6.

39 22 CHAP. 52. **perpetui temporis officia :** *his constant kindnesses ;* literally, *his kindnesses of uninterrupted time.*

39 24 **quanto . . . petisset :** indirect question depending on *testibus,* as if it were a noun in the gen.; it tells that of which the soldiers were *witnesses.*

39 25 **Vatinium :** cf. note on **4** 4.

39 25 **Aulum Clodium :** a man of whom little is known. He was a friend of Scipio, who introduced him to Caesar. When Caesar learned that Scipio was in Macedonia, he sent Clodius to him with a letter, in which he said that he had tried to come to terms with Pompey, but had failed because he had not had suitable agents ; that he thought Scipio was just the man to accomplish this. It is needless to say that Clodius returned without accomplishing his purpose.

40 1   **ad Oricum :** *in the neighborhood of Oricum.*

40 1   **cum Libone :** *Lucius Scribonius Libo,* commander of Pompey's fleet. Pompey's son Sextus had married Libo's daughter. In the Civil War he sided with Pompey, as was natural, and went with him into Greece, where he took an active part in the war. On the death of Bibulus, commander of Pompey's fleet, Libo was made admiral. After Caesar's death he followed the fortunes of Sextus Pompey, but left him on seeing the hopelessness of his cause. He was consul with Marcus Antonius in 34 B.C. Caesar had a conference with him near Oricum to see if terms of peace could be agreed upon, but without success.

40 6   **signum :** *the signal* for the advance against the enemy. Chap. 51 (**39** 20) tells us that the signal for the charge was to be given with a flag.

40 7   CHAP. 53. **Crastinus :** not otherwise known.

40 8   **primum pilum duxerat :** *had been first centurion of the first century ;* cf. note on *principem priorem,* **21** 21.

40 10   **manipulares mei qui fuistis :** *ye who served in my maniple.*

40 11   **constituistis :** sc. *dare.*

40 20   CHAP. 54. **concursum :** *the charge,* literally, *the running together.* A certain distance (about a quarter of a mile) was deemed necessary for the charging lines to gain sufficient impetus for the shock. This, of course, made the weapons hurled during the charge more effective. *Concursus* is used when there are two armies, while *impetus* is used (as below) of the *attack* or *charge* of one army upon another.

40 22   **aciemque :** *but,* etc.

40 23   **C. Triari :** not much is known of him ; Caesar mentions him as one of the two commanders of Pompey's fleet from Asia Minor.

40 24   **militum :** sc. *Caesaris.*

40 25   **in suis . . . dispositi :** *drawn up in ranks ;* sc. *sui* for *dispositi* to agree with.

41 1   **dispersos :** sc. *hostes.*

41 2 **immissis telis :** 370; H. 429.

41 3 **fore :** depends on *sperabat.*

41 3 **duplicato cursu :** *by having to run twice as far ;* abl. abs.

41 10 **ut . . . tollerent :** subject of *institutum est ;* 563. d and 566; H. 564. II.

41 10 **signa :** nom.

41 13 CHAP. 55. **infestis pilis :** *with threatening javelins,* referring probably to the position in which they were held, i.e. raised ready for hurling.

41 14 **non concurri :** *that no charge was being made ;* impersonal.

41 22 **exceperunt :** sc. *scutis ; received with their shields,* i.e. *warded off.*

41 24 **equites . . . procucurrerunt :** under the command of Labienus.

41 25 **ut erat imperatum :** cf. *persuasi,* etc., **37** 6.

42 1 **loco motus cessit :** *fell back.*

42 4 **sex cohortium :** *consisting of six cohorts ;* 344; H. 440. 3. The gen. depends on *quam.* Cf. note on **39** 15.

42 5 **Illi :** referring to the men who made up the *quarta acies ;* 280. a; H. 397. Cf. *illi,* **12** 2.

42 7 **nemo consisteret :** Labienus has quickly forgotten his oath ; cf. **38** 4.

42 10 **destituti :** *abandoned* by the cavalry.

42 10 **inermes :** *without defense,* as they had no defensive armor or weapons suitable to meet the attack of Caesar's *quarta acies,* which was made up of heavy infantry.

42 10 **sine praesidio :** *with no force to protect them,* the cavalry having fled.

42 11 **cohortes :** i.e. Caesar's six *cohorts.* Plutarch says that Caesar ordered his men not to hurl their javelins, as they usually did, but to use them as pikes for thrusting. This was probably to enable them to protect themselves more effectively against the cavalry, and not, as Plutarch says, to wound the young nobles in the face, a thing the latter held in special horror.

42 17 CHAP. 56. **alii :** seems to have reference to the men implied in *cohortes,* line 11.

42 19 fefellit : impersonal.

42 19 quin . . . oriretur : used as if some negative expression of doubt, like *neque vero Caesari erat dubium*, preceded. The whole may be rendered : *Nor indeed was Caesar deceived in thinking that,* etc.

42 21 ut ipse . . . pronuntiaverat : cf. *monuitque,* **39** 17.

42 26 eam partem : sc. *suarum copiarum*.

42 27 cui : 367 ; H. 426. 1. What other case does *confido* sometimes take ? For the difference, see the lexicon.

43 2 praetoriam portam : cf. note on *castraque metari,* **3** 12.

43 4 si . . . acciderit : 516. *a, c,* and *d* ; H. 574. 2.

43 6 praetorium : cf. note on *praetorium,* **34** 15.

43 8 CHAP. 57. intra vallum : i.e. of their own camp.

43 11 etsi magno aestu : 420. 3 ; H. 489. 1 and 2.

43 12 ad meridiem : the battle was fought on August 9, so the heat at noon must have been intense.

43 14 relictae : cf. *reliquas* [cohortes], **38** 21.

43 16 barbarisque auxiliis : as the Thracians were barbarians, this must be rendered *and other barbarian auxiliaries*.

43 18 de reliqua fuga : *cogitare* with the acc. has the same meaning.

43 22 ducibus : in apposition with *centurionibus,* etc.

43 23 in altissimos montes : i.e. in the same direction as the cavalry had fled ; cf. **42** 9.

43 25 CHAP. 58. structas : *all finished*.

44 1 Luci Lentuli : Lucius Cornelius Lentulus was praetor in 58 B.C., and consul in 49 B.C. ; he strongly opposed Caesar. He was slain in Egypt along with Pompey.

44 1 non nullorum : *some others ;* cf. note on *barbarisque auxiliis,* **43** 16.

44 2 protecta hedera : i.e. against the sun's rays ; cf. note on *ad meridiem,* **43** 12.

44 4 de eventu . . . timuisse : *feared about the issue.* What is the force of *timere* with the acc. ? What with the dat. ?

44 5 qui conquirerent : 535. e ; H. 592.

44 5 non necessarias : what figure of speech makes a statement by denying its opposite ? Cf. *non iniquo,* **36** 18.

44 7 **exercitu :** dat.

44 7 **obiciebant :** *were wont to reproach Caesar's army with ;* literally, *to throw in their faces ;* cf. note on *obicere,* **32** 2. Caesar sometimes allowed his men to commit excesses, for Plutarch says his men got intoxicated with the wine they found at the capture of *Gomphi.* Kraner infers from Suetonius' life of Caesar that Caesar thought they would fight all the better if they were indulged now and then. The nobles in Pompey's camp forgot their own luxurious manner of living when they reproached Caesar's veterans.

44 10 **insignibus imperatoriis :** "the purple cloak (cf. note on *veste,* **16** 1) and the toga trimmed with purple." He did not wish to be discovered. This desertion of his army was an act of cowardice. Compare Caesar's conduct after his defeat at Dyrrachium under similar circumstances.

44 16 **tantum . . . fefellisse :** *that he was so mistaken in his opinion ; se* is object ; cf. **23** 16.

44 19 CHAP. 59. **a militibus contendit :** *earnestly begged his men.*

44 23 **iugis eius :** 429. a ; H. 476.

44 24 **versus :** 599. d ; H. 676.

45 3 **subluebat :** compare the force of *sub* in composition here with that in *subnubilam,* **16** 7.

45 13 CHAP. 60. **passisque palmis :** modifies *proiecti.*

45 13 **flentes :** agrees with the subject of *petiverunt* and is equivalent to an adverb modifying *petiverunt.*

45 16 **omnes :** he enrolled the common soldiers in his own army and fined those whose position warranted it, but put to death the senators and equites of importance, except a few.

45 17 **qui :** Lodge's *Gildersleeve's Latin Grammar,* 315. N. 2 ; for the use of this indefinite, see 149. b ; H. 512. 1.

45 17 **neu :** 224. II. e ; H. 568. 6.

45 17 **quid sui :** *anything of theirs,* referring to the subject of *desiderarent,* which refers to *eorum.* As a further mark of his considerateness, he is said to have thrown Pompey's letters unopened into the fire.

45 18 **Hac adhibita diligentia :** *having made these arrangements with great care.*

45 19   alias : *the other*.

45 22   Chap. 61.   milites : 407. c and N.; H. 471. 4.

45 25   mentionem . . . fecimus : cf. **40** 7.

45 25   in os adversum : *square in the face ;* literally, *into the face turned towards* the one striking.

46 1   Sic : is explained by *eo . . . fuisse.*

46 3   meritum : and so he did, for he was an *evocatus* and might have remained peacefully at home, but preferred, at Caesar's call, to volunteer his services.   Cf. Chap. 53.

46 5   sed : the *number of prisoners* is contrasted with the *number that fell*, and so we have *sed* used.   In English we should be more likely to say " and " or " while."

46 6   cohortes : cf. **38** 26.

46 8   signaque militaria : cf. note on *signa*, **3** 10.

46 8   ex proelio : *after the battle ;* literally, *out of the battle.*

46 10   vires . . . defecissent : cf. *viribus deficeretur*, **21** 14, and the note thereon.

46 13   Chap. 62.   quascumque in partes : *in whatever direction ;* it is the *limit of motion* of *persequendum.*

46 14   recepisset : what would have been the tense in the direct discourse ? 484. c ; H. 644. 2.

46 18   Amphipoli : a town in Macedonia on the river Strymon, about three miles from the sea.   The river flowed nearly around it, hence its name from the Greek, ἀμφί, *around*, and πόλις, *city*.   It was one of the most important places on the north Aegean Sea belonging to Athens.

46 19   iuniores : men from seventeen to forty-five years old ; these were considered of military age and were liable to be drafted for military duties.   Those over forty-five were too old for regular service, but were sometimes drafted in emergencies ; they were called *seniores*, as distinguished from the *iuniores*.   Cf. note on *delectibus*, **37** 27.

46 20   iurandi causa : *to take the military oath.*   The tribunes of the soldiers dictated the oath according to a prescribed formula ; it required the soldiers to meet at the command of the consuls and not leave the *signa* without their orders.   It was sworn on the *signa*.

which were looked upon as sacred, and was the most sacred of all oaths. The commander could by law put to death any man who violated this oath.

46 20   **utrum . . . an . . . :** a double indirect question, subject of *existimari poterat*.

46 24   **conaretur :** *was really trying*, equivalent to *really proposed*.

46 24   **ad ancoram . . . constitit :** the equivalent of *in ancoris exspectavit*, *Gallic War*, Book IV. Chap. 23.

46 27   **Mytilenas :** capital of Lesbos, renowned for its beautiful situation. In the beginning of the war Pompey had sent hither his wife, Cornelia, and his younger son, Sextus. They embarked with him when he reached Mytilenae. Cf. Plutarch's *Life of Pompey*.

47 2   **Cyprum :** formerly this island had belonged to Egypt, but now it formed part of the province of Cilicia. For the case of *Cyprum*, cf. 427. 2 ; H. 419. 2.

47 3   **Antiochensium :** Antioch was a magnificent city, capital of the Greek kingdom of Syria, and was founded about 300 B.C. It was in a beautiful valley on the Orontes river, and was one of the earliest strongholds of the Christians. It had received its independence from Pompey himself in 64 B.C.

47 6   **ne . . . adirent :** understand a word of *bidding* or the like from *nuntios* for it to depend upon.

47 9   CHAP. 63. **societatis :** sc. *publicanorum ; leagues,* or (business) *companies* of publicans, for collecting the revenues in the provinces. The publicans were usually of the equestrian order and purchased of the state the privilege of collecting the revenues in the different provinces. For this purpose they often formed companies and divided the profits.

47 10   **sumpta :** sc. *pecunia.*

47 12   **familiis societatum :** the revenue collectors must have had many slaves to help them ; hence *familiis*, the first meaning of which is *household slaves*, is here equivalent to *servis.*

47 13   **partim :** understand *quos* after the second *partim.*

47 14   **Pelusium :** a celebrated and strongly fortified city of Egypt on the eastern, or Pelusiac, branch of the Nile.

47 15   **Ptolemaeus :** the ten-year-old king of Egypt, son of

Ptolemaeus Dionysus (usually called Auletes, i.e. the Flute-Player) and brother of the famous Cleopatra, who was six years his senior. See note on *de Pompei morte,* **49** 24.

47 19 **eius :** i.e. *Ptolemaei.*

47 20 **misit :** sc. some word like *nuntios,* and cf. note on *ne . . . adirent* in line 6.

47 20 **pro hospitio :** Ptolemaeus Dionysus was expelled by the Alexandrians in 58 B.C., and went to Rome for aid. Through Pompey's influence Aulus Gabinius, pro-consul in Syria, was led to restore him to his throne. It was this favor on which Pompey relied for a friendly reception from his son.

47 20 **Alexandrīa :** abl. It was one of the most celebrated and most important cities of Egypt, founded by Alexander the Great, 332 B.C. It was opposite the island *Pharos,* on which stood an immense lighthouse (hence the French *phare, lighthouse, beacon*). The city contained a magnificent library founded by Ptolemy Soter and said to have consisted at one time of several hundred thousand volumes. The greater part of the library was destroyed by Christians in 391 A.D.

47 21 **illius :** i.e. *Ptolemaei.*

47 26 **eius exercitu :** i.e. *Pompei exercitu.*

47 27 **Gabinius :** *Aulus Gabinius,* who proposed the law by which Pompey was given the chief command in the war against the pirates. For restoring Ptolemy to his throne he was tried on a charge of treason and at the same time on a charge of bribery. He was convicted on the latter, and banished from Rome. He died 48 B.C.

47 27 **belloque :** i.e. *the war* to restore Dionysus to his kingdom.

48 1 CHAP. 64. **tunc :** *on this occasion,* i.e. when Pompey asked to be received and protected.

48 1 **amici regis :** these were Pothīnus, the king's minister, Achillas, commander of the king's army, and Theodŏtus of Chios, the young king's tutor. The latter especially urged Pompey's death.

48 2 **in curatione erant regni :** *had charge of the kingdom,* i.e. *were regents,* since the king was a minor.

48 6 **ex amicis,** etc.: *enemies grow out of friends,* i.e. *friends become foes.*

48 6 **exsistunt:** for the tense, cf. 465. (3); H. 532. 2.

48 8 **clam:** contrasted with *palam.*

48 10 **L. Septimium:** not otherwise known.

48 10 **ad interficiendum:** what other construction is more commonly used with *mitto* to express purpose?

48 11 **ipse:** i.e. *Pompeius.*

48 12 **quadam notitia:** *a slight acquaintance.*

48 12 **bello praedonum:** for many years the Mediterranean had been infested with bands of pirates, who had their headquarters in Crete and Cilicia and had grown so bold as even to attack places near Rome. In 67 B.C. Pompey was appointed sole commander in the war against them (cf. note on Gabinius, **47** 27), and in three months had destroyed them or driven them from the sea.

48 13 **ordinem duxerat:** *had been centurion.* In Caesar's works *ordo* is a common synonym of *centuria ;* hence *ordinem ducere, to lead a century,* or *to be a centurion ;* cf. note on *legiones,* **1** 6.

48 13 **naviculam parvulam:** notice the diminutives. It was said that the water was not deep enough near the shore for a larger boat, but some galleys lying close in proved that this was not so.

48 15 **L. Lentulus:** cf. note on **44** 1.

48 17 CHAP. 65. **in Asiam:** *to Asia Minor.* He went by way of Thrace and the Hellespont. It is said that while he was crossing the Hellespont with a small force Caius Cassius Longinus, one of Pompey's naval commanders, pursued him, but was so much surprised when Caesar demanded his surrender that he complied. Caesar pardoned him and conferred many favors upon him, but Cassius returned his favors by conspiring against him and helping to murder him.

48 17 **T. Ampium** (*Balbum*): a friend of Pompey and foe of Caesar. He had held several offices. After Caesar came into power, he banished but afterwards pardoned him.

48 18 **Epheso:** *from Ephesus ;* but we should say (*from the temple of Diana*) *at Ephesus.* The Latin idiom often requires two expressions, or even more, denoting the place from which or the place to which, while the English allows only one.

48 20 **in summa:** *as to the amount.*

48 22 **duobus temporibus:** the other occasion referred to is the following: when Scipio (cf. note on *obsesso Scipione*, **31** 9) was in Asia Minor he started to do the same thing that Ampius here attempted. He had called together the senators as witnesses of the sum, since he intended to restore it later, when he received a letter from Pompey informing him of the straits in which the latter found himself in Greece, and bidding him march to his relief at once. This he did without touching the money, and Caesar claims that indirectly he saved the treasure.

48 23 **Elide:** capital and chief city of one of the three divisions of Elis, a country in the western part of the Peloponnesus.

48 24 **repetitis,** etc.: *on reckoning and counting the days back to that on which,* etc.

49 3 **exercitus:** *of an army.*

49 4 **civitas:** i.e. *cives.*

49 5 **Ptolemaide:** a celebrated city on the coast of Phoenicia, and one of the oldest cities of that country. It is the French St. Jean d' Acre, so well known from the Crusades.

49 5 **Pergami:** a renowned city of Asia Minor, capital of the kingdom of Pergamus, and later of the Roman province of Asia. One of its famous citizens was the physician Galen.

49 6 **occultis ac reconditis:** neuter, to represent the gender of ἄδυτα in line 7.

49 8 **tympana:** a sort of drum, sometimes like a modern tambourine, sometimes more like a modern kettledrum, but small enough to hold in the hand. It was covered with ox-hide or ass-hide, and was beaten with the hand or with a stick.

49 8 **Trallibus:** a city of Asia Minor with a flourishing commerce. It was on a tributary of the Maeander river near the borders of Ionia and Caria. Caesar probably mentions these different miracles because he wishes it understood that, since he had twice saved the treasure in the temple of Diana at Ephesus, the gods were showing their approval of him and his successes.

49 13 CHAP. 66. **Cypri**: cf. note on **47** 2.

49 13 **Aegyptum**: H. 419. 2 ; Lodge's *Gildersleeve's Latin Grammar*, 337. N. 1.

49 14 **necessitudines regni**: *friendly relations with the kingdom ;* cf. note on *pro hospitio*, **47** 20.

49 15 **cum legione una**: cf. *legionem unam*, **46** 16.

49 16 **Achaia** : on the dissolution of the Achaean League, 146 B.C., the Romans formed all of Greece south of Thessaly into a Roman province with this name.

49 17 **Q. Fufio** (*Caleno*): a strong partisan of Caesar. He had been tribune of the people and praetor, and was one of Caesar's lieutenants in the Gallic War and in the Civil War. He adhered faithfully to Caesar, and after the latter's death became attached to Mark Antony.

49 18 **Rhodiis**: a famous maritime nation. The island of *Rhodes* in the eastern Aegean Sea is best known to us perhaps from the celebrated Colossus which bestrode the entrance to its harbor.

49 19 **milia tria**: only *three thousand*.

49 23 **dubitaverat**: what is the difference in meaning between *dubitare* with the *infinitive* and *dubitare* with *quin* and the *subjunctive ?*

49 24 **de Pompei morte** : Caesar passes very briefly over the death of Pompey, but we learn the particulars from other sources. After the disastrous Battle of Pharsalia Pompey fled to Egypt, hoping to gain the sympathy and aid of the Egyptians, or at least such protection as they could afford. Dionysus, commonly called Auletes, had died 51 B.C., leaving the throne of Egypt to his two children, Ptolemy and Cleopatra. The latter was expelled and fled to Syria, but soon returned with an army to claim her rights. When Pompey came in his flight to Alexandria and sought help, Ptolemy sent a boat to bring him from his ship to land. Pompey bade his friends farewell and stepped on board, quoting from Sophocles : " He who goes to meet a tyrant is his slave, even if he be free." Just as he was disembarking, he was stabbed in the back by Septimius (**48** 15). His wife and son saw the deed from the ship, but could do nothing to help him. He was slain Sept. 28, 48 B.C. ; had he lived one day longer, he would have been 58 years old.   His head was cut off and presented to Caesar on the latter's arrival.   Caesar was deeply moved at this unfortunate ending of the struggle, and caused Pompey's murderers to be put to death.   Caesar fell a slave to the charms of Cleopatra, who was so famous for her beauty, espoused her cause, and became involved in a war to restore her to her rights.   Ptolemy was at first in Caesar's power, but escaping put himself at the head of his troops.   He was defeated by Caesar, and while trying to escape was drowned in the river.   This struggle is known as the *Alexandrine War*.

"The tragedy of his death and the splendour of his achievements have made Pompey a great figure in history.   A true Roman in his faults and virtues alike, Pompey was a better man and an abler soldier than his detractors allow.   In an age of lax morality and of unblushing peculation, he was a good husband and father, and upright in his dealings.   In war he proved himself a respectable strategist, an able tactician, and a great organiser of victory, though even there he lacked the penetration to divine the plans of his opponent and the genius to inspire his followers with devotion.   In politics he was a man of second-rate capacity in a first-rate position. Splendidly adapted for the part devised for him by the quick wit of Cicero, that of ornamental chief of an optimate Republic, the irony of fate placed him in a position with which there was no paltering, where he must be king or nothing.   It was his misfortune to be born too late or too early, and to serve as a foil for a more brilliant rival."

INDEX TO NOTES.

WORD–GROUPS.

1 AC-, *sharp, pierce.*

ācer, *sharp.*
ācriter, *sharply.*
aciēs, *edge.*
oculus, *eye.*

2 AC-, *swift.*

equus, *horse.*
eques, *horseman.*
equester, *of a horseman.*
equitātus, *cavalry.*
aqua, *water.*
aquor, *get water.*

AG-, *drive.*

agō, *drive.*
adigō, *drive to.*
cōgō (coïgō), *drive together.*
exigō, *drive out.*
redigō, *drive back.*
castīgō, *punish.*
dēfatīgō, *tire out.*
āctuārius, *easily driven.*
ager, *field.*
agmen, *army on the march.*
coāctum, *felt.*
coagmentum, *joint.*

AR-, *fit.*

arma, *arms.*
armō, *arm.*

armātī, *armed men.*
armātūra, *armor.*
inermis, *unarmed.*

ARC-, *shut in, keep off.*

arx, *fortress.*
exercitātus, *busied, trained.*
exercitus, *trained body of men.*

AV-, *mark, delight, desire.*

autumnus, *autumn.*
audeō, *dare.*
audācia, *daring.*
audācter, *boldly.*
negōtium (nec ōtium for avtium), *business.*
negōtior, *do business.*
negōtiātor, *merchant.*

AVG-, *grow.*

augeō, *increase.*
adaugeō, *add to.*
auctōritās, *power.*
auxilium, *help.*

CAD-, *fall.*

cadō, *fall.*
accidō, *fall to, happen.*
incidō, *fall in.*
cāsus (cadtus), *fall, chance.*
cadāver, *dead body.*

occāsiō (occadtio), *falling in the way of*, *opportunity*.
occāsus (occadtus), *falling*, *setting*.
cēdō, *give place, go*.
accēdō, *go to*.
antecēdō, *go before*.
concēdō, *give way*.
discēdō, *go apart*.
discessus (discedtus), *departure*.
excēdō, *go out*.
incēdō, *advance*.
intercēdō, *go between*.
prōcēdō, *go forward*.
succēdō, *go under, approach*.

1 CAL-, *call*.

conclāmō, *shout together*.
clāmor, *shouting*.
clārē, *clearly*.
classis, the people called together, *class ; fleet*.
classicum, *trumpet-call*.

2 CAL-, *cover, hide*.

occultō, *conceal*.
occultus, *hidden, secret*.
occultē, *secretly*.
clam, *secretly*.

CAP-, *take, hold*.

capiō, *take*.
accipiō, *receive*.
dēcipiō, *deceive*.
excipiō, *take out*.
incipiō, *take in hand, begin*.
percipiō, *get*.
praecipiō, *take beforehand*.
recipiō, *take back*.

receptus, *retreat*.
suscipiō, *undertake*.
captīvus, *captive in war*.
deinceps, *one after another*.
mancipium, *taking by the hand ; slave*.
particeps, *sharer*.
prīnceps, *foremost*.
prīncipātus, *supremacy*.
occupō, *take possession of*.
praeoccupō, *preoccupy*.
praecipuē, *chiefly*.
caput, *head*.
anceps, *two-headed, double*.
praeceps, *headlong*.
praecipitō, *throw headlong*.

CAV-, *watch, ware*.

causa, *cause*.
recūsō, *refuse*.
recūsātiō, *refusal*.
cūrō, *care for*.
cūrātiō, *caring for*.

CEL-, CER-, *strike, drive, run*.

perculsus, *struck with consternation*.
celer, *swift*.
celeriter, *quickly*.
celeritās, *speed*.
procul, *at a distance*.
concelebrō, *frequent ; proclaim*.
concurrō, *run together*.
concursus, *running together*.
cursus, *speed ; course*.
discurrō, *run to and fro*.
excursus, *charge*.
occurrō, *run against*.
praecurrō, *run before*.

prŏcurrō, *run forward.*
succurrō, *run to help.*

1 CER-, CRE-, *make.*

creō, *make.*
recreō, *make anew.*
crēber, *close together.*
crēbrō, *repeatedly.*
incrēbrēscō, *increase.*
percrēbrēscō, *spread abroad.*
corpus, *body.*

2 CER-, CRE-, *part.*

cernō, *distinguish ; see.*
certus, *settled, certain.*
dēcernō, *decide by combat.*
dēcertō, *fight.*
sēcrētō, *secretly.*

1 CI-, *rouse.*

citō, *rouse.*
incitō, *urge on.*
incitātus, *hurried.*
incitātiō, *ardor.*
sollicitor, *stir up.*

2 CI-, *lie.*

cīvis, *citizen.*
cīvitās, *state.*
conquiēscō, *rest.*
requiēscō, *rest.*
quiētus, *quiet.*
quiētē, *quietly.*

1 DA-, *give.*

dō, *give.*
dōnum, *gift.*
dōnō, *present.*
dēdō, *give up.*

dēditiō, *surrender.*
prōdō, *betray.*
reddō, *give back.*
trādō, *hand over.*
sacerdōs, *priest.*
sacerdōtium, *priesthood.*

2 DA-, *put.*

addō, *join.*
crēdō, *believe.*
incrēdibilis, *incredible.*
ēditus, *elevated.*
reconditus, *hidden.*
mandō, *intrust.*
commendō, *enjoin on.*

DAC-, DIC-, *show, point.*

doceō, *show ; teach.*
abdicō, *give up.*
praedicō, *make known ; relate.*
dīcō, *say, tell.*
praedīcō, *tell beforehand ; admonish.*
dictātor, *dictator.*
dictātūra, *dictatorship.*
ēdictum, *proclamation.*
condiciō, *agreement, terms.*
iūdicō, *judge.*
iūdicium, *judgment.*

DIV-, DI-, DIAV-, *shine.*

Diāna, *Diana.*
diēs, *day.*
hodiē, *to-day.*
cotīdiē, *daily.*
cotīdiānus, *daily.*
merīdiēs, *midday.*
merīdiānus, *of noon.*
prīdiē, *day before.*

postrīdiē, *day after.*
biduum (for bidivom), *two days.*
diurnus, *by day.*
interdiū, *in the daytime.*
diū, *long.*
adiūtor, *helper.*
iūnior, *younger.*

DVA-, DVI-, *apart, two.*

duo, *two.*
duodecim, *twelve.*
ducentī, *two hundred.*
dubito, *hesitate.*
bis (for dviies), *twice.*
bīnī, *two by two.*
biduum, *two days.*
bellum (for duellum), *war.*
bellō, *wage war.*
bellicōsus, *warlike.*

DVC-, *lead.*

dux, *leader.*
dūcō, *lead.*
abdūcō, *lead away.*
addūcō, *lead to ; induce.*
circumdūcō, *lead around.*
condūcō, *lead together, collect.*
dēdūcō, *withdraw.*
ēdūcō, *lead out.*
intrōdūcō, *lead in.*
obdūcō, *draw before.*
perdūcō, *carry along.*
prōdūcō, *lead forth.*
redūcō, *lead back.*
trādūcō, *lead across.*

EM-, *take.*

coëmō, *buy up.*
exemplum, *example.*

praemium (for praeimium), *reward.*
sūmō (for subimo), *take.*
cōnsūmō, *use up, exhaust.*
sūmptus, *expense.*

ES-, *be, live.*

sum (for esum), *be.*
absum, *be away.*
adsum, *be at hand.*
dēsum, *be wanting.*
intersum, *be between ; be present at.*
praesum, *be over, be before.*
subsum, *be near.*
supersum, *be left, remain.*
absēns, *absent.*
praesēns, *at hand, present.*
praesentia, *present time.*

FA-, *shine, show.*

profiteor, *declare publicly.*
fānum, *sanctuary.*
fāma, *report.*
īnfāmia, *ill report.*
fās, *right.*

FAC-, *put, make.*

faciō, *make, do.*
facinus, *deed.*
facilis, *capable of being done.*
facultās, *capability, means.*
difficilis, *hard.*
difficultās, *difficulty.*
adficiō, *do to ; treat.*
cōnficiō, *do thoroughly, accomplish.*
dēficiō, *fail.*
efficiō, *cause.*

interficiō, *kill.*
perficiō, *achieve.*
praeficiō, *put before, put over.*
praefectus, *commander.*
prōficiō, *effect.*
reficiō, *make anew ; recruit.*
satisfaciō, *give satisfaction.*
beneficium, *favor.*
beneficiāriī, *favorites.*
officium, *service ; duty.*
sīgnificātiō, *signal.*
proficīscor, *set out.*
profectiō, *departure.*

FEN-, FEND-, *strike.*

dēfendō, *ward off, defend.*
dēfēnsiō (defendtio), *defense.*
dēfēnsor (defendtor), *defender.*
offendō, *strike against ; blunder.*
offēnsiō (offendtio), *striking against ; defeat.*
cōnfestim, *at once.*

1 FER-, *bear.*

ferō, *bear.*
adferō, *bring to.*
cōnferō, *bring together.*
dēferō, *take down ; report.*
differō, *put off.*
efferō, *bring forth.*
īnferō, *bring in.*
offerō, *present.*
praeferō, *hold forth.*
prōferō, *bring forward.*
referō, *carry back.*
trānsferō, *bear across ; move.*
aquilifer, *eagle-bearer.*
sīgnifer, *standard-bearer.*
fortasse, *perhaps.*

forte, *by chance.*
fortūna, *chance.*

2 FER-, FRE-, *hold, fix.*

ferē, *closely ; nearly.*
frētus, *sustained, relying.*
fīrmus, *steadfast.*
fīrmō, *strengthen.*
cōnfīrmō, *encourage.*
īnfīrmus, *weak.*
fortis, *brave.*
fortiter, *bravely.*

1 FID-, FĪD-, *bind, trust.*

fidēs, *faith.*
fidūcia, *confidence.*
cōnfīdō, *trust.*
diffīdō, *be distrust)ul.*

2 FID-, *split.*

fīnis (for fidnis), *boundary.*
fīniō, *bound, finish.*
dēfīniō, *define.*
fīnitimus, *neighboring.*

FVG-, *flee.*

fuga, *flight.*
fugiō, *flee.*
cōnfugiō, *flee for refuge.*
perfugiō, *desert.*
perfuga, *deserter.*
profugiō, *escape.*
refugiō, *run away.*
fugitīvus, *runaway.*

GEN-, GN-, GNA-, *beget.*

genus, *birth; kind.*
gēns, *stock ; people.*

(g)nāscor, *be born.*
innātus ((g)nātus), *inborn.*
nātiō, *origin ; race.*
nātūra, *birth ; nature.*
nātūrāliter, *by nature.*

GNA-, GNO-, *know.*

cōgnōscō, *learn.*
nōtus, *known.*
incōgnitus, *unknown.*
nōtitia, *acquaintance.*
īgnōminia, *dishonor.*
nōmen, *name.*
īgnōrō, *not know.*
īgnōrantia, *ignorance.*
notō, *mark.*

HAB-, *have, hold.*

habeō, *have, hold.*
adhibeō, *hold toward.*
prohibeō, *hold back ; forbid.*
dēbeō (for dehibeo), *withhold ; owe.*
praebeō (for praehibeo), *hold forth, afford.*

HED-, HEND-, *seize, hold.*

prehendō and prēndō, *seize.*
comprehendō, *seize.*
dēprehendō, *catch.*
reprehendō, *hold back ; rebuke.*
praeda (for praeheda), *booty.*
praedō, *robber.*

I-, *go.*

adeō, *go to.*
aditus, *approach.*
dēpereō, *perish.*

ineō, *go upon ; begin.*
intereō, *be lost.*
introeō, *go into.*
prōdeō, *go forward.*
redeō, *go back.*
reditus, *return.*
subeō, *undergo.*
trānseō, *go across.*
circuitus, *way around.*
exitus, *way out.*
praeteritus, *past.*
comes, *associate.*
comitātus, *company.*
comitia, *election.*
initium, *beginning.*
subitus, *sudden.*
subitō, *suddenly.*
praetor (for praeitor), *leader ; praetor.*
iter, *route ; march.*

IAC-, *throw.*

iaciō, *throw.*
adiciō, *throw on.*
coniciō, *throw together, hurl.*
circumiciō, *throw around.*
dēiciō, *throw down.*
disiciō, *scatter.*
ēiciō, *throw out.*
intericiō, *put between.*
obiciō, *throw before.*
prōiciō, *throw forward ; yield.*
rēiciō, *drive back.*
subiciō, *throw under ; expose.*
trāiciō, *throw across.*
coniectō, *put together, infer.*
coniectūra, *inference.*
obiectō, *throw in the face, taunt.*
obiectātiō, *reproach.*

IV-, IVG-, *bind, yoke.*

iugum, *yoke; ridge.*
iūmentum, *beast of burden.*
adiungō, *join to.*
coniungō, *join together.*
cūnctus (for coiunctus), *all to-gether.*
iūstus, *fair.*
iūrō, *take oath.*
iniūria, *injustice.*
iūxtā, *at the side of.*
iūdicō, *judge.*
iūdicium, *judgment.*

1 LEG-, *gather.*

legō, *gather, pick out.*
conligō, *collect.*
dēligō, *pick out, choose.*
dēlēctus (delegtus), *levy.*
ēligō, *pick out.*
intellegō, *perceive, understand.*
dīligenter, *carefully.*
dīligentia, *care.*
legiō, *levy; legion.*
legiōnārius, *legionary.*
legūmen, *pulse.*

2 LEG-, *run, spring.*

levis (for legvis), *light.*
leviter, *lightly.*
levō, *lift up; lighten.*
sublevō, *raise up; support.*
longus, *long.*
longē, *long; far.*
longīnquus, *prolonged.*
longurius, *long pole.*

3 LEG-, *lie, be fixed.*

lēx, *law.*
lēgātus, *one legally appointed; envoy.*
lēgātiō, *embassy.*

LIB-, *desire.*

līber, *free man.*
līberē, *freely.*
līberō, *set free.*
lībertās, *freedom.*
līberālitās, *generosity.*
līberāliter, *generously.*
libenter, *willingly.*

LIC-, LIQV-, *let, leave.*

licet, *it is lawful.*
relinquō, *leave behind.*
reliquus, *remaining.*

MA-, MAD-, *measure, moderate.*

modus, *measure.*
modo, *by a measure; only.*
commodus, *suitable.*
incommodum, *disadvantage.*
remedium, *cure.*

MAC-, MAG-, *big.*

magis, *more.*
magistrātus, *rank of master; magistracy.*
māgnus, *great.*
māgnitūdō, *extent.*
māior (for magior), *greater.*
māximē, *in the highest degree.*

MAN-, MEN-, *mind, stay.*

maneō, *stay.*
remaneō, *stay behind.*
meminī, *remember.*
mentiō, *calling to mind; mention.*
Minerva, *Minerva.*
moneō, *remind, warn.*
admonitus, *advice.*
dēmōnstrō, *show.*

MIT-, *send, throw.*

mittō, *make go, send.*
admittō, *send to.*
āmittō, *send away; lose.*
committō, *bring together, join; intrust.*
dēmittō, *let down.*
dīmittō, *send here and there; abandon.*
ēmittō, *send forth.*
immittō, *send in or against.*
intermittō, *send between; interrupt.*
praemittō, *send ahead.*
remittō, *send back; relax.*
remissus, *relaxed; mild.*
submittō, *send under; send as aid.*
submissus, *let down; humble, moderate.*

1 MV-, MOV-, *move.*

moveō, *move.*
admoveō, *move up to.*
permoveō, *move deeply.*
submoveō, *drive back.*
mōmentum (for movimentum), *motion.*
commūtō (for commovito), *change.*
commūtātiō, *change.*

2 MV-, *shut, fasten.*

mūrus, *wall.*
moenia, *city walls.*
mūniō, *wall in.*
circummūniō, *fortify around.*
commūniō, *fortify strongly.*
praemūniō, *fortify in front.*
mūnītiō, *fortification.*
commūnis, *common.*
mūnus, *office; gift.*

NA-, NAV-, *wet, swim.*

nāvis, *ship.*
nauta (for navita), *sailor.*
nāvicula, *little boat.*
nāvigātiō, *sailing.*

NEC-, NOC-, *kill, hurt.*

necō, *kill.*
nox, *night.*
noctū, *by night.*
nocturnus, *nightly.*

NV-, *now.*

nunc, *now.*
novus, *new.*
renovō, *renew.*
nūntius (for noventius), *bearer of tidings.*
nūntiō, *announce.*
dēnūntiō, *pronounce.*
prōnūntiō, *proclaim.*
renūntiō, *report.*

PA-, *feed.*

pater, *father.*
pāscō, *feed.*
pābulum, *fodder.*
pābulor, *forage.*

pābulātiō, *foraging.*
pānis, *bread.*

PAC-, PAG-, *fix, make fast.*

pāx, *compact ; peace.*
pācō, *make peaceful ; subdue.*
pactiō, *agreement.*
pecus, *cattle.*
pecūnia, *money.*
pecūniārius, *of money.*
pūgna, *battle.*
pūgnō, *fight.*
expūgnō, *take by storm.*
oppūgnō, *attack.*
oppūgnātiō, *attack, siege.*
prōpūgnō, *rush out to fight.*
repūgnō, *fight back, resist.*

1 PAR-, PER-, *through, fare, reach, try.*

per, *through.*
pār, *equal.*
pariter, *equally.*
perītus, *skilled.*
perīculum, *trial ; danger.*
perīculōsus, *dangerous.*
experior, *try.*
porta, *gate.*
portus, *harbor.*
opportūnitās, *fitness.*

2 PAR-, POR-, *part, breed.*

pars, *part.*
partim, *partly.*
partior, *divide.*
pariō, *bring forth ; produce.*
properō, *hasten.*
imperō, *command.*
imperium, *authority, power.*

imperātum, *order.*
imperātor, *commander.*
imperātōrius, *of a commander.*
pāreō, *obey.*
aperiō, *uncover.*
reperiō, *find.*
comportō, *bring together.*
importō, *bring in.*
supportō, *bring up, convey.*
trānsportō, *take across.*
oportet, *it is proper.*

PAV-, *little.*

paucī, *few.*
paucitās, *fewness.*
parvus, *small.*
parvulus, *very small.*
paulō, *by a little.*
paulātim, *by degrees.*
paulisper, *for a little while.*

PED-, *tread.*

pēs, *foot.*
impediō, *hinder, obstruct.*
impedītus, *obstructed ; difficult.*
impedīmentum, *hindrance ;* plu., *baggage.*
expedītus, *unobstructed ; unencumbered.*

PLE-, PLO-, PLV-, *fill.*

compleō, *fill.*
expleō, *fill up.*
oppleō, *fill completely.*
plēnus, *full.*
plērīque, *most.*
plērumque, *for the most part.*
locuplēs, *rich in lands.*
plūs, *more.*

plūrimus, *most.*
complūrēs, *many.*
amplus, *high ; ample.*
amplius, *more.*
amplissimē, *most generously.*
populus, *people.*

PLEC-, *weave, fold.*

amplector, *twine around.*
complector, *embrace.*
duplex, *twofold.*
duplicō, *double.*
explicō, *unfold ; settle.*
suppliciter, *like a suppliant.*

POT-, *master.*

potius, *rather.*
possum (for potsum), *be able.*
potior, *get possession of.*
potestās, *power.*

PRO-, PRI-, PRAE-, *before.*

prō, prōd-, *before.*
procul, *at a distance.*
prōtinus, *right on.*
prior, *former.*
prius, *sooner.*
prīstinus (for priustinus), *former.*
prīmus, *first.*
prīmum, *in the first place.*
prīmō, *at first.*
imprīmīs, *among the first.*
prīnceps (for primiceps), *first ;
    first centurion.*
prīncipātus, *first place ; suprem-
    acy.*
prīmipīlus, *first centurion.*
prae-, *before.*
praeter, *before ; beyond.*

praeteritus, *past.*
praetereā, *besides.*
praetor, *leader, praetor.*
prīvō, *deprive.*
prīvātus, *private citizen.*

QVAES-, *seek.*

quaerō, *seek.*
conquīrō, *hunt up.*
quaestor, *questioner, quaestor.*
quaestus, *gain.*

RAP-, RVP-, *snatch, break.*

dīripiō, *tear asunder ; plunder.*
corrumpō, *destroy.*
ērumpō, *break out.*
ēruptiō, *rushing out.*
inrumpō, *rush in.*
interrumpō, *break off.*

REG-, *stretch, guide.*

dērigō, *direct.*
dērēctus, *straight.*
cōnsurgō (for consubrigo), *rise.*
regiō, *direction ; region.*
rēx, *king.*
rēgius, *royal.*
rēgnum, *kingdom.*

SAC-, SEC-, SCI-, SCID-, *split,
    distinguish.*

saxum, *stone.*
dēsecō, *cut down.*
sciō, *know.*
cōnscientia, *consciousness.*
caedēs (for scaedes), *slaughter.*
caespes, *cut sod.*
abscīdō, *cut off.*
excīdō, *cut down.*

SAL-, SER-, save.

salūs, *health ; safety.*
salūtō, *greet.*
cōnsōlor, *cheer.*
servō, *save.*
cōnservō, *keep safe ; spare.*
reservō, *save.*

SCAND-, climb.

ascendō, *climb.*
cōnscendō, *embark upon.*
dēscendō, *come down.*
trānscendō, *cross.*
scālae, *ladder.*

SCARP-, SCALP-, cut, scratch.

scrībō, *write.*
cōnscrībō, *write together ; enlist.*
dēscrībō, *mark off.*
praescrīptum, *previous direction.*
culpa, *blame ; error.*

SEC-, follow.

sequor, *follow.*
cōnsequor, *overtake.*
īnsequor, *follow up.*
persequor, *pursue.*
prōsequor, *follow.*
subsequor, *follow after.*
secundus, *following ; favorable.*
secundum, *following ; beside.*
sētius (for sectius), *less.*
socius, *companion.*
societās, *association.*

SED-, SID-, sit.

obsideō, *besiege.*
obsidiō, *siege.*
obses, *hostage.*

praesidium, *protection ; guard.*
subsidium, *aid.*
īnsidiae, *ambush.*
cōnsīdō, *settle.*

SEM-, SIM-, together, like.

semper, *always.*
similis, *like.*
similiter, *in a like manner.*
similitūdō, *likeness.*
simul, *at the same time.*
simulācrum, *statue (likeness).*

SENT-, feel.

sentiō, *perceive.*
dissēnsiō (dissenttio), *difference.*
cōnsēnsus (consenttus), *agreement.*

SPEC-, see, spy.

speciēs, *look.*
cōnspiciō, *perceive.*
cōnspectus, *sight.*
dēspiciō, *look down on.*
perspiciō, *perceive clearly.*
respiciō, *look back on ; gaze at.*
spectō, *look at.*
exspectō, *look out for.*
exspectātiō, *expectation.*
suspīciō, *suspicion.*
cōnspicor, *catch sight of.*
suspicor, *suspect, conjecture.*
speculātor, *spy ; scout.*

STA-, stand.

cōnstō, *stand ; depend on.*
dīstō, *stand apart.*
īnstō, *stand on.*
praestō, *stand before.*

cōnsistō, *stand still.*
dēsistō, *cease.*
exsistō, *come forth.*
resistō, *stand back ; resist.*
statuō, *set up, fix.*
cōnstituō, *place together ; decide.*
dēstituō, *leave alone.*
īnstituō, *set in ; undertake.*
īnstitūtum, *custom.*
restituō, *replace.*
statua, *statue.*
statim, *on the spot, at once.*
statiō, *standing place.*
statīvus, *stationary, permanent.*

TA-, TEN-, *stretch.*

tabernāculum, *tent.*
contubernium, *tent.*
tener, *soft.*
attenuō, *make thin, weaken.*
tendō, *stretch.*
contendō, *stretch, strive.*
dētendō, *unstretch.*
distendō, *stretch out.*
extendō, *exert.*
ostendō, *show.*
temptō, *try.*
ostentō, *show.*
ostentātiō, *display.*
sustentō, *hold up, support.*
teneō, *hold.*
contineō, *hold together ;*
continēns, *unbroken ;* noun, *mainland.*
contentus, *satisfied.*
dētineō, *check.*
distineō, *keep apart.*
obtineō, *hold fast.*
pertineō, *extend, reach.*

retineō, *hold back.*
sustineō, *withstand ; support.*
intentus, *eager.*

TAG-, *touch.*

attingō, *touch, reach.*
contingō, *touch closely ; border on.*
integer, *untouched, fresh.*

1 TEM-, *cut.*

templum, *place marked off, temple.*
tempus, *section of time.*
contemptiō, *scorn.*

2 TEM-, TIM-, *stun.*

temerē, *rashly.*
timeō, *fear.*
timor, *fear.*

TVR-, *harry, crowd.*

dēturbō, *thrust down.*
perturbō, *confuse.*
perturbātiō, *disorder.*
turmātim, *by troops.*

VA-, VEN-, *go, come.*

vadum, *ford.*
veniō, *come.*
circumveniō, *surround.*
conveniō, *come together.*
inveniō, *come upon, find.*
perveniō, *come up, arrive.*
adventus, *arrival.*
ēventus, *outcome.*
cōntiō (for coventio), *assembly ; speech.*
cōntiōnor, *harangue.*

VAG-, VEH-, *move, carry.*

circum**veh**or, *sail around.*
praeter**veh**or, *ride* or *sail past.*
vectūra, *transportation.*
vēxillum, *flag.*

VERT-, *turn.*

vertō, *turn.*
āvertō, *turn aside.*
animad**vert**ō, *notice ; punish.*
animad**vers**iō (animad**vert**tio),
    punishment.
con**vert**ō, *turn.*
re**vert**or, *return.*
versus, *towards.*
versor, *be busied.*
ad**vers**us, *turned towards, facing.*
ad**vers**us, *against.*
ad**vers**ārius, *adversary.*
contrō**vers**ia (contro**vert**tia), *dis-
    pute.*
dī**vers**us, *turned away, opposite.*
trāns**vers**us, *crosswise.*
ūni**vers**us, *all together.*
rūrsum (for re**vors**um), *again.*

VIC-, *conquer.*

vincō, *conquer.*
dē**vinc**ō, *subdue completely.*

victor, *conqueror.*
victōria, *victory.*

VID-, *see.*

videō, *see.*
prō**vid**eō, *foresee.*
impro**vīs**us, *unexpected.*
imprūdēns (for impro**vid**ens), *un-
    suspecting.*

VOC-, *call.*

vōx, *voice.*
vocō, *call.*
ē**voc**ō, *call forth.*
ē**voc**ātus, *called out; volunteer
    veteran.*
re**voc**ō, *call back.*

VOL-, *will, wish.*

volō, *wish.*
voluntās, *will.*
voluntārius, *voluntary.*
voluptās, *pleasure.*
mālō (mag**vol**o), *prefer.*
nōlō (nōn **vol**ō), *be unwilling.*
-**ve,** *or (if you please).*
vel, *or (if you will).*

SUFFIXES.

NOTE.— In this list of derivatives, references preceded by A. & G. are to Allen and Greenough's New Latin Grammar; those preceded by H., to Harkness' Complete Latin Grammar. The list is not exhaustive, but merely gives some of the best illustrations found in the text.

A. NOUNS.

a. FROM NOUNS.

Diminutives.	*Occupations.*	*Characteristic* or *condition.*
-ellum.	-iō.	-tās.
castellum.	centuriō.	cīvitās.
		societās.
-culus.	-ārius.	-tūs.
mūsculus.	sagittārius.	virtūs.
-cula.	*Office* or *condition.*	*Rank* or *office.*
nāvicula.	-ium.	-ātus.
-culum.	hospitium.	cōnsulātus.
tabernāculum.	sacerdōtium.	magistrātus.
		prīncipātus.

b. FROM ADJECTIVES.

Quality.

-ia.	contrōversia.	īgnōrantia.	persevērantia.
adrogantia.	dīligentia.	inopia.	praesentia.
audācia.	frequentia.	patientia.	vigilia.

-tia.
amīcitia.
laetitia.
nōtitia.

-tās.
alacritās.
celeritās.

cupiditās.
dīgnitās.
facultās.
fēlīcitās.
inīquitās.
liberālitās.
lībertās. |
necessitās.

opportūnitās.
paucitās.
potestās.
propīnquitās.

-tūdō.
altitūdō.

cōnsuētūdō.
lassitūdō.
lātitūdō.
māgnitūdō.
multitūdō.
necessitūdō.
similitūdō.

c. From Verbs and Roots.

Agent.

-tor.
adiūtor.
dēfēnsor.[1]
dictātor.
explōrātor.
funditor.[2]
imperātor.
negōtiātor.
quaestor.
senātor.[2]
speculātor.
victor.

Act.

-tūra.
armātūra.
coniectūra.
vectūra.

-tus.
apparātus.

aditus.
adventus.
cōnātus.
cōnsēnsus.[1]
cōnspectus.
cursus.[3]
dēlēctus.
exercitus.
hortātus.
ictus.
occāsus.[1]

-tiō, -iō.
commūtātiō.
contemptiō.[4]
cūrātiō.
dēditiō.
dēfēnsiō.[1]
legiō.
mūnītiō.
occāsiō.[1]
oppūgnātiō.

ōrātiō.
ostentātiō.
pābulātiō.
perturbātiō.
profectiō.
suspīciō.

Act or state.

or.
error.
timor.

-iēs.
speciēs.

-ium.
beneficium.
conloquium.
comitium.
initium.
studium.

*Means, involun-
tary subject, act,
or result.*

-men.
agmen.
flūmen.

-mentum.
coagmentum.
dētrīmentum.
impedīmentum.
mōmentum.
pavīmentum.
tegimentum.
tormentum.

[1] A. & G. 15. 5 ; H. 52. 1.
[2] A. & G. 236. a. ¶ 2 ; H. 334. 4.
[3] A. & G. 15. 5 ; cf. H. 253. 2.
[4] A. & G. 15. 11.

B. ADJECTIVES.

a. From Nouns.

Fulness, abun-
dance, or *supply.*
-*ōsus.*
montuōsus.[1]
perīculōsus.

-*cōsus.*
bellicōsus.

-*lentus.*
opulentus.

-*tus.*
honestus.

Material.

-*eus.*
vīmineus.

Characteristic.
-*ānus.*
antesīgnānus.
decumānus.
merīdiānus.
oppidānus.

-*āris.*
cōnsulāris.
familiāris.
manipulāris.
mīlitāris.
singulāris.

-*ārius.*
beneficiārius.
frūmentārius.
legiōnārius.
necessārius.
pecūniārius.

voluntārius.

-*ius.*
imperātōrius.
praetōrius.
rēgius.
senātōrius.

-*timus.*
fīnitimus.
maritimus.

-*ticus.*
domesticus.

Proper adjectives.
-*ānus.*
Hispānus.
Pompēiānus.
Rōmānus.
Trānspadānus.

-*īnus.*
Dyrrachīnus.
Latīnus.

-*ius.*
Ephesius.
Rhodius.

-*icus, -ticus.*
Asiāticus.
Gallicus.
Italicus.
Syriacus.

-*ēnsis.*
Antiochēnsis
Byllidēnsis.
Ciliciēnsis.
Gomphēnsis.

b. From Adjectives.

Diminutive.
-*ulus,* parvulus.

c. From Verbs and Roots.

Capability.
-*bilis.*
incrēdibilis.

-*lis.*
facilis.
inūtilis.

Inclination.
-*tīvus.*
fugitīvus.
statīvus.

[1] Formed as if the noun were of Declension IV. Cf. *fluctuōsus.*

d. From Adverbs and Prepositions.

| contrārius. | diurnus. | prīstinus. |
| cotīdiānus. | nocturnus. | repentīnus. |

C. ADVERBS.

a. From Adjectives.

-*ē.*[1]	māximē.	fortiter.
aegrē.	occultē.	graviter.
aequē.	praecipuē.	īnsolenter.
amplissimē.	tardē.	leviter.
angustē.		libenter.
clārē.	-*ter.*[2]	nātūrāliter.
cōnsīderātē.	ācriter.	pariter.
lātē.	audācter.	similiter.
līberē.	celeriter.	suppliciter.
longē.	dīligenter.	vehementer.

b. Case Forms used as Adverbs.[3]

diū.	multum.	praesertim.	statim.
eō.	necessāriō.	prīmō.	tūtō.
eōdem.	noctū.	prīmum.	utrum.
forte.	partim.	quā.	vērō.
modo.	paulātim.	quō.	
multō.	paulō.	sōlum.	

c. Phrases.[4]

cotīdiē.	prīdiē.	posteā.
hodiē.	interdiū.	praetereā.
postrīdiē.	imprīmīs.	proptereā.

---

[1] A. & G. 214. a.   [2] A. & G. 214. b.   [3] A. & G. 215.   [4] A. & G. 216.

D. VERBS.

a. FROM NOUNS.

aquor.	hiemō.	moror.	spērō.
armō.	intrō.	negōtior.	spoliō.
bellō.	labōrō.	pācō.	superō.
cūrō.	laudō.	praecipitō.	tribuō.
dōnō.	līgnor.	proelior.	volnerō.
fīniō.	locō.	pūgnō.	
glōrior.	mētor.	sonō.	

b. FROM VERBS.

Inceptives.	*Intensives and Frequentatives.*	
cōgnōscō.	citō.	dēlectō.
cōnsuēscō.	cōgitō.	spectō.
exārēscō.	commūtō.	sustentō.
mātūrēscō.	coniectō.	versor.[1]
percrēbrēscō.	dēcertō.	

[1] A. & G. 15. 5 ; H. 52. 1.

PREFIXES.

a. SEPARABLE.

claudō.
circum-clūdō.
ex-clūdō.
in-clūdō.
inter-clūdō.
prae-clūdō.

dūcō.
ab-dūcō.
ad-dūcō.
circum-dūcō.
con-dūcō.
dē-dūcō.

ē-dūcō.
intrō-dūcō.
ob-dūcō.
per-dūcō.
prō-dūcō.
trā-dūcō.

eō.
ad-eō.
dē-per-eō.
in-eō.
inter-eō.
intro-eō.

prōd-eō.
sub-eō.
trāns-eō.

ferō.
ad-ferō.
cōn-ferō.
dē-ferō.
ef-ferō.
īn-ferō.
of-ferō.
prae-ferō.
prō-ferō.

trāns-ferō.

iaciō.
ad-iciō.
circum-iciō
con-iciō.
dē-iciō.
ē-iciō.
inter-iciō.
ob-iciō.
prō-iciō.
sub-iciō.
trā-iciō.

b. INSEPARABLE.

dif-ferō.
dis-iciō.
in-ermis.

in-īquus.
īn-solitus.
in-ūsitātus.

in-ūtilis.
red-eō.
re-dūcō.

re-ferō.
rē-iciō.
sē-clūdō.

VOCABULARY.

N.B.—For abbreviations, see page 51.

A.

A., see Aulus.

Ā, see ab.

ab (before vowels and some consonants), **ā** (before consonants), **abs**, prep. with abl., *away from, from, of*, 1, 3, 5, etc.; *by*, 1, 2, 5, etc.

ab-dicō, 1 [DIC-, *show*], *disown, resign, abdicate*, 1.

ab-dūcō, 3, -dūxī, -ductus, *lead away, draw away*, 41.

abscīdō, 3, -cīdī, -cīsus (abs, *from* + caedō, *cut*) [SCID-, *split*], *cut off, separate*, 35.

absēns, -entis, adj. (absum, *be away*), *absent*, 45.

abs-trahō, 3, -trāxī, -trāctus [TRAG-, *drag*], *drag away, exclude, cut off*, 41.

ab-sum, abesse, āfuī, āfutūrus, v. n., *be away, be distant*, 9, 16, 17, etc.

ab-undō, 1, -āvī, —, v. n., *stream over, overflow, abound*, 14, 16.

ab-ūtor, 3, -ūsus, v. dep. n., *use up, waste, spill*, 52.

ac, conj. (see atque), *and also, and*, 1, 4, 9, etc.; after words of comparison, *as*, 23, 35.

Acarnānia, -ae, F., *Acarnania*, a country in western Greece, 21.

ac-cēdō (adc-), 3, -cessī, -cessus, v. n., *go to, approach*, 26, 48; *be added*, 42; *fill, inspire*, 35.

accidō, 3, -cidī, —, v. n. (ad, *to* + cadō, *fall*), *fall to, happen, come to pass*, 8, 11, 24, etc.

accipiō, 3, -cēpī, -ceptus (ad, *to* + capiō, *take*), *take to oneself, receive, suffer*, 35, 36, 40, etc.; *hear*, 48.

ācer, ācris, ācre, adj. [AC-, *sharp*], *sharp, keen, fierce*, 35.

Achāia, -ae, F., *Achaea*, the Roman province of Achaea, including all of Greece south of Thessaly, 66.

Achillās, -ae, M., *Achillas*, one of Pompey's murderers, 64.

aciēs, aciēī and aciē, F. [AC-, *sharp*], *edge ; line of battle*, 8, 20, 30, etc. ; *battle, battlefield*, 56, 57.

ācriter, ācrius, ācerrimē, adv. (ācer, *sharp*), *sharply, keenly, fiercely*, 12, 17, 55, etc.

āctuārius, -a, -um, adj. (agō, *drive*), *easily driven ; swift*, 25, 62.

ad, prep. with acc., *to*, 1, 3, 5, etc. ; *to, until*, 17, 56, 57 ; *towards, against*, 4, 7 ; *near, at*, 1, 4, 7, etc. ; *for*, 5, 10, 17, etc. ; *according to*, 5, 15, 17, etc. ; *in the sight of*, 23 ; *about, to the number of*, 19.

ad-augeō, 2, -auxī, -auctus, *add to, increase, eke out*, 21.

Adbucillus, -ī, M., *Adbucillus*, an Allobrogian, 22.

addō, 3, -didī, -ditus [DA-, *put*], *put to, add, join*, 16, 20, 22, etc.

ad-dūcō, 3, -dūxī, -ductus, *lead to*, 43 ; *move, influence*, 12, 23, 64.

ad-eō, -īre, -iī (-īvī), -itus *go to*, 41, 47, 62, etc. ; *approach, apply to*, 22.

adeō (ad, *to* + eō, *thither, to that point*), adv., *to that degree, so far, so much so*, 21, 32, 45.

ad-ferō (aff-), -ferre, attulī (adt-), adlātus (all-), *bring to, bring, cause*, 17, 19, 23, etc.

adficiō (aff-), 3, -fēcī, -fectus (ad, *to* + faciō, *do*), *do to ; treat, visit, afflict*, 16, 27.

adhibeō, 2, -hibuī, -hibitus (ad, *to* + habeō, *hold*), *hold towards, apply, exercise*, 60.

ad-hortor, 1, *exhort, encourage*, 8.

adiciō, 3, -iēcī, -iectus (ad, *to* +

iaciō, *throw*), *throw on*, 16 ; *add*, 29.

adigō, 3, -ēgī, -āctus (ad, *to* + agō, *drive*), *drive to, drive home, throw*, 20 ; pass., *reach*, 17, 20.

aditus, -ūs, M. (adeō, *go to*), *a going to, approach, means of approach*, 9, 12, 16, etc.

ad-iungō, 3, -iūnxī, -iūnctus [IVG-, *bind*], *join to, add*, 51.

adiūtor, -ōris, M. (adiuvō, *help*), *he who helps, adjutant*, 25.

ad-mīror, 1, *wonder at, admire*, 48.

ad-misceō, 2, -miscuī, -mixtus, *mix with, add*, 15, 38.

ad-mittō, 3, -mīsī, -missus, *send to ; commit*, 27.

admonitus, -ūs, M. (admoneō, *advise*), *advising, advice, suggestion*, 54.

ad-moveō, 2, -mōvī, -mōtus, *move to, bring up*, 26.

ad-orior, 4, -ortus, *rise up against, fall upon, attack*, 7, 11, 14, etc.

adrogantia (arr-), -ae, F., *presumption, arrogance*, 22.

ad-sum, adesse, adfuī (affuī), v. n., *be at hand, be present*, 32, 46.

adulēscēns, -entis, M. (pres. part. of adolēscō, *grow up*), *young man*, between the ages of 15 and 25 years, 46.

adventus, -ūs, M. (adveniō, *arrive*), *coming to, arrival*, 2, 4, 17, etc. ; *approach*, 3, 7, 28, etc.

adversārius, -ī, M. (adversus, *opposite*), *adversary, enemy*, 1, 42.

adversus, -a, -um, adj. (perf. part.

of advertō, *turn to*), *turned towards, facing,* 13, 61; adversō flūmine, *up stream,* 7; *unfavorable,* 36, 43.

adversus, prep. with acc. (advertō, *turn to*), *against, up,* 13.

ἄδυτα (Greek), adyta, plu. noun, *inmost recesses, sanctuaries,* 65.

aeger, aegra, aegrum, adj., *sick,* 38, 41.

Aeginium, -ī, N., *Aeginium,* a fortress in Epirus, on the border of Thessaly, 42.

aegrē, adv. (aeger, *sick*), *painfully, with difficulty,* 26.

Aegyptus, -ī, F., *Egypt,* 64, 66.

aequē, adv. (aequus, *equal*), *equally, in an equal degree,* 66.

aequus, -a, -um, adj., *equal, level,* 12, 20; *favorable,* 36; *calm, equable;* aequō animō, *calmly, patiently,* 1, 8.

aes, aeris, N., *copper, bronze,* 63.

aestimō, 1, *value, estimate,* 6.

aestus, -ūs, M. [AID-, *burn*], *heat,* 16, 57.

aetās, -ātis, F., *age,* 63, 64.

Aetōlia, -ae, F., *Aetolia,* a province of Greece, 24.

Afrānius, -ī, M., *Lucius Afranius,* one of Pompey's lieutenants, 50.

Āfricus, -ī, M., *the southwest wind* (blowing from Africa), 6.

ager, agrī, M. [AG-, *drive*], *field, country,* 9, 22, 43, etc.

agger, -eris, M. (ad, *to* + GES-, *carry*), *what has been brought to a place, heap, rubbish* to fill

a moat, 25, 26; *earthwork, rampart,* 26, 32.

aggredior (adg-), 3, -gressus (ad, *to* + gradior, *walk*), *approach,* 16; *attack,* 30, 41, 48; *begin, set about,* 43.

agmen, -inis, N. [AG-, *drive*], that which is led, *army on the march, line,* 38, 47; prīmum agmen, *the van,* 8; novissimum agmen, *the rear,* 38.

agō, 3, ēgī, āctus [AG-, *drive*], put in motion, *drive,* 13; *do, perform,* 5, 17, 42; *aim at,* 5; *treat, treat of, discuss,* 52, 59; grātiās agere, *give thanks, express gratitude,* 45, 53.

alacritās, -ātis, F. (alacer, *eager*), *eagerness, zeal,* 54.

Alesia, -ae, F., *Alesia,* a town in Gaul, 14.

Alexandrīa, -ae, F., *Alexandria,* the principal city of Lower Egypt, founded by Alexander the Great, 63, 64, 66.

aliquamdiū, adv. (aliquam, *somewhat* + diū, *long time*), *for a while, for some time,* 33.

aliquī, -qua, -quod, indef. adj. (AL-, ALI-, *other* + quī, *some, any*), *some, any,* 14, 17, 23, etc.

aliquis, -qua, -quid, indef. pron. (AL-, ALI-, *other* + quis, *some one*), *some one, something,* 21.

alius, -a, -ud, adj. [AL-, ALI-, *other*], *other, another,* 1, 8, 13, etc.; aliī . . . aliī, *some . . . others,* 32, 39.

Allobrox, -ogis, M., *one of the*

Allobroges, a people of Gaul, 46; commonly plu., 22, 26, 42.

alō, 3, aluī, altus or alitus [AL-, *feed*], *feed, support*, 21.

alter, -tera, -terum, adj. [AL-, ALI-, *other*], *other of two, another*, 14, 18, 20, etc.; *the other*, 5, 50; *the next*, 5, 6, 7; alter . . . alter, *the one . . . the other*, 17.

altercor, 1, v. n. (alter, *other*), *alternate in discussion, dispute, wrangle*, 5.

alteruter, -utra, -utrum, adj. (alter, *other* + uter, *which of two?*), *either, one or the other*, 52.

altitūdō, -inis, F. (altus, *high*), *height*, 20, 26.

altus, -a, -um, adj. (perf. part. of alō, *nourish*), *grown great, high, deep*, 40, 43, 55, etc.

Amantīnī, -ōrum, M., *Amantini*, inhabitants of Amantia in Illyria, 3.

ambō, -ae, -ō, num. adj., *both*, 7.

amīcitia, -ae, F.(amīcus, *friendly*), *friendship*, 22, 23, 42, etc.

amīcus, -ī, M. [AM-, *love*], *friend*, 63, 64.

ā-mittō, 3, -mīsī, -missus, *let go away; lose*, 13, 19, 30, etc.

Amphipolis, -is, F., *Amphipolis*, a city in Macedonia, on the Strymon, 62.

Ampius, -ī, M., *Titus Ampius*, one of Pompey's followers, 65.

amplector, 3, -plexus (am-, *around* + PLEC-, *fold*), *twine around; encompass*, 11.

amplissimē, adv., superl. of amplē, *most generously*, 19.

amplius, adv., comp. of amplē, *more*, 19, 61.

amplus, -a, -um, adj. (am-, *around* + PLE-, PLV-, *fill*), *ample, high, important*, 22.

an, conj., introducing the second part of a disjunctive question, *or*, 62; sometimes with no question preceding, *What, did you not?* 49.

anceps, -cipitis, adj. (an-, in ambō, *both*+CAP-, in caput, *head*), *two-headed; double, twofold*, 26, 35.

ancora, -ae, F., *anchor*, 62.

Androsthenēs, -is, M., *Androsthenes*, a governor of Thessaly, 43.

angulus, -ī, M., *angle, corner*, 29.

angustē, adv. (angustus, *narrow*), *narrowly, closely*, 12.

angustiae, -ārum, F. (angustus, *narrow*), *narrowness, narrow passage*, 16, 32, 33, etc.; *scarcity, want*, 8, 14.

angustus, -a, -um, adj. [ANG-, *squeeze*], *narrow*, 8, 21, 32; *scanty*, 10.

animadversiō, -ōnis, F. (animadvertō, *punish*), *punishment*, 23.

animadvertō, 3, -vertī, -versus (animus, *mind* + advertō, *turn to*), *turn the mind towards; notice, observe*, 8, 13, 16, etc.

animus, -ī, M., *mind, feelings*, 1, 5, 8, etc.; plu., *spirit, courage*, 37.

annus, -ī, M., *year*, 1, 14, 22, etc.

ante, prep. with acc., *before*, of time, 24, 38, 43; of space, 65;

as adv., *before, previously,* 25, 27, 33, etc.

ante-cēdō, 3, -cessī, ——, *go before, precede,* 43, 45; v. n., *go ahead, get the start,* 38, 42.

antesīgnānus, -ī, M. (ante, *before* + sīgnum, *standard*), *a soldier who fought before the standards, skirmisher,* 38, 46.

Antiochēnsēs, -ium, M., *Antiochians,* people of Antioch, 62.

Antiochīa, -ae, F., *Antioch,* chief town of Syria, 62, 65.

antīquitus, adv. (antīquus, *old*), *in former times, of old,* 54.

antīquus, -a, -um, adj. (cf. ante, *before*), *ancient, former,* 20.

Antōnius, -ī, M., *Mark Antony,* one of Caesar's most faithful friends, 6, 7, 13, etc.

aperiō, 4, -eruī, -ertus, *uncover; open,* 2, 44.

apertus, -a, -um, adj. (perf. part. of aperiō, *open*), *open, clear,* 46; *exposed,* 48, 55.

Apollōnia, -ae, F., *Apollonia,* a town of Illyria, 2, 3, 4, etc.

Apollōniātēs, -ium, M., *Apollonians,* inhabitants of Apollonia, 3, 4.

apparātus (adp-), -ūs, M. (apparō, *prepare*), *preparation; munitions, supplies,* 8, 11.

appellō (adp-), 1, *address,* 64; *call, name,* 1, 6, 9, etc.

ap-propīnquō (adp-), 1, v. n., *approach, draw near,* 4, 6, 7, etc.

Apsus, -ī, M., *Apsus,* a river in Illyria, 4, 5, 7, etc.

apud, prep. with acc., *before, in the presence of, with, to,* 1, 10, 12, etc.; *before the tent of,* 45; *on the side of, under,* 53, 64.

aqua, -ae, F. [AC-, *swift*], *water,* 3, 16, 59.

aquila, -ae, F., *eagle,* the standard of the legion, 27, 61.

aquilifer, -ferī, M. (aquila, *eagle* + FER-, *bear*), *standard bearer,* 27.

aquor, 1, v. n. (aqua, *water*), *get water,* 29, 59.

arbitrō, 1, -āvī, ——, *consider, believe,* 1; more commonly

arbitror, 1, *consider, believe, think,* 23, 31.

arbor, -ŏris, F., *tree,* 15, 21.

ārdeō, 2, ārsī, ārsus, v. n., *burn, glow, be inflamed,* 37, 52.

argentum, -ī, N., *silver, silver plate,* 58.

arma, -ōrum, N. [AR-, *fit*], *implements, arms, weapons,* 2, 4, 5, etc.

armātī, -ōrum, M. (perf. part. of armō, *arm*), *armed men, soldiers,* 44.

armātūra, -ae, F. (armō, *arm*), *armor, equipment,* 25; levis armātūra, *light infantry,* 12, 25.

armō, 1 (arma, *arms*), *arm, equip,* 63, 65.

arx, arcis, F. [ARC-, *shut in*], *fortress, stronghold,* 3, 29, 62.

ascendō (adsc-), 3, -scendī, -scēnsus (ad, *to* + scandō, *climb*) [SCAND-, *climb*], *mount, climb,* 32; *man,* 2.

Asia, -ae, F., *Asia Minor,* 9, 19, 65, etc.

Asiāticus, -a, -um, adj. **(Asia),** *Asiatic, of Asia,* 66.

Asparagium, -ī, N., *Asparagium,* a town near Dyrrachium and under its sway, 7, 8, 39.

asper, aspera, asperum, adj., *rough, rugged,* 9, 10.

at, conj., introducing a contrast to what precedes, *but, but on the other hand,* 2, 4, 14, etc. ; *but, now,* 17, 34.

Athamānia, -ae, F., *Athamania,* a district in Epirus, 41.

atque, also **ac** (before consonants only), conj., *and also, and,* emphasizing what follows, 1, 2, 3, etc. ; **simul atque,** *as soon as,* 6.

at-tenuō (adt-), 1 [TA-, TEN-, *stretch*], *make thin, weaken, reduce,* 51.

attingō (adt-), 3, -tigī, — (ad, *to* + tangō, *touch*) [TAG-, *touch*], *touch, reach,* 1.

auctōritās, -ātis, F. (auctor, *producer*), *power, authority,* 10, 45.

audācia, -ae, F. (audāx, *bold*), *daring, boldness,* 64.

audācter, audācius, audācissimē, adv. (audāx, *bold*), *boldly,* 13.

audeō, 2, ausus, *dare, venture,* 10, 23, 33, etc.

audiō, 4, *hear, hear of,* 3, 15, 49, etc. ; *listen to,* 5.

augeō, 2, auxī, auctus [AVG-, *grow*], *increase, spread,* 27, 43, 45, etc.

Aulus, -ī, M., *Aulus,* a Roman praenomen, 5, 34, 52.

Auster, -trī, M., *the south wind,* 6.

aut, conj., introducing an alternative where there is a real difference between the things offered, *or,* 17 ; **aut . . . aut,** *either . . . or,* 8, 11, 14, etc.

autem, conj. (postpositive), *but, however,* 12, 20, etc.; *moreover,* 2, 14, 16, etc.

autumnus, -ī, M., *autumn,* 49.

auxilium, -ī, N. [AVG-, *grow*], *help, aid,* 17, 35, 41, etc. ; plu., **auxilia,** *sources of aid, reinforcements,* 2, 43; *auxiliary troops, troops,* 4, 57, 66.

Avāricum, -ī, N., *Avaricum,* a town in Gaul, 14.

ā-vertō, 3, -vertī, -versus, *turn from, turn away, divert, avert,* 16, 22, 26, etc.

B

Balbus, -ī, M., *Cornelius Balbus,* a follower of Caesar, 5.

barbarus, -a, -um, adj., *barbarous, barbarian,* 22, 57.

bellicōsus, -a, -um, adj. (bellum, *war*), *warlike,* 36.

bellō, 1, v. n. (bellum, *war*), *wage war,* 16.

bellum, -ī, N. (for duellum) [DVA-, DVI-, *two*], *war,* 8, 9, 11, etc.

bene, melius, optimē, adv. (bonus, *good*), *well,* 4, 61.

beneficiāriī, -ōrum, M. (beneficium, *favor*), *privileged men,
favorites*, 50.

beneficium, -ī, N. (beneficus, *favor-
ing*), *favor, kindness*, 6, 42, 57.

biduum, -ī, N. (bi- [DVI-], *two* +
DIV-, *shine*), *period of two days*,
6, 62.

bīnī, -ae, -a, num. adj. distributive [DVI-, *two*], *two by two, two
each, two*, 5.

bis, num. adv. [DVI-, *two*], *twice*,
65.

bonus, -a, -um, melior, optimus,
adj., *good, valuable*, 16, 22 ;
N. as noun, **bonum**, *profit, advantage*, 36; plu., **bona**, *property, goods*, 45.

brevis, -e, adj. [BREG-, *break*],
short, 8.

Brundisium, -ī, N., *Brundisium*,
a seaport town in Calabria, 1,
6, 49.

Byllidēnsēs, -ium, M., *Byllidenses*,
inhabitants of Byllis in Illyria,
3.

C

C., centum, 100.

C., see Gāius.

cadāver, -eris, N. (cadō, *fall*), *dead
body, corpse*, 16.

cadō, 3, cecidī, cāsūrus, v. n.
[CAD-, *fall*], *fall*, 54 ; *turn out,
happen*, 36; *fall, perish*, 19, 61.

caedēs, -is, F. [for scaedes, from
SCID-, *split*], *slaughter*, 28, 56.

Caesar, -aris, M., *Caius Julius
Caesar*, 1, 2, 3, etc.

caespes, -itis, M. [SCID-, *split*],
cut sod, turf, 58.

calamitās, -ātis, F., *loss, misfortune, adversity*, 63, 64.

Calēnus, -ī, M., *Quintus Fufius
Calenus*, one of Caesar's lieutenants, 6.

Candāvia, -ae, F., *Candavia*, a
district of Illyria, 2, 42.

canō, 3, cecinī, — [CAN-, *sound,
sing*], *sing, sound*, 45.

Canulēius, -ī, M., *Lucius Canu-
leius*, one of Caesar's lieutenants, 9.

capiō, 3, cēpī, captus [CAP-, *take,
hold*], *take, seize*, 2, 11, 22, etc.;
receive, sustain, 13 ; *form*, 7, 8,
10, etc.

captīvus, -ī, M. (capiō, *take*), *captive in war, prisoner*, 34, 44.

Capua, -ae, F., *Capua*, chief city
of Campania, 34.

caput, -itis, N. [CAP-, *take, hold*],
head, 5 ; *life*, 62.

cārus, -a, -um, adj., *dear, esteemed*,
22.

castellum, -ī, N. (castrum, *fortress*), *stronghold, redoubt, fort*,
4, 9, 10, etc.

castīgō, 1 (castus, *pure* + AG-,
drive), *set right, punish, reprove*,
23.

castrum, -ī, N. [SCAD, CAD-, *cover*],
fortress ; plu., **castra**, *camp*, 4,
5, 7, etc.

cāsus, -ūs, M. (cadō, *fall*), *fall ; chance, event, fate*, 4, 27, 35, etc. ; *exigency*, 40 ; *misfortune*, 17 ; cāsū, *by chance*, 63.

causa, -ae, F. [CAV-, *watch, care*], *cause, reason*, 6, 12, 14, etc. ; causā, with gen., *for the sake of*, 9, 18, 34, etc.

cēdō, 3, cessī, cessus, v. n. [CAD-, *fall*], *go away, withdraw, retreat*, 17, 55.

celer, celeris, celere, adj. [CEL-, *strike, drive, run*], *swift, speedy*, 32.

celeritās, -ātis, F. (celer, *swift*), *speed*, 33, 41, 42, etc.

celeriter, adv. (celer, *swift*), *quickly*, 30, 38, 51 ; *immediately, soon*, 15, 16, 43, etc.

centō, -ōnis, M., *patchwork, matting*, 11.

centum, C., indecl. num. adj., *hundred*, 19, 50, 53, etc.

centuria, -ae, F. (centum, *hundred*), *division of a hundred men ; century, company*, 53.

centuriō, -ōnis, M. (centum, *hundred*), *commander of a* centuria *; captain, centurion*, 4, 5, 19, etc.

cernō, 3, crēvī, certus (-crētus) [CER-, CRE-, *part*], *separate ; distinguish, make out, perceive*, 8, 28, 32.

certus, -a, -um (perf. part. of cernō, *decide*), *fixed, certain*, 5, 9 ; certior fīō, *I am informed*, 2, 8, 17, etc.

cēterī, -ae, -a, adj. plu., *the rest, the other*, 22.

chara, -ae, F., *chara*, perhaps a kind of wild cabbage, 15.

Cilicia, -ae, F., *Cilicia*, province in Asia Minor, 62.

Ciliciēnsis, -e, adj. (Cilicia, *Cilicia*), *Cilician, from Cilicia*, 50.

circiter, adv., *about*, 19, 29, 30, etc.

circuitus, -ūs, M. (circueō, *go around*), *way around, circuit, compass*, 7, 8, 11, etc.

circum, prep. with acc., *around, round about*, 10.

circumclūdō, 3, -clūsī, -clūsus (circum, *around* +claudō, *shut*), *shut in, surround*, 7.

circum-dūcō, 3, -dūxī, -ductus, *lead around*, 24.

circum-eō (circueō), -īre, -īvī or -iī, -itus (circuitus), *go around, surround, outflank*, 55, 56.

circum-fundō, 3, -fūdī, -fūsus, *pour around ;* pass., *crowd around*, 26.

circumiciō, 3, -iēcī, -iectus (circum, *around* + iaciō, *throw*), *throw around, put about*, 12.

circum-mūniō, 4, *fortify around, surround*, 29, 59.

circum-vāllō, 1, *wall around, surround, blockade*, 10.

circum-vehor, 3, -vectus [VEH-, *carry*], *sail around*, 26.

circum-veniō, 4, -vēnī, -ventus, *come around, surround, outflank*, 11, 26, 48, etc.

citerior, -us, adj. (comp. of citer, *on this side*), *nearer ;* Gallia citerior, *hither* or *Cisalpine*

Gaul, i.e. on the Roman side of the Alps, 49.

citō, 1 (cieō, *put in motion*) [CI-, *rouse*], *rouse*; **citātus**, *at full speed*, 58.

citrā, prep. with acc., *on this side of*, 13.

cīvis, -is, M. or F. [CI-, *lie*], *citizen, fellow-citizen*, 5, 62.

cīvitās, -ātis, F. (cīvis, *citizen*), *community of citizens, state*, 2, 3, 4, etc.; *citizens*, 65.

clam, adv. [CAL-, *cover, hide*], *secretly*, 3, 7, 64.

clāmor, -ōris, M. [CAL-, *call*], *shout, cry*, 54, 65.

clārē, adv. (clārus, *clear*), *clearly, distinctly*, 56.

classicum, -ī, N., *a trumpet-call*, 45.

classis, -is, F. [CAL-, *call*], *division of the people, class; fleet*, 6, 9, 36.

claudō, 3, clausī, clausus [CLAV-, *lock*], *shut, close*, 2, 44.

Cleopatra, -ae, F., *Cleopatra*, queen of Egypt, 63.

cliēns, -entis, M., *retainer, follower*, 23.

clīvus, -ī, M. [CLI-, *lean*], *slope, hill*, 13.

Clōdius, -ī, M., *Aulus Clodius*, a friend of Scipio, 52.

Cn., see Gnaeus.

co-, see com-.

coāctum, -ī, N. (cōgō, *collect*), plu., **coācta**, *felted cloths, felt*, 11.

coagmentum, -ī, N. (cōgō, *join*), *joint, crevice*, 65.

co-emō, 3, -ēmī, -ēmptus [EM, *take*], *buy up, purchase*, 23.

coepī, coeptus (pres. **coepiō**, 3, archaic), *begin*, 2, 3, 12, etc.

cōgitō, 1 (co-, *together* + AG-, *say*), *reflect, think*, 35, 57; *plan*, 47, 48.

cōgnōscō, 3, -gnōvī, -gnitus (co-, *together* + (g)nōscō, *learn*) [GNO-, *know*], *learn, ascertain*, 3, 4, 7, etc.

cōgō, 3, coēgī, coāctus (co-, *together* + agō, *drive*), *drive together, collect*, 36, 43, 63; *compel, force*, 13, 16, 21, etc.

cohors, -hortis, F., *cohort*, division of 360 men, 16, 17, 18, etc.

co-hortor, 1, *exhort, encourage, urge*, 13, 43, 45, etc.

collis, -is, M. [CEL-, *rise*], *hill*, 10, 11, 12, etc.

colōnia, -ae, F. (colō, *till*) [COL-, *till*], *colony*, 49.

com- (con-, co-), forms taken by cum in composition, *together, with*.

comes, -itis, M. (com-, *with* + I-, *go*), *associate, sharer, partner*, 43.

comitātus, -ūs, M. (comitor, *attend*), *number of attendants, company, escort*, 24, 58.

comitium, -ī, N. (com-, *with* + I-, *go*), *place of assembly*; plu., **comitia**, *an assembly of people* for voting, *election*, 1, 45.

commeātus (conm-), -ūs, M. (commeō, *go back and forth*), *provisions, supplies*, 8, 9, 10, etc.

com-memorō (conm-), 1, *call to mind, recount, relate*, 29, 52.

commendō (conm-), 1 (com-, *together* + mandō, *put in hand*), *intrust, commend*, 60.

commīlitō, -ōnis, M., *fellow-soldier*, 34.

com-mittō (conm-), 3, -mīsī, -missus, *bring together, join*, 38; *commit, intrust*, 23, 37; *allow*, 27.

commodus, -a, -um, adj. (com-, *together* + modus, *measure*), *full; suitable, good*, 25, 47, 59.

com-mūniō (conm-), 4, *fortify, secure, intrench*, 9, 10, 17.

commūnis (conm-), -e, adj. (com-, *together* + MV-, *shut*), *common*, 35.

commūtātiō (conm-), -ōnis, F. (commūtō, *change*), *change*, 31, 35.

com-mūtō (conm-), 1, *change*, 28, 36.

com-parō (conp-), 1, *prepare, make ready, get together*, 13, 41, 62.

com-pellō (conp-), 3, -pulī, -pulsus, *drive together, force, drive*, 8, 57.

complector (conpl-), 3, -plexus (com-, *together* + PLEC-, *fold*), *embrace, include*, 26.

com-pleō (conpl-), 2, -ēvī, -ētus [PLE-, *fill*], *fill full, fill*, 25, 26; *man*, 44.

complūrēs (conpl-), -a or -ia, adj. (com-, *together* + plūs, *more*), *more than one; several, many*, 4, 5, 13, etc.

com-portō (conp-), 1, *carry together, collect, bring*, 3, 9, 25.

compositiō (conp-), -ōnis, F. (compōnō, *bring together*), *adjustment, agreement*, 5.

com-prehendō (conp-), 3, -hendī, -hēnsus, *seize, arrest*, 13, 64.

comprimō (conp-), 3, -pressī, -pressus (com-, *together* + premō, *press*), *press together; check, restrain*, 28.

con-, see com-.

cōnātus, -ūs, M. (cōnor, *try*), *attempt, endeavor, enterprise*, 6.

con-cēdō, 3, -cessī, -cessus, *grant, concede, give up*, 23, 43.

con-celebrō, 1, *publish, proclaim*, 35.

concinō, 3, -cinuī, —, v. n. (con-, *together* + canō, *sound*), *sound*, 54.

con-clāmō, 1, *cry out together, shout*, 1; *give signal for packing up*, 38.

con-currō, 3, -currī or -cucurrī, -cursus, v. n. [CER-, *run*], *run together, assemble*, 43; *rush together, meet*, 48; *charge*, 51, 55.

concursus, -ūs, M. (concurrō, *run together*), *onset, charge*, 35, 54.

condiciō, -ōnis, F. (con-, *together* + DIC-, *show*), *conditions, terms*, 41.

con-dūcō, 3, -dūxī, -ductus, *lead together, collect*, 4.

cōn-ferō, cōnferre, contulī, conlātus (coll-), *bring together, gather*, 8; *compare*, 44; *transfer*, 44; sē cōnferre, *betake one-*

self, go, 56 ; **conlāta,** *near, opposite,* 42.

cōnfestim, adv. (con-, *together* + FEN-, FEND-, *strike*), *at once, immediately,* 16, 39, 47.

cōnficiō, 3, -fēcī, -fectus (con-, *together* + faciō, *do, make*), *do thoroughly, bring to an end, finish, accomplish,* 14, 17, 23, etc. ; *use up, exhaust,* 54, 57, 59, etc.

cōn-fīdō, 3, -fīsus, v. n. [FID-, *trust*], *trust, be assured, be confident,* 15 ; *rely on, have confidence in,* 37, 43, 56, etc.

cōn-fīrmō, 1, *strengthen, encourage, reassure,* 27, 32, 41, etc. ; *ratify, corroborate,* 30; *assert,* 48, 49; **cōnfirmātus,** *confident,* 46.

cōn-fugiō, 3, -fūgī, —, v. n., *flee for refuge, take refuge,* 57.

congiārium, -ī, N., *a largess in oil, in money,* 19.

coniciō or **cōiciō,** 3, -iēcī, -iectus (con-, *together* + iaciō, *throw*), *throw together, hurl,* 13, 16, 19, etc.

coniectō, 1 (coniciō, *throw together*), *conjecture, infer,* 66.

coniectūra, -ae, F. (coniciō, *throw together*), *conjecture, inference,* 41.

con-iungō, 3, -iūnxī, -iūnctus [IVG-, *bind*], *join together, unite,* 4, 7, 26, etc.

con-laudō (coll-), 1, *praise highly, extol,* 19.

conligō (coll-), 3, -lēgī, -lēctus (con-, *together* + legō, *gather*), *collect ;* sē conligere, *recover,* 28.

con-locō (coll-), 1, *place, station, set, store,* 7, 11, 50, etc.

conloquium (coll-), -ī, N. (conloquor, *speak together*), *conference, parley,* 5, 15, 52.

con-loquor (coll-), 3, -locūtus, v. dep. n., *speak with, converse with,* 23, 63.

cōnor, 1, *undertake, attempt, try,* 2, 14, 21, etc.

con-quiēscō, 3, -quiēvī, -quiētus, v. n., *rest, stop,* 38.

conquīrō, 3, -quīsīvī, -quīsītus (con-, *together* + quaerō, *seek*), *hunt up, seek,* 9, 58.

cōnscendō, 3, -scendī, -scēnsus (con-, *together* + scandō, *climb*) [SCAND-, *climb*], *mount, embark upon,* 1, 58, 64.

cōnscientia, -ae, F. (cōnsciō, *be conscious*), *consciousness ; moral sense, sense of guilt,* 23.

cōn-scrībō, 3, -scrīpsī, -scrīptus, *enlist, levy,* 24.

cōnsecrō, 1 (con-, *together* + sacrō, *consecrate*), *dedicate,* 65.

cōnsēnsus, -ūs, M. (cōnsentiō, *agree*), *consent, agreement,* 62.

cōn-sequor, 3, -secūtus, *follow, overtake, come up with,* 38, 40, 66.

cōn-servō, 1, *keep safe, preserve, spare,* 2, 19, 27, etc.

cōnsīderātē, adv. (cōnsīderātus, *deliberate*), *deliberately,* 45.

cōn-sīdō, 3, -sēdī, -sessus, v. n. [SID-, *sit*], *settle, encamp, take up a position,* 17, 39, 60.

cōnsilium, -ī, N. (con-, *together* +

SAL-, *leap*), assembly, council, 45, 48, 49; *plan*, 7, 8, 9, etc.

cōn-sistō, 3, -stitī, —, v. n. [STA-, *stand*], stand still, halt, stand one's ground, 4, 32, 55, etc.; take one's stand, post oneself, 17, 51, 57, etc.

cōn-sōlor, 1 [SAL-, *save*], encourage, cheer, 60.

cōnspectus, -ūs, M. (cōnspiciō, *see*), sight, 17, 34, 38.

cōnspiciō, 3, -spexī, -spectus (con-, *together* + SPEC-, *see*), see, perceive, 33.

cōnspicor, 1 (con-, *together* + SPEC-, *see*), get sight of, perceive, 27, 42.

cōnspīrātus, -a, -um, adj. (perf. part. of cōnspīrō, *breathe together*), acting together, in unison, 13.

cōn-stat, 1, -stitit, v. n. impersonal [STA-, *stand*], it is clear, it is agreed, 19, 65.

cōn-sternō, 3, -strāvī, -strātus [STER-, STRA-, *strew*], strew over, thatch, cover, 58.

cōnstituō, 3, -stituī, -stitūtus (con-, *together* + statuō, *set up*), station, draw up, 20, 51; establish, 9; fix upon, determine, decide, 4, 5, 11, etc.

cōn-stō, 1, -stitī, -stātūrus, v. n. [STA-, *stand*], stand firm; depend, 51.

cōn-suēscō, 3, -suēvī, -suētus, v. n., *become accustomed*; perf., be accustomed, 14.

cōnsuētūdō, -inis, F. (cōnsuēscō,

become accustomed), custom, practice, 24, 28, 46, etc.; familiarity, intimacy, 42.

cōnsul, -ulis, M. (con-, *together* + SAL-, *leap*), consul, 1, 3.

cōnsulāris, -is, M. (cōnsul, *consul*), one of consular rank, ex-consul, 45.

cōnsulātus, -ūs, M. (cōnsul, *consul*), office of consul, consulship, 45.

cōnsulō, 3, -suluī, -sultus, v. n. (con-, *together* + SAL-, *leap*), take counsel, take thought, 17, 32.

cōnsultum, -ī, N. (cōnsultus, perf. part. of cōnsulō, *decide*), decree, decision, 50.

cōn-sūmō, 3, -sūmpsī, -sūmptus, use up, exhaust, 14, 21, 55; carry off, kill, 49.

cōn-surgō, 3, -surrēxī, -surrēctus, v. n. [REG-, *stretch*], rise, stand up, 60.

contemptiō, -ōnis, F. (contemnō, *despise*), contempt, scorn, 23.

con-tendō, 3, -tendī, -tentus, v. n., stretch for, hasten, 4, 7, 41, etc.; strive, 52; contend, dispute, 45; beg, 59.

contentus, -a, -um, adj. (perf. part. of contineō, *hold together*), contented, satisfied, 17.

continēns, -entis, adj. (pres. part. of contineō, *hold together*), unbroken, uninterrupted, 26, 59; *following* without interruption, 46; as noun, F. (sc. terra), mainland, 6, 49.

contineō, 2, -tinuī, -tentus (con-,

together + **teneō**, *hold*), *hold fast, keep, retain, hem in,* 7, 12, 17, etc.; *keep back, hold in check,* 14, 16.

contingō, 3, -tigī, -tāctus (con-, *together* + **tangō**, *touch*) [TAG-, *touch*], *touch closely, border on,* 20, 29.

cōntiō, -ōnis, F. (for coventio from co-, *together* + VEN-, *come*), *assembly ; speech,* 36, 37.

cōntiōnor, 1, v. n. (cōntiō, *speech*), *harangue, make an address,* 1, 45.

contrā, adv., *on the contrary ;* with atque, *contrary to, otherwise than,* 3 ; prep. with acc., *facing, over against, next,* 13, 26, 39, etc.; *against, in opposition to,* 2, 37.

contrārius, -a, -um, adj. (contrā, *against*), *situated over against, facing, opposite,* 12, 26.

contrōversia, -ae, F. (contrōversus, *disputed*), *dispute, debate,* 45.

contubernium, -ī, N. (con-, *together* + taberna, *hut*), *tent,* 39.

contumēlia, -ae, F., *insult,* 34.

con-tundō, 3, -tudī, -tūsus or -tūnsus, *bruise, grind,* 21.

con-veniō, 4, -vēnī, -ventus, *come together, assemble, gather,* 5, 9, 14, etc.

con-vertō, 3, -vertī, -versus, *turn, face,* 26, 55; sē convertere, *turn about,* 65.

cōpia, -ae, F., *abundance, supply,* 14, 15, 16, etc. ; plu., **cōpiae,** *supplies, resources,* 41 ; *troops, forces,* 4, 7, 8, etc.

Coponius, -ī, M., *Caius Coponius,* one of Pompey's officers, 6.

Corcȳra, -ae, F., *Corcyra,* island in the Ionian Sea, 21.

corium, -ī, N., *hide,* 11.

Cornēlius, -ī, M., *Cornelius,* a Roman nomen, 5.

cornū, -ūs, N. [CAR-, *hard*], *horn ; wing of an army,* 30, 31, 32, etc.

corpus, -oris, N. [CER-, *make*], *body,* 32.

cor-rogō (conr-), 1, *collect by entreaty,* 62.

cor-rumpō (conr-), 3, -rūpī, -ruptus [RVP-, *break*], *destroy, waste,* 21 ; *carry away,* 27.

cortex, -icis, M. and F. [CAR-, *hard*], *bark,* 15.

cotīdiānus, -a, -um, adj. (cotīdiē, *daily*), *daily,* 16, 46, 47.

cotīdiē, adv. (quot, *how many* + diēs, *day*), *daily, every day,* 14, 16, 24, etc.

Crāstinus, -ī, M., *Crastinus,* a volunteer veteran in Caesar's army, 53, 61.

crātēs, -ium, F. plu., *hurdles,* 13, 43.

crēber, crēbra, crēbrum, adj. [CER-, CRE-, *make*], *close together, frequent, repeated,* 5, 12, 15.

crēbrō, adv. (crēber, *frequent*), *repeatedly, often,* 5.

crēdō, 3, -didī, -ditus (CRAT-, *faith* + DA-, *put*), *believe, suppose,* 33.

creō, 1 [CER-, CRE-, *make*], *make, create, choose, appoint,* 1.

culpa, -ae, F. [SCALP-, *cut*], *error, blame, fault,* 35, 36.

cum, prep. with abl., *with, together with,* 5, 7, 8, etc.

cum or **quom,** conj., of time, *when, while,* 2, 4, 5, etc.; *whenever,* 11 ; **cum . . . tum,** *not only . . . but also, both . . . and,* 9, 14, 16, etc.; of cause, *since,* 12, 19, 31, etc.; of concession, *although,* 24, 40.

cūnctus, -a, -um, adj. (for co(n)iūnctus, perf. part. of coniungō, *join together*), *all together, all, entire,* 42, 45, 50.

cupiditās, -ātis, F. (cupidus, *eager*), *eagerness,* 37.

cupiō, 3, cupīvī, cupītus [CVP-, *wish*], *long, desire,* 30, 40.

cūrātiō, -ōnis, F. (cūrō, *care for*), *charge,* 64.

cūrō, 1 [CAV-, *watch, ware*], *care for;* with gerundive, *have a thing done,* 22, 44.

cursus, -ūs, M. (currō, *run*) [CER-, *run*], *running, speed,* 13, 32, 55 ; *voyage, course, march,* 14, 54.

custōdia, -ae, F. (custōs, *keeper*), *watch, guard,* 24 ; *custody, prison,* 64.

Cyprus, -ī, F., *Cyprus,* island south of Asia Minor, 62, 66.

D

dē, prep. with abl., *down from, from, for,* 19, 29 ; of time, *during, at,* 25, 38, 40 ; *concerning, about,* 2, 5, 9, etc.

dēbeō, 2, -uī, -itus (for dehibeo, dē, *from* + habeō, *hold*), *withhold ; owe, be bound, ought,* 5, 17, 36, etc.

decem, X., indecl. num. adj., *ten,* 26, 32, 50, etc.

dē-cernō, 3, -crēvī, -crētus, v. n., *decide by combat ; contend,* 8.

dē-certō, 1, v. n. [CER-, CRE-, *part*], *fight out ; contend,* 5, 41 ; **proeliō dēcertāre,** *fight a decisive battle,* 11, 17, 20, etc.

decimus, -a, -um, X., num. adj. (decem, *ten*), *tenth,* 51, 53.

dēcipiō, 3, -cēpī, -ceptus (dē, *from* + capiō, *take*), *catch, deceive,* 45.

dēclīvis, -e, adj. (dē, *down* + clīvus, *slope*), *sloping ;* N. as noun, *slope,* 12, 17.

decumānus, -a, -um, adj. (decimus, *tenth*), *of the tenth* cohort ; with porta, the main entrance of a camp, *rear gate,* 32, 39, 58.

dēdecus, -oris, N. (dē, *from, dis-* + decus, *honor*), *disgrace, disgraceful act,* 27.

dēditiō, -ōnis, F. (dēdō, *give up*), *surrender,* 59, 60.

dē-dō, 3, -didī, -ditus [DA-, *give*], *give up, yield, surrender,* 2, 61.

dē-dūcō, 3, -dūxī, -ductus, *lead away, withdraw,* 25, 28, 32, etc.

dē-fatīgō, 1, *tire out, exhaust,* 47.

dēfendō, 3, -fendī, -fēnsus (dē,

from + FEND-, *strike*), *ward off ; protect, defend*, 2, 26, 27, etc.

dēfēnsiō, -ōnis, F. (dēfendō, *defend*), *defense, protection*, 57.

dēfēnsor, -ōris, M. (dēfendō, *defend*), *defender*, 26.

dē-ferō, -ferre, -tulī, -lātus, *bear down, drive*, 7 ; *take*, 27 ; *report*, 7, 22, 24, etc.

dēfessus, -a, -um, adj. (perf. part. of dēfetīscor, *grow weary*), *worn out, exhausted*, 56.

dēficiō, 3, -fēcī, -fectus (dē, *from* + faciō, *make*), v. n., *be wanting, fail*, 21 ; v. a., *desert, fail*, 27, 61.

dē-finiō, 4, *define, fix, settle*, 45.

dēiciō, 3, -iēcī, -iectus (dē, *down* + iaciō, *throw*), *throw down, dislodge*, 17, 26.

deinceps, adv. (dein, *next* + CAP-, *take*), *one after another, in succession*, 20.

dēlectō, 1, *delight, charm, please*, 45.

dēlēctus, -ūs, M. (dēligō, *choose*), *levy, draft*, 49, 62.

dēleō, 2, -ēvī, -ētus, *destroy*, 33.

dēligō, 3, -lēgī, -lēctus (dē, *from* + legō, *gather*), *pick out, choose*, 63.

dē-minuō, 3, -uī, -ūtus, *make smaller, lessen*, 30.

dēmissus, -a, -um, adj. (perf. part. of dēmittō, *lower*), *low-lying, low*, 16.

dē-mittō, 3, -mīsī, -missus, *let down, lower, drive*, 16.

dē-mōnstrō, 1, *set forth, show, mention*, 25, 26, 29, etc.

dē-moror, 1, *retard, delay*, 38.

dēnique, adv., *finally*, 35, 36.

dē-nūntiō, 1, *announce, direct, order*, 48.

dē-pellō, 3, -pulī, -pulsus, *drive out, move, dislodge*, 18, 36.

dē-pereō, -īre, -iī, —, v. n., *perish, be lost*, 49.

dē-pōnō, 3, -posuī, -positus, *put down, lay, leave*, 39, 41 ; *give up, abandon*, 63.

dē-poscō, 3, -poposcī, — [PREC-, *pray*], *demand, ask*, 47.

dē-prehendō, 3, -hendī, -hēnsus *seize, catch, surprise*, 38.

dērēctus, -a, -um, adj. (perf. part of dērigō, *set straight*), *straight, direct*, 42.

dērigō, 3, -rēxī, -rēctus (dē, *from* + regō, *stretch*) [REG-, *stretch*], *set straight, direct, aim*, 7.

dēscendō, 3, -scendī, -scēnsus, v. n. (dē, *down* + scandō, *climb*) [SCAND-, *climb*], *come down, descend*, 28, 60.

dē-scrībō, 3, -scrīpsī, -scrīptus, *mark off, assign*, 9.

dē-secō, 1, -secuī, -sectus [SEC-, *split*], *cut down, part*, 21.

dē-serō, 3, -seruī, -sertus, *leave, desert, abandon*, 4.

dēsīderō, 1, *long for, desire, need, require*, 24, 37 ; *lose*, 19, 34, 60, etc.

dē-sīgnō, 1, *point out, indicate*, 58.

dē-sinō, 3, -siī (but dēstitī is

used instead), -situs, *leave off,
cease, forbear,* 5.

dē-sistō, 3, -stitī, -stitus, v. n.
[STA-, *stand*], *cease, desist,* 6.

dē-spērō, 1, *have no hope of, de-
spair of, give up,* 2, 9.

dēspiciō, 3, -spexī, -spectus (dē,
down + SPEC-, *see*), *look down
upon, despise,* 22, 63, 64; *express
contempt for,* 49.

dēstituō, 3, -stituī, -stitūtus (dē,
down + statuō, *set*), *leave alone,
abandon,* 55.

dē-sum, -esse, -fuī, v. n., *be wanting, fail, be unequal to, miss,* 42,
55, 58.

dē-tendō, 3, —, -tēnsus, *unstretch ; take down, strike,* 47.

dētineō, 2, -uī, -tentus (dē, *from*
+ teneō, *hold*), *detain, check,*
38.

dē-trahō, 3, -trāxī, -trāctus
[TRAG-, *draw*], *draw away,
take away, take off,* 51, 58.

dētrīmentum, -ī, N. (dēterō, *wear
away*), *loss, defeat,* 12, 13, 28,
etc.

dē-turbō, 1 [TVR-, *crowd*], *thrust
down, drive,* 30.

dē-vincō, 3, -vīcī, -victus, *overcome, subdue completely,* 49.

dexter, -tera or -tra, -terum or
-trum, adj., *right, on the right,*
31, 32, 48, etc.

di-, see dis-.

Diāna, -ae, F. [DIV-, *shine*],
Diana, goddess of light, 65.

dīcō, 3, dīxī, dictus [DIC-, *show*],
say, declare, 4, 12, 45, etc.

dictātor, -ōris, M. (dictō, *dictate*)
dictator, 1.

dictātūra, -ae, F. (dictō, *dictate*),
office of dictator, dictatorship, 1.

diēs, diēī or diē, M. (sometimes
F. in sing.) [DIV-, *shine*], *day,*
1, 2, 4, etc.

dif-, see dis-.

dif-ferō, -ferre, distulī, dīlātus,
put off, postpone, 23, 47.

difficilis, -e, adj. (dis-, *not* +
facilis, *easy*), *not easy, hard,
difficult,* 8, 23, 48.

difficultās, -ātis, F. (difficilis, *difficult*), *difficulty,* 17.

dif-fīdō, 3, -fīsus, v. n. [FID-,
trust], *be distrustful, lose confidence,* 56, 59.

dīgnitās, -ātis, F. (dīgnus, *worthy*),
worth, authority, honor, 53.

dīligenter, adv. (dīligēns, *careful*), *carefully, with great pains,*
44, 56.

dīligentia, -ae, F. (dīligēns, *careful*), *care, assiduity, watchful-
ness,* 9, 24, 27, etc.

dīmicō, 1, *fight, contend,* 10, 11,
26, etc.

dī-mittō, 3, -mīsī, -missus, *send
here and there,* 42, 62 ; *let go,
abandon,* 15, 32, 36, etc.

dīripiō, 3, -ripuī, -reptus (dī-,
apart + rapiō, *snatch*) [RAP-,
snatch], *tear asunder ; lay
waste, plunder,* 43.

dis- (dī-, dif-), inseparable prefix,
apart ; not, un-.

dis-cēdō, 3, -cessī, -cessus, v. n.,
go apart ; go away, depart,

7, 8, 11, etc.; *withdraw, come off*, 13, 14.

discessus, -ūs, M. (**discēdō**, *depart*), *departure, withdrawal*, 39, 43.

dis-currō, 3, -currī or -cucurrī, -cursus, v. n. [CER-, *run*], *run to and fro*, 65.

disiciō, 3, -iēcī, -iectus (**dis-**, *apart* + **iaciō**, *throw*), *throw asunder, scatter*, 13.

dīspergō, 3, -spersī, -spersus (**dī-**, *apart* + **spargō**, *strew*), *scatter, disperse*, 50, 54.

dis-pōnō, 3, -posuī, -positus, *put here and there, distribute*, 50; *arrange, draw up*, 54.

dissēnsiō, -ōnis, F. (**dissentiō**, *differ*), *difference, strife*, 50.

dis-tendō, 3, -tendī, -tentus, *stretch out, break, throw into confusion*, 54.

distineō, 2, -tinuī, -tentus (**dis-**, *apart* + **teneō**, *hold*), *keep asunder*, 11, 18.

dī-stō, 1, —, —, v. n. [STA-, *stand*], *stand apart, be distant*, 63.

dis-trahō, 3, -trāxī, -trāctus [TRAG-, *draw*], *draw asunder, break*, 54.

diū, diūtius, diūtissimē, adv. [DIV-, *shine*], *long, a long time*, 57, 62.

diurnus, -a, -um, adj. (**dius** akin to **diēs**, *day*), *daily, by day*, 4.

dīversus, -a, -um, adj. (perf. part. of **dīvertō**, *turn away*), *opposite, contrary, different*, 7, 8, 30.

dīvidō, 3, -vīsī, -vīsus (**dī-**, *apart* + VID-, *split*), *force apart; divide*, 59.

dō, dare, dedī, datus [DA-, *give*], *give*, 3, 13, 14, etc.; **operam dare**, *take pains, serve*, 36, 53.

doceō, 2, docuī, doctus [DAC-, *show*], *show, teach, explain, inform of*, 16, 42, 43, etc.

dolor, -ōris, M. (**doleō**, *suffer*), *grief, vexation*, 37.

domesticus, -a, -um, adj. (**domus**, *house*), *of the household; one's own*, 23.

Domitius, -ī, M., *Cnaeus Domitius Calvinus*, one of Caesar's lieutenants, 41, 42, 51, etc.

domus, -ūs, F. [DOM-, *build*], *house, home*, 9, 45 ; **domī**, *at home*, 22; **domum**, *homewards*, 22, 49.

dōnō, 1 (**dōnum**, *gift*), *present*, 19.

dōnum, -ī, N. [DA-, *give*], *gift*, 19.

dubitō, 1 [DVA-, *apart, two*], *hesitate*, 49, 66.

ducentī, -ae, -a, **CC.**, num. adj. (DVA-, *two* + **centum**, *hundred*), *two hundred*, 19, 61, 66.

dūcō, 3, dūxī, ductus [DVC-, *lead*], *lead*, 25, 29, 32, etc. ; *protract*, 9, 17.

duo, duae, duo, **II.**, num. adj. [DVA-, *two*], *two*, 7, 17, 18, etc.

duodecim, **XII.**, indecl. num. adj. (DVA-, *two* + **decem**, *ten*), *twelve*, 1, 28.

duplex, -icis, adj. [DVA-, *two* + PLEC-, *fold*], *twofold, double*, 19, 26, 30.

duplicō, 1 (duplex, *twofold*), . *double*, 39, 54.

dūrus, -a, -um, adj., *hard, ad-. verse,* 56.

dux, ducis, M. [DVC-, *lead*], *leader, guide,* 57 ; *commander, chief,* 35, 36.

Dyrrachīnus, -a, -um, adj. (Dyrra-chium, *Dyrrachium*), *of Dyrra-chium, Dyrrachian,* 43, 46, 49, etc. ; masc. plu., *inhabitants of Dyrrachium,* 7.

Dyrrachium, -ī, N., *Dyrrachium,* a town of Illyria, on the coast, 2, 4, 6, etc.

E

ē, see ex.

ēdictum, -ī, N. (ēdīcō, *proclaim*), *proclamation, edict,* 62.

ēditus, -a, -um, adj. (perf. part. of ēdō, *raise*), *elevated, high,* 9, 10.

ē-dūcō, 3, -dūxī, -ductus, *lead out,* 6, 7, 8, etc.

efferō, -ferre, extulī, ēlātus (ex, *out* + ferō, *carry*), *carry out ; raise, exalt, extol,* 49.

efficiō, 3, -fēcī, -fectus (ex, *out* + faciō, *make*), *make, cause, form, construct,* 10, 11, 15, etc. ; *ac-complish,* 43, 46, 62.

effodiō, 3, -fōdī, -fossus (ex, *out* + fodiō, *dig*), *dig out ; ran-sack,* 9.

egēns, -entis, adj. (pres. part. of egeō, *need*), *poor, needy,* 22.

ego, meī ; plu. nōs, nostrūm or nostrī, personal pron., *I, me, we, us,* 5, 23, 27, etc.

ēgredior, 3, -gressus, v. dep. n. (ē, *out* + gradior, *walk*), *come out, go out,* 28, 38, 40; v. transitive, *go out from, leave,* 18.

Egus, -ī, M., *Egus,* an Allobro-gian, 22, 42.

ēiciō, 3, -iēcī, -iectus (ē, *out* + iaciō, *throw*), *cast out ;* sē ēicere, *rush out,* 58.

ēlātus, -a, -um, adj. (perf. part. of efferō, *exalt*), *exalted, puffed up,* 22, 42.

ēliciō, 3, -licuī, — (ē, *out* + -laciō, *entice*), *draw out, entice,* 47.

ēligō, 3, -lēgī, -lēctus (ē, *out* + legō, *gather*), *pick out, choose,* 46, 53.

Ēlis, -idis, F., *Elis,* capital of Elis, province in Peloponnesus, 65.

ē-mittō, 3, -mīsī, -missus, *send out, send forth,* 39.

enim, conj. (postpositive), *for,* 1, 8, 10, etc.

ē-numerō, 1, *count over, count,* 65.

eō, īre, īvī or iī, itum, v. n. [I-, *go*], *go ;* intrō eō, see introeō.

eō, adv. (is, *that*), *to that place, thither,* 1, 4, 6, etc.

eōdem, adv. (īdem, *the same*), *to the same place,* 8, 25, 28, etc.

Ephesius, -a, -um, adj. (Ephesus,

Ephesus), *Ephesian, of Ephesus*, 65.

Ephesus, -ī, F., *Ephesus*, city in Ionia, 65.

Ēpīrus (-os), -ī, F., *Epirus*, province in northern Greece, 3, 4, 9, etc.

eques, equitis, M. (**equus**, *horse*), *horseman, knight, cavalryman*, 9, 10, 14, etc.

equester, -tris, -tre, adj. (**eques**, *horseman*), *of cavalry, equestrian*, 38, 46.

equitātus, -ūs, M. (**equitō**, *ride*), *cavalry*, 1, 10, 21, etc.

equus, -ī, M. (**AC-**, *swift*), *horse*, 16, 21, 56, etc.

ergō, adv., *therefore, then*, 5.

ēricius, -ī, M. (**ēr**, *hedgehog*), *a beam set with spikes, chevaux-de-frise*, 30.

error, -ōris, M., *wandering, error, mistake*, 36.

ē-rumpō, 3, -rūpī, -ruptus, v. n. [RVP-, *break*], *break out, rush forth*, 11.

ēruptiō, -ōnis, F. (**ērumpō**, *rush forth*), *sally, sortie*, 21, 25.

et, conj., *and*, 1, 2, 3, etc.; **et . . . et**, *both . . . and*, 11, 27, 30, etc.

etiam, adv. (**et**, *and* + **iam**, *now*), *now too, still, even*, 2,4, 5, etc.; *also, likewise*, 14, 15, 16, etc.; **nōn sōlum . . . sed etiam**, *not only . . . but also*, 22, 36.

etsī, conj. (**et**, *even* + **sī**, *if*), *although*, 11, 57, 59.

ēventus, -ūs, M. (**ēveniō**, *come out*), *outcome, issue*, 56, 58.

ēvocātus, -a, -um, adj. (perf. part. of **ēvocō**, *call out*), *enlisted;* M. as noun, *volunteer veteran*, 19, 50, 53.

ē-vocō, 1, *call out, summon*, 65,66.

ex or (before consonants only) **ē**, prep. with abl., *out of, from, of*, 1, 2, 4, etc.; *after*, 61; *because of*, 41; *in accordance with*, 10, 17, 23, etc.

exanimō, 1 (**exanimus**, *lifeless*), *put out of breath, fatigue*, 54.

ex-ārēscō, 3, -āruī, —, v. n., *dry up, become dry*, 16.

ex-audiō, 4, *hear clearly, distinguish*, 56, 65.

ex-cēdō, 3, -cessī, -cessus, v. n., *go out, retire, withdraw*, 12, 29, 55.

excellēns, -entis, adj. (pres. part. of **excellō**, *surpass*), *surpassing, preëminent*, 61.

excīdō, 3, -cīdī, -cīsus (**ex**, *out* + **caedō**, *cut*), *cut down*, 30.

excipiō, 3, -cēpī, -ceptus (**ex**, *out* + **capiō**, *take*), *take up, follow*, 49; *receive, meet*, 54, 55.

exclūdō, 3, -clūsī, -clūsus (**ex**, *out* + **claudō**, *shut*), *cut off, separate*, 41, 62.

ex-cubō, 1, -cubuī, -cubitus, v. n., *camp out, keep watch*, 16, 26.

excursus, -ūs, M. (**excurrō**, *run out*), *dash, charge*, 54.

exemplum, -ī, N. (**ex**, *out* + **EM-**, *take*), *example; warning*, 43.

exercitātus, -a, -um, adj. (perf. part. of **exercitō**, *exercise*), *trained, disciplined*, 36, 55.

exercitus, -ūs, M. (exerceō, *train*), *trained body of men, army,* 4, 7, 8, etc.

exigō, 3, -ēgī, -āctus (ex, *out* + agō, *drive*), *drive out ; demand, exact,* 3.

exīstimō, 1 (ex, *out* + aestimō, *value*), *estimate ; consider, think,* 8, 9, 12, etc.

exitus, -ūs, M. (exeō, *go out*), *way out, escape,* 32.

expedītus, -a, -um, adj. (perf. part. of expediō, *set free*), *free, unencumbered, without baggage,* 1, 38, 40, etc. ; *unobstructed, clear,* 7, 38, 42 ; *complete,* 33.

ex-pellō, 3, -pulī, -pulsus, *drive out, dislodge,* 36, 63.

experior, 4, -pertus (ex, *out* + PAR-, PER-, *try*), *try, make trial of,* 23.

expleō, 2, -plēvī, -plētus (ex, *out* + pleō, *fill*) [PLE-, *fill*], *fill up, make up,* 50.

ex-plicō, 1, -āvī or -uī, -ātus or -itus [PLEC-, *fold*], *unfold, deploy,* 55 ; *set in order, arrange,* 38, 41.

explōrātor, -ōris, M. (explōrō, *examine*), *scout,* 8, 42.

ex-pōnō, 3, -posuī, -positus, *put out, display,* 58 ; *disembark, land,* 1, 2, 26 ; *set forth, explain, relate,* 5, 42.

ex-poscō, 3, -poposcī, —, *ask earnestly, beg,* 52.

ex-pūgnō, 1, *take by storm, carry,* 8, 33, 43.

ex-sistō (existō), 3, -stitī, -stitus, v. n. [STA-, *stand*], *step out, come forth, arise,* 64, 65.

exspectātiō (exp-), -ōnis, F. (exspectō, *await*), *expectation,* 5.

ex-spectō (exp-), 1, *look for, await, wait for,* 2, 4, 41, etc. ; *expect,* 23.

ex-struō (ext-), 3, -strūxī, -strūctus, *build up, raise,* 20.

ex-tendō, 3, -tendī, -tentus or -tēnsus, *stretch out ;* sē extendere, *exert oneself,* 40.

(exter or exterus, -a, -um), adj. (ex, *out*), *outward ; of another country, foreign,* 10.

exterior, -us, adj. (comp. of exter, *outward*), *outer,* 26.

extrā, prep. with acc. (exter, *outward*), *outside, out of,* 22, 28, 35 ; *contrary to,* 47 ; adv., *outside, without,* 32.

extrēmus, -a, -um, adj. (superl. of exter, *outward*), *outermost, extreme, last,* 11 ; *edge of,* 13.

F

facilis, -e, adj. [FAC-, *make*], *capable of being done, easy,* 12 ; N. facile as adv., *easily,* 17, 21, 47, etc.

facinus, -oris, N. [FAC-, *make*], *deed, act, crime,* 23.

faciō, 3, fēcī, factus [FAC-, *make*], *make, do, cause,* 1, 2, 3, etc. ;

potestātem facere, *give a chance,* 8 ; **iter facere,** *march,* 41, 42 ; **proelium facere,** *fight a battle,* 19, 42, 46, etc.

facultās, -ātis, F. (**facilis,** *easy*), *opportunity, means, resources,* 23, 43, 59.

fallō, 3, fefellī, falsus [FAL-, *trip*], *deceive, disappoint,* 30, 48, 56, etc.

falsus, -a, -um, adj. (perf. part. of **fallō,** *deceive*), *false, incorrect,* 22, 35, 61.

fāma, -ae, F. [FA-, *shine, show*], *report, rumor,* 10, 35, 42, etc. ; *reputation,* 20.

famēs, -is, F., *hunger, famine,* 15.

familia, -ae, F. (**famulus,** *attendant*), *household establishment, family, servants,* 63.

familiāris, -is, M. (**familia,** *household*), *friend, companion,* 42.

fānum, -ī, N. [FA-, *shine, show*], *sanctuary, temple,* 65.

fās (used in nom. and acc. singular only), N. [FA-, *shine, show*], *divine law ;* **fās est,** *it is lawful, right,* 65.

fascis, -is, M. [FASC-, *twist*], *bundle ;* plu. **fascēs,** *fasces,* bundle of rods with an axe, carried before the highest magistrates by the lictors, 34.

fēlīcitās, -ātis, F. (**fēlīx,** *happy*), *happiness, good fortune, luck,* 6, 36.

ferē, adv. [FER-, *hold*], *closely ; generally,* 14 ; *nearly, almost, about,* 7, 11, 13, etc.

fēriae, -ārum, F., *holidays, festival,* 1.

ferō, ferre, tulī, lātus [FER-, TOL-, TLA-, *bear, lift*], *bear, bring,* 35, 41, 65 ; *require,* 10 ; *prompt,* 24 ; pass., *be borne, rush,* 41 ; *bear, endure,* 8, 14, 17, etc. ; **graviter ferre,** *take to heart,* 36.

fidēs, fideī, F. [FID-, *bind, trust*], *faith, confidence, faithfulness,* 27, 34 ; *promise, good faith,* 45.

fidūcia, -ae, F. [FID-, *bind, trust*], *confidence, assurance,* 35, 58.

fīlius, -ī, M. [FĪ-, *nurse*], *son,* 19, 22, 34.

fīniō, 4 (**fīnis,** *limit*), *put an end to, finish,* 17.

fīnis, -is, M. [FID-, *split*], *limit, end,* 1, 4, 40 ; plu., **fīnēs,** *boundaries, territory,* 4.

fīnitimus, -a, -um, adj. (**fīnis,** *limit*), *bordering, neighboring, near,* 3, 4, 9, etc.

fīō, fierī, factus (used as pass. of **faciō**), *be made, be done, become, take place,* 1, 7, 12, etc. ; **certior fīō,** *I am informed,* 2, 8, 17, etc.

fīrmō, 1 (**fīrmus,** *firm*), *strengthen, encourage, reassure,* 28.

fīrmus, -a, -um, adj. [FER-, *hold, fix*], *firm, unflinching, steadfast,* 48, 50.

Flaccus, -ī, M., *Valerius Flaccus,* one of Pompey's officers, 19.

Fleginās, -ātis, M., *Caius Fleginas,* a Roman knight, 34.

fleō, 2, flēvī, flētus, v. n., *weep, shed tears,* 60.

flō, 1, v. n. [FLA-, *blow*], *blow*, 6, 14.

flūmen, -inis, N. (fluō, *flow*), *river*, 4, 5, 7, etc.

fodiō, 3, fōdī, fossus [FOD-, *dig*], *dig*, 16.

folium, -ī, N. [FOL-, *blow*], *leaf*, 21.

fōns, fontis, M. [FV-, FVD-, *pour*], *spring, well*, 16.

forāmen, -inis, N. [FOR-, *bore*], *opening, hole*, 19.

fore, fut. inf. of sum.

fortasse, adv., *perhaps, possibly*, 17, 23.

forte, adv. (abl. of fors, *chance*), *by chance*, 6.

fortis, -e, adj., *strong, brave*, 22, 24, 61.

fortiter, adv. (fortis, *brave*), *bravely*, 30, 61.

fortūna, -ae, F. (cf. fors, *chance*), *chance, fate, fortune*, 4, 6, 23, etc.

fossa, -ae, F. (fodiō, *dig*), *ditch, fosse*, 13, 26, 32, etc.

frāter, -tris, M., *brother*, 22.

fraudō, 1 (fraus,„*cheating*), *steal, embezzle*, 22, 23.

frequentia, -ae, F. (frequēns, *numerous*), *large assembly, crowd, throng*, 5.

frētus, -a, -um, adj. [FER-, FRE-, *hold, fix*], *relying, trusting*, 22.

frōns, frondis, F., *foliage*, 21.

frūmentārius, -a, -um, adj. (frūmentum, *grain*), *abounding in grain, of grain, grain-*, 36, 58; rēs frūmentāria, *grain supply*, 8, 9, 10, etc.

frūmentum, -ī, N. [FRVG-, *enjoy*], *grain*, 9, 10, 11, etc.; plu., frūmenta, *crops*, 14, 15, 16, etc.

frūstrā, adv. [FRVD-, *strike*], *in vain, to no purpose, without good reason*, 40, 49, 54.

Fufius, -ī, M., *Quintus Fufius Calenus*, one of Caesar's faithful lieutenants, 66.

fuga, -ae, F. [FVG-, *flee*], *flight*, 4, 32, 34, etc.; ex fugā, *in flight*, 57, 58, 62.

fugiō, 3, fūgī, —, v. n. [FVG-, *flee*], *flee*, 27, 32, 33, etc.

fugitīvus, -ī, M. (fugiō, *flee*), *runaway, deserter*, 5.

Fulvius, -ī, M., *Fulvius Postumus*, an under-officer of Caesar, 25.

fūmus, -ī, M. [FV-, *smoke*], *smoke*, 28.

funditor, -ōris, M. (funda, *sling*), *slinger*, 11, 12, 13, etc.

G

Gabīnius, -ī, M., *Aulus Gabinius*, friend of Pompey, 63.

Gāius, Gāī, M., *Caius*, a Roman praenomen, 23, 34, 54.

galea, -ae, F., *helmet*, 25, 26.

Gallia, -ae, F., *Gaul*, 9, 22, 42, etc.

Gallicus, -a, -um, adj. (Gallī, *the Gauls*), *Gallic, pertaining to the Gauls*, 22.

Gallus, -ī, M., *Tuticanus Gallus*, one of Caesar's followers, 34.

gēns, gentis, F. [GEN-, *beget*], *race, tribe, people*, 14, 43.

genus, generis, N. [GEN-, *beget*], *stock, class, kind, character*, 14, 15, 16, etc.

Genūsus, -ī, M., *Genusus*, a river in Illyria, 38, 39.

Gergovia, -ae, F., *Gergovia*, a town in Celtic Gaul, 36.

Germānī, -ōrum, M., *the Germans*, 18.

Germānia, -ae, F., *Germany*, 49.

Germiniī, -ōrum, M., *Germinii*, a people on the coast of Epirus, 1.

gerō, 3, gessī, gestus [GES-, *carry*], *bear, manage, carry on, do, perform, wage*, 4, 10, 42, etc.; rēs gesta, *exploit*, 66.

gladius, -ī, M., *sword*, 55, 61.

glōria, -ae, F. [CLV-, *hear*], *fame; pride, vanity*, 42.

glōrior, 1 (glōria, *pride*), *boast*, 12.

Gnaeus, -ī, M., *Cnaeus*, a Roman praenomen, 41, 51.

Gomphēnsis, -e, adj. (Gomphī, *Gomphi*), *of Gomphi*, 44; plu., M., *the Gomphians, people of Gomphi*, 44.

Gomphī, -ōrum, M., *Gomphi*, a town in Thessaly, 43.

Graecus, -ī, M., *a Greek*, 2, 7, 62, etc.

Granius, -ī, M., *Aulus Granius*, a follower of Caesar, 34.

grātia, -ae, F. [GRA-, *favor*], *favor, gratitude, thanks*, 36, 45, 53.

gravis, -e, adj., *heavy, severe, serious*, 27, 37.

graviter, adv. (gravis, *heavy*), *heavily;* graviter ferre, *take to heart*, 36.

H

habeō, 2, -uī, -itus [HAB-, *have*], *have, hold*, 1, 2, 5, etc.; *pronounce, make*, 36, 37; iter habēre, *be on the way, march*, 2, 41, 42, etc.; grātiam habēre, *be grateful*, 36; *hold, consider*, 13, 22, 24; ratiōnem habēre, *take account*, 19.

harūndō (arūn-), -inis, F., *reed*, 21.

hedera, -ae, F., *ivy*, 58.

Hēraclīa (-ēa), -ae, F., *Heraclea*, a city in Macedonia, 42.

herba, -ae, F., *grass*, 21.

hīberna, -ōrum, N. (hiems, *winter*), *winter quarters*, 2.

hīc, haec, hōc, demonstrative pron., *this, these*, 1, 4, 5, etc.; as personal pron., *he, she, it*, 3.

hīc, adv. (cf. hīc, *this*), *in this place, here*, 30.

hiemō, 1, v. n. (hiems, *winter*), *pass the winter, winter*, 4.

hiems, hiemis, F., *winter*, 9.

Hirrus, -ī, M., *Lucilius Hirrus*, a follower of Pompey, 45.

Hispānia, -ae, F., *Spain,* 14, 36.

Hispānus, -a, -um, adj., *Spanish,* 50.

hodiē, adv. (hō(c) diē), *to-day,* 53.

homō, -inis, M., *human being, man,* 20, 22, 27, etc.

honestus, -a, -um, adj. (honōs, *honor*), *honorable,* 24.

honōs or **honor,** -ōris, M., *honor, respect,* 14, 22, 24, etc.

hōra, -ae, F., *hour,* 42, 43.

hordeum, -ī, N., *barley,* 14, 21.

horreum, -ī, N., *storehouse, magazine of supplies,* 9.

hortātū, abl. of (hortātus, -ūs), M.

(hortor, *incite*), *instigation, exhortation,* 48.

hortor, 1, *urge, incite, encourage,* 6, 36, 49, etc.

hospes, -itis, M., *host, friend,* one bound by the ties of hospitality, 62.

hospitium, -ī, N. (hospes, *friend*), *relation of guest and host, guest-friendship,* 63.

hostis, -is, M. and F., *stranger; enemy,* often plu., 13, 14, 22, etc.

humilis, -e, adj. (humus, *ground*), *low,* 26.

I

iaciō, 3, iēcī, iactus [IAC-, *throw*], *throw, hurl,* 15, 26, 48.

iam, adv., *already, now, at length,* 6, 15, 25, etc.

Iānuārius, -a, -um, adj. (Iānus, *Janus*), *of January,* 1.

ibī, adv., *there, in that place,* 2, 3, 4, etc.

ictus, -ūs, M. (icō, *strike*), *blow,* 26.

īdem, eadem, idem, demonstrative pron. (is, *that*), *the same,* 2, 4, 6, etc.; *the same man, he also,* 5.

idōneus, -a, -um, adj., *fit, suitable, convenient,* 7, 13, 44, etc.

īgnis, -is, M., *fire;* plu., īgnēs, *camp fires,* 7, 16.

īgnōminia, -ae, F. (in, *not* + (g)nōmen, *name, repute*), *dishonor, disgrace,* 37.

īgnōrantia, -ae, F. (īgnōrāns, *igno-*

rant), *ignorance, unfamiliarity,* 31.

īgnōrō, 1 (in, *not* + GNO-, *know*), *not know, be ignorant of,* 7, 8, 42.

ille, illa, illud, demonstrative pron., *that, those,* 23, 49, etc.; as personal pron. emphatic, *he, she, it,* 2, 3, 5, etc.

illīc, adv. (ille, *that*), *in that place, there,* 62.

illō, adv. (ille, *that*), *to that place, thither,* 41.

Īllyricum, -ī, N., *Illyria,* the country east of the Adriatic Sea, 41.

im-mittō (inm-), 3, -mīsī, -missus, *send in; throw against, discharge,* 5, 54.

impedīmentum (inp-), -ī, N. (impediō, *hinder*), *hindrance,* 13;

plu., impedīmenta, *baggage, baggage train*, 1, 38, 39, etc.

impediō (inp-), 4 (in, *upon* + PED-, *tread*), *entangle, block up, hinder*, 12, 13, 20, etc.

impedītus (inp-), -a, -um, adj. (perf. part. of impediō, *block up*), *blocked, obstructed, difficult*, 38, 40, 50.

imperātor (inp-), -ōris, M. (imperō, *command*), *commander, general*, 12, 17, 34, etc.

imperātōrius (inp-), -a, -um, adj. (imperātor, *general*), *of a general, general's*, 58.

imperātum (inp-), -ī, N. (imperātus, perf. part. of imperō, *command*), *order*, 44.

imperium (inp-), -ī, N. (cf. imperō, *command*), *order; authority, power, command*, 2, 37, 45, etc.

imperō (inp-), 1 [PAR-, *part, breed*], *command, order*, 1, 3, 9, etc.

impetrō (inp-), 1 (in, *in* + patrō, *bring about*), *obtain one's request, get*, 34, 59.

impetus (inp-), -ūs, M. (in, *upon* + PET-, *fly*), *attack, onset*, 6, 13, 17, etc.

im-plōrō (inp-), 1 [PLV-, *wash, flow*], *entreat* (with tears), *ask*, 45.

im-pōnō (inp-), 3, -posuī, -positus, *put in, put on board*, 1, 25, 63; *put on*, 26; *impose*, 37, 40.

im-portō (inp-), 1, *bring in, import*, 9.

imprīmīs (in prīmīs), adv., *among the first, particularly*, 52.

imprōvīsus (inpr-), -a, -um, adj. (in, *not* + prōvīsus, *foreseen*), *unexpected;* ex imprōvīsō, *unexpectedly*, 42.

imprūdēns (inpr-), -entis, adj. (in, *not* + prūdēns, *foreseeing*), *unaware, unsuspecting*, 7.

in, prep. with abl. or acc.; with abl., *in, on*, 1, 2, 4, etc.; *among*, 5, 19; with acc., *into, to, towards, for, against*, 2, 3, 6, etc.; in diēs, *from day to day*, 46.

in-cēdō, 3, -cessī, -cessus, v. n., *advance, come up, arise*, 11; *be infused in, fill*, 37.

incendō, 3, -cendī, -cēnsus (in, *to* + candō, *set fire*), *kindle, inflame, rouse*, 54.

incidō, 3, -cidī, —, v. n. (in, *in* + cadō, *fall*), *fall in, fall upon*, 4, 32.

incipiō, 3, -cēpī, -ceptus (in, *in* + capiō, *take*), *take in hand, begin*, 5, 15.

incitātiō, -ōnis, F. (incitō, *urge on*), *ardor, enthusiasm*, 54.

incitātus, -a, -um, adj. (perf. part. of incitō, *urge on*), *hurried, at full speed*, 13, 55.

in-citō, 1, *urge on, stir, stimulate*, 41, 54.

inclūdō, 3, -clūsī, -clūsus (in, *in* + claudō, *shut*), *inclose*, 29, 30.

incōgnitus, -a, -um, adj. (in, *not* + cōgnitus, *known*), *unknown, not known*, 49.

incolumis, -e, adj., *unharmed, unimpaired, safe,* 1, 2, 14, etc.

incommodum, -ī, N. (incommodus, *inconvenient*), *disadvantage, injury, harm, loss,* 26, 36, 37, etc.

in-crēbrēscō (-bēscō), 3, -crēbruī, —, v. n. (cf. crēber, *frequent*), *grow strong, increase,* 6.

incrēdibilis, -e, adj. (in, *not +* crēdibilis, *credible*), *incredible, extraordinary,* 6, 48.

inde, adv., *from there, thence,* 12, 62; *thereupon, then,* 10.

industria, -ae, F. (industrius, *diligent*), *diligence, zeal,* 36.

industriē, adv. (industrius, *diligent*)· *diligently, assiduously,* 57·

in-eō, -īre, -īvī and -iī, -itus, *go upon, enter upon, begin,* 20; *form,* 64.

inermis, -e, adj. (in, *not +* arma, *arms*), *unarmed, without weapons,* 55·

īnfāmia, -ae, F. (īnfāmis, *of ill repute*), *ill report, disgrace,* 37.

īnferior, -us, adj. (comp. of īnferus, *below*), *lower, smaller, inferior,* 13, 14, 46.

īn-ferō, -ferre, intulī, inlātus (ill-), *bring in, bring,* 30; *produce, cause, make,* 28, 35, 38, etc.

īnfestus, -a, -um, adj., *unsafe, dangerous, hostile, threatening,* 42; *īnfestīs sīgnīs, with flying colors,* 55·

īnfimus, -a, -um, adj. (superl. of īnferus, *below*), *lowest,* 47·

īnfīrmus, -a, -um, adj. (in, *not +* fīrmus, *strong*), *weak, not strong,* 14, 66.

(īnflātē), īnflātius, adv. (īnflātus, *puffed up*), *pompously, with exaggeration,* 42.

īnfringō, 3, -frēgī, -frāctus (in, *in +* frangō, *break*), *break, check,* 54·

inimīcus, -ī, M. (in, *not +* amīcus, *friend*), *enemy,* 64.

inīquitās, -ātis, F. (inīquus, *uneven*), *unevenness, disadvantage,* 35·

inīquus, -a, -um, adj. (in, *not +* aequus, *even*), *uneven, unfavorable, dangerous,* 17, 47·

initium, -ī, N. (ineō, *go in*), *beginning,* 32, 50, 56, etc.

iniūria, -ae, F. (iniūrius, *unlawful*), *wrong, evil deed, injustice,* 22.

iniussū, abl. of (iniussus, -ūs), M. (in, *not +* iussū, *order*), *without command,* 51.

innātus, -a, -um, adj. (perf. part. of innāscor, *be born in*), *inborn, inherent, innate,* 54.

inopia, -ae, F. (inops, *without resources*), *want, scarcity, poverty,* 14, 15, 16, etc.

inquam, v. defective (postpositive), *say,* 27, 47, 48, etc.

in-rumpō (irr-), 3, -rūpī, -ruptus, v. n. [RVP-, *break*], *rush in, force a way in,* 30.

īn-sequor, 3, -secūtus, *follow up, pursue,* 17, 33, 38·

īnsidiae, -ārum, F. (in, *against +*

SED-, *sit*), *ambush, ambuscade*, 7, 33.

īnsīgne, -is, N. (īnsīgnis, *marked*), *badge, decoration*, 34, 58.

īnsolenter, adv. (īnsolēns, *haughty*), *haughtily, insolently*, 13.

īnsolitus, -a, -um, adj. (in, *not* + solitus, *accustomed*), *unaccustomed, unused*, 47.

īnstar, indecl., N., *image; the equivalent of, about*, 29.

īnstituō, 3, -stituī, -stitūtus (in, *on* + statuō, *place*), *make, construct*, 13, 51, 55; *ordain*, 54; *begin, undertake*, 10, 59.

īnstitūtum, -ī, N. (īnstitūtus, perf. part. of īnstituō, *ordain*), *practice, custom*, 38, 46, 51.

īn-stō, 1, -stitī, -stātūrus, v. n. [STA,- *stand*], *stand upon, press on*, 12, 13, 55.

īn-struō, 3, -strūxī, -strūctus, *build in; set in order, array, draw up*, 8, 13, 20, etc.; *equip, supply*, 24.

īnsuētus, -a, -um, adj. (in, *not* + suētus, *accustomed*), *unaccustomed, unused*, 16.

integer, -gra, -grum, adj. (in, *not* + TAG, *touch*), *untouched, unimpaired, fresh*, 14, 29, 39, etc.

intellegō, 3, -lēxī, -lēctus (inter, *between* + legō, *choose*), *perceive, understand*, 23.

intentus, -a, -um, adj. (perf. part. of intendō, *strive*), *intent, eager*, 5.

inter, prep. with acc., *between,*

among, 1, 5, 26, etc.; inter sē, *with one another, together*, 5, 45.

inter-cēdō, 3, -cessī, -cessus, v. n., *come between, intervene, pass*, 45.

interclūdō, 3, -clūsī -clūsus (inter, *between* + claudō, *shut*), *shut out, cut off, intercept*, 8, 9, 32.

interdiū, adv. (inter, *between* + DIV-, *shine*), *by day, in the daytime*, 7.

inter-eō, -īre, -iī, -itūrus, v. n., *be lost, perish*, 16, 34, 49.

interficiō, 3, -fēcī, -fectus (inter, *between* + faciō, *make*), *kill*, 13, 18, 23, etc.

intericiō, 3, -iēcī, -iectus (inter, *between* + iaciō, *throw*), *throw between, put between*, 50; pass., *be interposed, intervene*, 21, 32.

interim, adv. (cf. inter, *between*), *meanwhile, meantime*, 5, 11, 17, etc.

interior, -us, adj. (comp. of interus, *within*), *inner*, 11, 26, 29.

inter-mittō, 3, -mīsī, -missus, *send between, leave off, interrupt*, 4, 8, 58; pass., *intervene*, 20, 21, 26, etc.

interpellō, 1, *hinder, prevent*, 33, 36, 65.

inter-pōnō, 3, -posuī, -positus, *put between, let pass, interpose*, 3, 37, 38.

inter-rogō, 1, *ask, inquire*, 34.

inter-rumpō, 3, -rūpī, -ruptus [RVP-, *break*], *break apart, break off, interrupt*, 5.

inter-sum, -esse, -fuī, —, v. n., *be between, intervene*, 5 ; *take part in, be present at*, 49.

intrā, prep. with acc. (cf. **inter**, *between*), *within*, 11, 13, 16, etc.

intrō, adv. (cf. **inter**, *between*), *within ;* cf. **introeō**.

intrō, 1 (cf. **inter**, *between*), *enter, go into*, 11.

intrō-dūcō, 3, -dūxī, -ductus, *lead in, bring in*, 6.

intro-eō, -īre, -īvī and -iī, -itus, v. n., *go into*, 6.

intus, adv., *within, inside*, 32.

inūsitātus, -a, -um, adj. (**in**, *not* + **ūsitātus**, *usual*), *unusual, rare,* 14.

inūtilis, -e, adj. (**in**, *not* + **ūtilis**, *useful*), *unserviceable, unfit, ineffective*, 10.

in-veniō, 4, -vēnī, -ventus, *come upon, find*, 15, 19.

invicem or **in vicem**, adv., *in turn*, 60.

invītō, 1 (for **invocitō**, *call earnestly*), *invite, attract*, 39.

ipse, -a, -um, intensive pron., *self, myself, yourself, himself*, etc., 1, 6, 7, etc. ; *very*, 5.

is, ea, id, demonstrative pron., *this, that, these, those*, 1, 2, 5, etc. ; as personal pron., *he, she, it, they*, 1, 2, 3, etc.

ita, adv., *so, in this way*, 11, 17, 19, etc.

Ītalia, -ae, F., *Italy*, 1, 3, 4, etc.

Italicus, -a, -um, adj. (**Ītalia**, *Italy*), *Italian, from Italy*, 9.

itaque, conj. (**ita**, *so* + **que**, *and*), *and so, therefore*, 8, 16, 26, etc.

item, adv., *likewise*, 9, 29, 64, etc.

iter, itineris, N. [I-, *go*], *journey, march, route*, 2, 4, 7, etc.; **iter facere (habēre)**, *be on the way, march*, 2, 41, 42, etc.

iubeō, 2, iussī, iussus, *order, bid, command*, 1, 2, 4, etc.

iūdicium, -ī, N. (**iūdex**, *judge*), *judgment, decision, opinion*, 3, 23.

iūdicō, 1 (**iūdex**, *judge*), *judge, decide, form opinion*, 3, 41, 47, etc.

iugum, -ī, N. [IVG-, *yoke*], *yoke ; ridge, summit*, 59.

Iūlius, -ī, M., *Julius*, name of a Roman gens; *Caius Julius Cæsar*, 1.

iūmentum, -ī, N. [IVG-, *yoke*], *beast of burden, pack-animal*, 11, 16, 24.

iūnior, -us, adj. (comp. of **iuvenis**, *young*), *younger ;* as noun, *youth, young man* (between the ages of 17 and 46), 62.

iūrō, 1 (**iūs**, *that which is binding*), *swear, take oath*, 4, 49, 62.

iussū, abl. of (**iussus**, -ūs), M. (**iubeō**, *order*), *by order*, 2.

iūstus, -a, -um, adj. (**iūs**, *right*), *fair, regular*, 39.

iūxtā, prep. with acc., *very near, close to*, 8, 28.

L

L., see **Lūcius**.

Labiēnus, -ī, M., *Titus Atius Labienus*, Caesar's trusted lieutenant in the Gallic wars, now in the service of Pompey, 4, 5, 34, etc.

labor, -ōris, M., *toil, effort, labor,* 6, 14, 16, etc.; *toil, hardship,* 1, 8, 19, etc.

labōrō, 1 (labor, *labor*), *toil, struggle, be oppressed*, 27.

lāc, lactis, N., *milk*, 15.

laetitia, -ae, F. (laetus, *joyful*), *rejoicing, delight*, 49.

lapis, -idis, M., *stone*, 26, 65.

Lārīsa or **Lārissa**, -ae, F., *Larissa*, city of Thessaly, 43, 58, 59, etc.

Lārīsaeī, -ōrum, M., *people of Larissa, Larisseans*, 44.

lassitūdō, -inis, F. (lassus, *weary*), *weariness*, 54, 57, 61.

lātē, adv. (lātus, *wide*), *widely, extensively*, 42 ; longē lātēque, *far and wide*, 14.

Latīnus, -a, -um, adj. (Latium, *Latium*), *of Latium, Latin*, 1.

lātitūdō, -inis, F. (lātus, *wide*), *width, breadth*, 13, 26.

lātus, -a, -um, adj. [STLA-, *strew*], *broad, extended*, 11.

latus, -eris, N., *side, flank*, 48, 55.

laudō, 1 (laus, *praise*), *praise, approve*, 49.

laurea, -ae, F., *a wreath of laurel*, 34.

laus, laudis, F. [CLV-, *hear*], *praise*, 49.

lēgātiō, -ōnis, F. (lēgātus, *ambassador*), *embassy*, 63.

lēgātus, -ī, M. (perf. part. of lēgō, *send as ambassador*), *ambassador, envoy*, 3, 5, 43, etc.; *lieutenant*, 4, 5, 6, etc.

legiō, -ōnis, F. [LEG-, *gather*], *levy of soldiers, legion*, 1, 4, 12, etc.

legiōnārius, -a, -um, adj. (legiō, *legion*), *pertaining to a legion ;* M. plu. as noun, *legionary soldiers*, 26.

legō, 3, lēgī, lēctus [LEG-, *gather*], *pick out, choose, elect*, 22.

legūmen, -inis, N., *pulse, beans*, 14.

lēnitās, -ātis, F. (lēnis, *gentle*), *gentleness, leniency*, 60.

Lentulus, -ī, M., *Lentulus*, a Roman name ; *Lentulus Marcellinus*, an officer of Caesar, 25 ; *Lucius Cornelius Lentulus*, ex-consul, ex-praetor, a great enemy of Caesar, 58, 64.

levis, -e, adj. [LEG-, *run*], *light, slight, trifling*, 6, 12, 25.

leviter, adv. (levis, *light*), *lightly, not heavily*, 54.

levō, 1 (levis, *light*), *lighten, relieve*, 15.

lēx, lēgis, F. [LEG-, *be fixed*], *law*, 1.

libenter (lub-), adv. (libēns, *willing*), *willingly, gladly*, 16.

līber, -era, -erum, adj. [LIB-, *desire*], *free ;* M. as noun, *freeman*, 43.

līberālitās, -ātis, F. (līberālis, *gen-erous*), *generosity*, 1.

līberāliter, adv. (līberālis, *gener-ous*), *like a freeman, courteous-ly*, 64 ; *liberally*, 24.

līberē, līberius, līberrimē, adv. (līber, *free*), *freely, boldly*, 17, 28, 29, etc.

līberō, 1 (līber, *free*), *set free, de-liver*, 17, 23.

lībertās, -ātis, F. (līber, *free*), *free-dom*, 53.

Libō, -ōnis, M., *Lucius Scribonius Libo*, commander of Pompey's fleet, 52.

licet, 2, licuit and licitum est, v. impersonal [LIC-, *let*], *it is lawful, it is permitted ;* alicui licet, *one may*, 1, 5, 58.

līgnor, 1, v. n. (lignum, *wood*), *collect wood*, 39.

līmen, -inis, N. [LIC-, *crook*], *threshold, entrance*, 65.

Lissus, -ī, F., *Lissus*, town of Illyria, 6, 9, 41.

littera, -ae, F. [LI-, *smear*], *letter of the alphabet ;* plu., litterae, *letter, despatch*, 34, 35, 42.

lītus, -oris, N., *sea-shore, shore*, 9, 36.

locō, 1 (locus, *place*), *place, sta-tion*, 13.

locuplēs, -plētis, adj. (locus, *place* + PLE-, *fill*), *rich in lands, rich*, 22.

locus, -ī, M. (plu., loca, -ōrum, N.), *place, spot, ground, position*, 1, 7, 8, etc. ; *position, rank*, 24 ; locō, with gen., *in place of, as*, 9, 37.

longē, adv. (longus, *long*), *far*, 9, 16, 17, etc.; *long*, of time, 9 ; longē lātēque, *far and wide*, 14.

longīnquus, -a, -um, adj. (longus, *long*), *prolonged, continued*, 43.

longurius, -ī, M. (longus, *long*), *long pole*, 13.

longus, -a, -um, adj. [LEG-, *run*], *long*, 7, 21, 32, etc.; nāvis longa, *ship of war*, 9, 25, 66.

loquor, 3, locūtus, v. n. [LOQV-, *talk*], *speak, converse*, 5, 60.

Lūcīlius, -ī, M., *Caius Lucilius Hirrus*, one of Pompey's fol-lowers, 45.

Lūcius, -ī, M., *Lucius*, a Roman praenomen, 2, 3, 5, etc.

lūx, lūcis, F. [LVC-, *shine*], *light ;* prīmā lūce, *at daybreak*, 26, 60.

lūxuria, -ae, and lūxuriēs, —, acc. -em, F. (lūxus, *luxury*), *luxury, extravagance*, 58.

M

M., see **Mārcus**.

Macedonia, -ae, F., *Macedonia*, country between Thessaly and Thrace, 2, 42, 62.

maciēs, —, abl. maciē, F., *lean-ness, want of food*, 21.

magis, adv. comp. [MAG-, *big*], *more*, 57.

magistrātus, -ūs, M. (magister, *master*), *civil office, magistracy,* 22.

māgnitūdō, -inis, F. (māgnus, *large*), *extent, vastness,* 26, 66.

māgnus, -a, -um, māior, māximus, adj. [MAG-, *big*], *large, great,* 1, 5, 6, etc.; *loud,* 5; **māgnīs** (māiōribus) itineribus, *by forced marches,* 2, 7, 40; **māgnō opere,** *greatly,* 37, 46.

māior, comp. of māgnus.

mālō, mālle, māluī, — (magis, *more* + volō, *wish*), *wish rather, prefer,* 43.

malum, -ī, N., *anything bad, evil,* 33.

mancipium, -ī, N. (manus, *hand* + CAP-, *take*), *possession; a slave* (obtained by legal purchase), 1.

mandō, 1 (manus, *hand* + DA-, *put*), *intrust, bestow,* 22.

māne, adv., *in the morning,* 8.

maneō, 2, mānsī, mānsus [MAN-, *stay*], *remain, stay,* 29, 37.

manipulāris, -e, adj. (manipulus, *maniple*), *manipular;* M. as noun, *soldier of a maniple, comrade,* 53.

manus, -ūs, F. [MAN-, *measure*], *hand,* 11, 15, 32, etc.; *band, force,* 18.

Mārcellīnus, -ī, M., *Lentulus Marcellinus,* one of Caesar's officers, 25, 27, 28.

Mārcus, -ī, M., *Marcus,* a Roman praenomen, 5, 28, 34.

mare, maris, N., *sea,* 11, 16, 25, etc.

maritimus or **maritumus,** -a, -um, adj. (mare, *sea*), *relating to the sea;* **ōra maritima,** *sea-coast,* 2, 41.

mātūrēscō, 3, mātūruī, —, v. n. (mātūrus, *ripe*), *begin to be ripe, become ripe,* 15.

mātūritās, -ātis, F. (mātūrus, *ripe*), *ripeness, maturity,* 16.

mātūrus, -a, -um, adj. [MA-, *produce*], *ripe,* 44.

māximē or **māxumē,** adv., superl. of magis (māximus, *greatest*), *in the highest degree, especially,* 5, 10, 56; **quam māximē,** *as much as possible,* 11, 13.

māximus or **māxumus,** superl. of māgnus.

mediocris, -e, adj. (medius, *middle*), *middling, ordinary, fairly good,* 9, 13, 28, etc.

medius, -a, -um, adj. [MED-, *middle*], *middle, middle of, in the midst,* 5, 13, 25, etc.

melior, -us, comp. of bonus.

meminī, -isse, v. defective [MEN-, *mind*], *call to mind, remember,* 14.

mēnsis, -is, M. [MAN-, *measure*], *month,* 43, 63.

mentiō, -ōnis, F. [MEN-, *mind*], *mention,* 61.

mereor, 2, meritus, v. n. [SMAR-, MER-, *ascribe*], *deserve, merit,* 4, 19, 61.

merīdiānus, -a, -um, adj. (merī-diēs, *midday*), *of noon,* 39.

merīdiēs, —, -em, -ē, M. (for medi-dies, medius, *middle* + diēs, *day*), *midday, noon,* 57.

mētor, 1 (mēta, *goal*), *measure, mark off, pitch,* 4.

Mētropolis, -is, F., *Metropolis, town of Thessaly,* 43.

Mētropolītae, -ārum and -um, M., *Metropolitans, inhabitants of Metropolis,* 44.

metus, -ūs, M., *fear, dread,* 32.

mīles, -itis, M., *soldier,* 1, 2, 4, etc.; *foot-soldier,* 14, 24.

mīlitāris, -e, adj. (mīles, *soldier*), *of war, military,* 19, 34, 38, etc.; rēs mīlitāris, *art of war, war,* 24, 27.

mīlle, indecl. num. adj., *a thousand;* as noun, mīlle, sing., mīlia or mīllia, plu., N., *thousand,* 19, 46, 61; mīlle passuum, *a thousand paces, a mile,* 6, 11, 26, etc.

Minerva, -ae, F. [MEN-, *mind*], *Minerva, goddess of wisdom and of the arts and sciences,* 65.

minor, minus, comp. of parvus [MIN-, *small, less*].

minuō, 3, minuī, minūtus [MIN-, *less*], *make small, lessen,* 10, 15.

minus, adv., comp. of parum, *little,* superl., minimē (minor, *less*), *less,* 28; *not,* 25.

miser, -era, -erum, adj. [MIS-, *wretched*], *wretched,* 58.

mittō, 3, mīsī, missus [MIT-, *send, throw*], *make go, let go, send,* 3, 5, 7, etc.; *hurl, throw away,* 17, 55, 57.

modo, adv. (modus, *measure*), *merely,* 38; nōn modo . . . sed etiam, *not only . . . but also,* 21.

modus, -ī, M. [MAD-, *measure*], *measure, way, manner,* 5, 50, 52.

moenia, -ium, N. [MV-, *shut*], *walls, ramparts,* 43.

mōmentum, -ī, N. [MOV-, *move*], *motion; circumstance,* 31; *weight,* 33.

moneō, 2, -uī, -itus [MAN-, MEN-, *mind*], *warn, advise,* 23; *remind,* 51.

mōns, montis, M., *mountain, hill,* 47, 55, 57, etc.

montuōsus, -a, -um, adj. (mōns, *mountain*), *mountainous,* 9, 16.

mora, -ae, F. [SMAR-, MAR-, *think*], *delay,* 3, 32, 38, etc.

morior, 3, mortuus (fut. part. moritūrus), v. n. [MAR-, *die*], *die,* 27.

moror, 1 (mora, *delay*), *delay, put off,* 45; v. n., *delay, wait, loiter,* 9, 13, 66.

mors, mortis, F. [MAR-, *die*], *death,* 66.

mortuus, -a, -um, adj. (perf. part. of morior, *die*), *dead,* 53.

mōs, mōris, M., *way, manner, custom,* 52.

moveō, 2, mōvī, mōtus [MV-, MOV-, *move*], *set in motion, move,* 43, 47, 55; castra movēre, *break (up) camp,* 8, 47; locō movēre, *degrade,* 37; locō sē movēre, *stir from the spot, become disordered,* 54.

multitūdō, -inis, F. (multus, *much*), *great number, crowd,* 5, 10, 12, etc.

multō, adv. (multus, *much*), *by much, much,* 14, 28, 42, etc.

multum, plūs, plūrimum, adv. (multus, *much*), *much, greatly, earnestly,* 6, 15, 26, etc.; plūrimum posse, *have very great influence,* 31.

multus, -a, -um, plūs, plūrimus, adj., *much,* 17; plu., *many,* 5, 11, 22, etc.

mūniō, 4 (moenia, *walls*), *wall in, secure, protect, fortify,* 3, 12, 28, etc.; castra mūnīre, *build a camp,* 43.

mūnītiō, -ōnis, F. (mūniō, *fortify*), *act of fortifying,* 30; *fortification,* 10, 11, 12, etc.

mūnus, -eris, N. [MV-, *shut*], *service; gift,* 23.

mūrus, -ī, M. [MV-, *shut*], *city wall, wall,* 2, 44, 65.

mūsculus, -ī, M. (mūs, *mouse*), *shed, covered shed,* 43.

mūtō, 1 (for movito, from moveō, *move*), *change,* 29, 32, 46.

mūtuor, 1 (mūtuus, *borrowed*), *borrow,* 23.

Mytilēnae, -ārum, F., *Mytilenae,* capital of Lesbos, 62.

N

nam, conj., *for,* 5, 7, 14, etc.

namque, conj. (strengthened form of nam, *for*), *and with reason for, for in fact, for,* 46, 48, 61.

nancīscor, 3, nactus or nanctus [NAC-, *get*], *get, find,* 1, 6, 7, etc.; *overtake,* 58; *take advantage of,* 6, 20.

nāscor, 3, nātus, v. n. [GNA-, *beget*], *be born,* 24.

nātiō, -ōnis, F. [GNA-, *beget*], *origin; race of people, nation,* 10.

nātūra, -ae, F. [GNA-, *beget*], *nature,* 9, 10, 24.

nātūrāliter, adv. (nātūrālis, *natural*), *by nature, naturally,* 54.

nauta, -ae, M. (for navita, from nāvis, *ship*), *sailor,* 6.

nāvicula, -ae, F. (nāvis, *ship*), *little boat, skiff,* 64.

nāvigātiō, -ōnis, F. (nāvigō, *sail*), *sailing, voyage,* 21.

nāvis, -is, F. [NAV-, *wet, swim*], *ship,* 1, 6, 7, etc.; nāvēs solvere, *set sail,* 1, 6; nāvis āctuāria, *swift boat,* 25, 62; nāvis frūmentāria, *grain transport,* 58; nāvis longa, *man of war,* 9, 25, 66; nāvis onerāria, *transport,* 14. See notes on **7** 21 and **12** 4.

-ne, enclitic [NA-, *no*], used to ask a question, 5; in an indirect question, *whether,* 34, 45.

nē, conj. [NA-, *no*], *in order that not, that not, lest, that,* 2, 5, 7, etc.; as adv. with utī, *not,* 20; for nē quis, see quis.

nec, see neque.

necessāriō, adv. (necessārius, *unavoidable*), unavoidably, *according to necessity*, 16, 17, 41.

necessārius, -a, -um, adj. (necesse, *necessary*), necessary, 58, 62 ; M. as noun, *relative, friend*, 45.

necesse, adj., only nom. and acc. singular [NEC-, *bind*], *necessary, requisite, inevitable*, 29, 41, 49.

necessitās, -ātis, F. (necesse, *necessary*), necessity, *need*, 40.

necessitūdō, -inis, F. (necesse, *necessary*), necessity ; *close connection, friendship*, 66.

necō, 1 [NEC-, *kill*], kill (by poison, hunger, torture, etc.), 64.

negō, 1, *say "no," deny, refuse*, 2, 3.

negōtiātor, -ōris, M. (negōtior, *trade*), *merchant, banker*, 63.

negōtior, 1, v. n. (negōtium, *business*), *do business, trade*, 62.

negōtium, -ī, N. (nec, *and not* + ōtium, *leisure*), *business, affair*, 17, 24, 45, etc.

nēmō, nūllīus, nēminī, nēminem, nūllō, M. (nē, *not* + homō, *man*), *not a man, no one*, 19, 24, 37, etc. Cf. nūllus.

neque (nec), conj. (nē, *not* + que, *and*), *and not, nor*, 3, 4, 5, etc.; neque ... neque, *neither ... nor*, 3, 11, 27, etc.

nēve or neu, conj. (nē, *not* + -ve, *and*), *and not, and that not, nor*, with subjunctive, 36, 54, 60, etc.

nihil, indecl., N. (nē, *not* + hīlum, *a whit*), *nothing*, 21, 49, 58.

nihilum, -ī, N. (nē, *not* + hīlum, *a whit*), *nothing* ; nihilō sētius, *none the less*, 6.

nimius, -a, -um, adj. (nimis, *too much*), *excessive, too great*, 58.

nisi, conj. (nē, *not* + sī, *if*), *if not, unless, except*, 5, 11, 49.

nītor, 3, nīxus and nīsus, v. n. [CNI-, *bend*], *lean, depend on*, 10 ; *labor, strive*, 12.

noctū, adv. (old abl. of noctus for nox, *night*), *in the night, by night*, 7, 20, 25, etc.

nocturnus, -a, -um, adj. (nox, *night*), *nightly, by night*, 4, 58.

nōlō, nōlle, nōluī, — (nē or nōn, *not* + volō, *wish*), *be unwilling*, 41; nōlī (nōlīte), *do not*, 27, 49.

nōmen, -inis, N. [GNO-, *know*], *name*, 34, 62.

nōn, adv., *not*, 4, 6, 7, etc.

nōn-nūllus, -a, -um, adj., *some, several*, 5, 30, 37, etc.

Nōnae, -ārum, F. (nōnus, *ninth*), *the Nones*, ninth day before the Ides, — the seventh of March, May, July, October, fifth of other months, 1.

nōndum, adv. (nōn, *not* + dum, *yet*), *not yet*, 26, 43.

nōngentī, -ae, -a, num. adj. (novem, *nine* + centum, *hundred*), *nine hundred*, 34.

nōnus, -a, -um, IX., adj. (for novenus, from novem, *nine*), *ninth*, 12, 13, 25, etc.

nōs, see ego.

noster, nostra, nostrum, possessive adj. (nōs, *we*), *our*, 16, 17, 18, etc. ; M. plu. as noun, *our men*, 6, 11, 12, etc.

nōtitia, -ae, F. (nōtus, *known*), *acquaintance*, 64.

notō, 1 (nota, *mark*) [GNO-, *know*], *mark, censure*, 37.

nōtus, -a, -um, adj. (perf. part. of nōscō, *come to know*), *known, familiar*, 26 ; *famous*, 34.

novem, IX., indecl. num. adj., *nine*, 61.

novus, -a, -um, adj. [NV-, *now*], *new, recent*, 2, 14, 16, etc. ; novissimum agmen (novissimī), *the rear*, 38.

nox, noctis, F. [NOC-, *kill*], *night*, 4, 8, 16, etc.

nūllus, -a, -um, adj. (nē, *not* + ūllus, *any*), *not any, none, no,* 3, 5, 12, etc.; gen. and abl. singular are used for the corresponding forms of nēmō, 31 ; for nōn nūllus, see nōn-nūllus.

numerus, -ī, M. [NVM-, *allot*], *number*, 1, 11, 14, etc ; *number, rank, place*, 45.

nunc, adv., *now*, 27.

nūntiō, 1 (nūntius, *making known*), *announce, make known*, 27, 28, 32.

nūntius, -ī, M. (nūntius, *making known*), *bearer of tidings, messenger*, 7, 41, 43, etc.

Nymphaeum, -ī, N., *Nymphaeum, point and harbor of Illyria*, 6.

O

ob, prep. with acc., *over against, before ; on account of, because of*, 6, 12, 22, etc.

ob-dūcō, 3, -dūxī, -ductus, *draw before, extend*, 13.

obiciō, 3, -iēcī, -iectus (ob, *before* + iaciō, *throw*), *throw before, set up, put in the way*, 13, 20, 30, etc.; sē obicere, *oppose*, 29 ; *reproach with*, 58 ; obiectus, *opposed, opposing*, 35.

obiectātiō, -ōnis, F. (obiectō, *reproach*), *taunt, reproach*, 23.

obiectō, 1 (obiciō, *throw before*), *throw in the face of, taunt, reproach with*, 15.

obsecrō, 1 (ob, *before* + sacrō, *devote*), *entreat, implore*, 27.

obses, obsidis, M. and F. (ob, *before* + SID-, *sit*), *hostage*, 3.

obsideō, 2, -sēdī, -sessus (ob, *before* + sedeō, *sit*), *beset, besiege, blockade*, 10, 14, 41.

obsidiō, -ōnis, F. (ob, *before* + SID-, *sit*), *siege*, 14.

ob-struō, 3, -strūxī, -strūctus, *build against, stop up, barricade*, 16, 20.

ob-tegō, 3, -tēxī, -tēctus, *cover over, protect*, 5, 20.

obtineō, 2, -tinuī, -tentus (ob, *before* + teneō, *hold*), *hold fast, hold, possess*, 19, 22, 29, etc.

occāsiō, -ōnis, F. (occidō, *fall*), *opportunity, favorable moment,* 42, 47.

occāsus, -ūs, M. (occidō, *fall*),
falling, setting, 17, 43.

occultē, adv. (occultus, *secret*),
secretly, 30.

occultō, 1 (occulō, *cover*) [CAL-,
cover], *conceal, keep hidden,* 62.

occultus, -a, -um, adj. (perf. part.
of occulō, *cover*), *hidden, secret,*
7, 65.

occupō, 1 (ob, *before* + CAP-, *take*),
take possession of, seize, 2, 11,
12, etc.; occupātus, *busied. en-*
gaged, 59.

oc-currō (obc-), 3, -currī, -cursus,
v. n., *run up, run to meet, meet,*
42, 60; *head off,* 8, 59; *run*
against, 54.

octāvus, -a, -um, VIII., num. adj.
(octō, *eight*), *eighth,* 19, 51.

octingentī, -ae, -a, DCCC., num.
adj. (octō, *eight* + centum, *hun-*
dred), *eight-hundred,* 66.

octō, VIII., indecl. num. adj.,
eight, 39.

octōgintā, LXXX., indecl. num.
adj. (octō, *eight*), *eighty,* 51,
61.

oculus, -ī, M. [AC-, *sharp*], *eye,*
19.

odor, -ōris, M. [OD-, *smell*], *smell,*
odor, 16.

offendō, 3, -fendī, -fēnsus, v. n. (ob,
against + -fendo, *strike*) [FEND-,
strike], *hit; stumble, blunder,*
make a mistake, 35.

offēnsiō, -ōnis, F. (offendō, *hit*),
accident, misfortune, defeat, 14;
disfavor, discredit, 23.

of-ferō (obf-), -ferre, obtulī, oblā-

tus, *bring before, present, offer,*
expose, 36.

officium, -ī, N. (for opificium,
from opus, *work* + FAC-, *do*],
service, kindness, 23, 52; *duty,*
63; *business,* 63.

omnīnō, adv. (omnis, *all*), *in all,*
altogether, 13; *at all,* 19, 32.

omnis, -e, adj., *all, the whole,* 1,
2, 3, etc.

onerārius, -a, -um, adj. (onus,
burden), *burden bearing, for*
freight; with nāvis, *transport,*
14. See note on **12** 4.

opera, -ae, F. (opus, *work*), *service,*
means, aid, 19, 22; operam dare,
take pains, exert oneself, serve,
36, 53.

opīniō, -ōnis, F. (opīnor, *think*),
opinion, expectation, renown,
20, 30, 45, etc.

oportet, 2, oportuit, —, v. n. impersonal, *it is proper, it behooves,*
one ought, 45, 57.

oppidānus, -ī, M. (oppidum, *town*),
townsman, inhabitant, 2.

oppidum, -ī, N. (ob, *on* + PED-,
tread), *town, collection of dwell-*
ings, 2, 3, 8, etc.

oppleō, 2, -ēvī, -ētus (ob, intensive
+ -pleō, *fill*) [PLE-, *fill*], *fill*
completely, fill, 36.

oppōnō, 3, -posuī, -positus (ob,
before + pōnō, *put*), *set before,*
oppose, 7, 38, 51; *contrast,* 36.

opportūnitās, -ātis, F. (opportū-
nus, *fit*), *suitableness, advan-*
tage, 66.

oppositus, -a, -um, adj. (perf.

part. of **oppōnō**, *set before*), *opposite, on the border of*, 42.

opprimō, 3, -pressī, -pressus (ob, *against* + premō, *press*), *press hard, crush, overpower*, 30, 32, 34, etc.

oppūgnātiō, -ōnis, F. (oppūgnō, *assault*), *attack, siege*, 36, 43.

oppūgnō, 1 (ob, *against* + pūgnō, *fight*), *attack, lay siege to*, 41, 43, 57.

(ops), opis, F. [OP-, *work, help*], *help*; plu., **opēs**, *means, resources*, 63.

optimus, superl. of **bonus**.

opulentus, -a, -um, adj. (opēs, *wealth*), *rich*, 43.

opus, operis, N. [OP-, *work, help*], *work*, 12, 15, 16, etc.; *product of work, work, fortification*, 11, 16, 20, etc.; **māgnō opere**, *greatly*, 37, 46.

ōra, -ae, F. [OS-, *face*], *border, coast*, 2, 41.

ōrātiō, -ōnis, F. (ōrō, *speak*), *speech, discourse, talk*, 5, 52.

orbis, -is, M., *circle*; orbis terrārum, *world, universe*, 10, 35.

ōrdō, -inis, M., *row, rank, place*, 19, 37, 54, etc. ; **ōrdinem dūcere**, *be centurion*, 64 ; *turn*, 22.

Ōricum, -ī, N., *Oricum*, town of Epirus, 2, 3, 4, etc.

orior, 4, ortus, v. dep. n. [OR-, *rise*], *arise, start, proceed*, 56.

ōs, ōris, N. [OS-, *face*], *face*, 61.

ostendō, 3, -tendī, -tentus (obs, ob, *before* + tendō, *stretch*), *show, indicate, make known*, 41, 51, 65.

ostentātiō, -ōnis, F. (ostentō, *show*), *display*, 34.

ostentō, 1 (ostendō, *show*), *display, show, exhibit*, 24.

P

P., see **Pūblius**.

pābulātiō, -ōnis, F. (pābulor, *forage*), *collecting fodder, foraging*, 10, 21.

pābulor, 1 (pābulum, *fodder*), *forage, get provisions*, 11, 28, 39.

pābulum, -ī, N. [PA-, *feed*], *fodder*, 21.

pācō, 1 (pāx, *peace*), *make peaceful, subdue*, 36.

pactiō, -ōnis, F. (pacīscor, *agree*), *agreement, contract*, 5.

paene, adv., *nearly, almost*, 4, 20, 24, etc.

Palaestē, -ēs, F., *Palaeste*, town of Epirus, 1.

palam, adv., *openly*, 7, 22, 45, etc.

palma, -ae, F., *palm, hand*, 60 ; *palm-tree*, 65.

palūster, -tris, -tre, adj. (palūs, *swamp*), *marshy, swampy*, 16.

pandō, 3, pandī, passus [PAD-, *spread*], *spread out, open, extend*, 60.

pānis, -is, M. [PA-, *feed*], *bread, a loaf*, 15.

pār, paris, adj. [PAR-, *through*], *equal, like*, 41, 45.

parātus, -a, -um, adj. (perf. part. of **parō**, *prepare*), *ready, prepared*, 47, 48, 57.

pāreō, 2, pāruī, —, v. n. [PAR-, *part, breed*], *obey, submit to*, 44, 57.

pariō, 3, peperī, partus [PAR-, *breed*], *produce; acquire, win*, 32, 36, 45.

pariter, adv. (pār, *equal*), *equally, at the same time*, 18.

parō, 1, *make ready, prepare*, 25, 43.

pars, partis, F. [PAR-, *part*], *part, portion*, 8, 9, 20, etc.; *side, direction*, 12, 13, 14, etc.; *party, side*, 5; *degree*, 43, 46; **māgnā ex parte**, *in great measure*, 19; plu., **partēs**, *duty*, 17.

Parthī, -ōrum, M., *the Parthians*, a people of Scythia, 45.

Parthīnī, -ōrum, M., *the Parthini*, a people of Illyria, 2, 8, 9.

particeps, -cipis, M. (pars, *part* + CAP-, *take*), *sharer, accomplice*, 23, 45.

partim, adv. (old acc. of pars, *part*), *partly, in part*, 63.

partior, 4 (pars, *part*), *divide, share*, 45.

parvulus, -a, -um, adj. (parvus, *small*), *small*, 64; *trifling, slight*, 35.

parvus, -a, -um, minor, minimus, adj. [PAV-, *little*], *small, short, little*, 8, 10, 11, etc.

pāscō, 3, pāvī, pāstus [PA-, *feed*], *cause to eat, feed*, 11.

passus, -ūs, M. [PAT-, *go*], *step,*

pace, containing five Roman feet, 29, 30; **mīlle passuum**, *a thousand paces, a mile*, 6, 11, 26, etc.

pateō, 2, patuī, —, v. n. [PAT-, *open*], *be open, extend*, 26.

pater, patris, M. [PA-, *feed*], *father*, 63.

patiēns, -entis, adj. (pres. part. of patior, *suffer*), *long-suffering, enduring*, 58.

patientia, -ae, F. (patiēns, *enduring*), *endurance, patience*, 14.

patior, 3, passus, *bear, suffer, allow*, 12, 34, 54.

paucī, -ae, -a, adj. [PAV-, *little*], *few*, 21, 23, 29, etc.

paucitās, -ātis, F. (paucī, *few*), *fewness, small number*, 35.

paulātim, adv. (paulum, *a little*), *by degrees, gradually*, 55.

paulisper, adv. (paulum, *a little*), *a short time*, 30.

paulō, adv. (abl. of paulus, *little*), *by a little, a little*, 13, 26, 29, etc.

pavīmentum, -ī, N. (paviō, *beat*), *hard floor, pavement*, 65.

pāx, pācis, F. [PAC-, *fix*], *compact; treaty of peace, peace*, 5, 52.

pecūnia, -ae, F. (pecus, *cattle*), *wealth in cattle, money, funds*, 23, 62, 63, etc.

pecūniārius, -a, -um, adj. (pecūnia, *money*), *pecuniary, of money*, 22.

pecus, pecoris, N. [PAC-, *fix*], *cattle*, 14.

pellis, -is, F., *skin, hide; tent,* 4.

pellō, 3, pepulī, pulsus [PEL-, *drive*], *drive back, rout,* 30, 38, 42, etc.

Pēlūsium, -ī, N., *Pelusium,* city of Egypt, at the eastern mouth of the Nile, 63.

per, prep. with acc., *through, across, over,* 10, 12, 17, etc.; *through, by means of, by,* 7, 8, 9, etc.; *by, according to,* 1, 5; *of time, for, during,* 6, 27, 46, etc.

perangustus, -a, -um, adj. (per, *thoroughly* + angustus, *narrow*), *very narrow,* 16.

percipiō, 3, -cēpī, -ceptus (per, *thoroughly* + capiō, *take*), *get, obtain,* 46.

per-crēbrēscō (-bēscō), 3, -crēbruī (-buī), —, v. n., *become frequent; be spread abroad,* 10, 42.

perculsus, -a, -um, adj. (perf. part. of percellō, *overturn*), *struck with consternation, discouraged,* 14.

per-dūcō, 3, -dūxī, -ductus, *carry along, construct,* 10, 11, 29, etc.; *drag out, protract,* 57.

perexiguus, -a, -um (per, *thoroughly* + exiguus, *small*), *very small, very little,* 9, 49.

perficiō, 3, -fēcī, -fectus (per, *through* + faciō, *make*), *bring to an end, achieve, complete,* 1, 13, 24, etc.; *accomplish, bring about,* 23, 40.

perfuga, -ae, M. (per, *through* + FVG-, *flee*), *deserter,* 16, 26, 34.

per-fugiō, 3, -fūgī, —, v. n., *flee, desert,* 23, 24, 42, etc.

Pergamum, -ī, N., *Pergamum,* city in Mysia, 65.

perīculōsus, -a, -um, adj. (perīculum, *danger*), *dangerous,* 1.

perīculum, -ī, N. [PER-, *try*], *trial; danger, risk,* 1, 6, 10, etc.

perītus, -a, -um, adj. [PER-, *try*], *skilled, experienced,* 24, 36, 49, etc.

per-moveō, 2, -mōvī, -mōtus, *move deeply, influence, excite,* 14, 22, 37, etc.

permultus, -a, -um, adj. (per, *thoroughly* + multus, *much*), *very much, very many,* 10.

pernīcitās, -ātis, F. (pernīx, *swift*), *speed, swiftness,* 46.

perpetior, 3, -pessus (per, *through* + patior, *suffer*), *suffer, endure,* 14.

perpetuus, -a, -um, adj. (per, *through* + PAT-, *go*), *continuous, unbroken,* 11, 52.

per-sequor, 3, -secūtus, *pursue,* 62.

persevērantia, -ae, F. (persevērāns, *persevering*), *steadfastness, endurance,* 6.

perspiciō, 3, -spexī, -spectus (per, *through* + SPEC-, *see*), *see through, perceive clearly, ascertain,* 47.

per-suādeō, 2, -suāsī, -suāsus, v. n. [SVAD-, *sweet*], *persuade, prevail upon,* 48.

per-terreō, 2, -terruī, -territus, *frighten through and through, terrify,* 4, 37, 38, etc.

pertineō, 2, -tinuī, —, v. n. (per, *through* + teneō, *hold*), *stretch out, extend, reach,* 16, 25, 31, etc.; *pertain, relate,* 5.

perturbātiō, -ōnis, F. (perturbō, *disturb*), *disorder,* 36.

per-turbō, 1 (TVR-, *crowd*), *throw into disorder, confuse, disturb,* 2, 48.

per-veniō, 4, -vēnī, -ventus, v. n., *come up, arrive,* 1, 7, 8, etc.

pēs, pedis, M. [PED-, *tread*], *foot,* 20, 26, 32.

pestilentia, -ae, F. (pestilēns, *infected*), *plague, malaria,* 49.

petō, 3, petīvī or petiī, petītus [PET-, *fly*], *make for, go to, seek,* 2, 52, 55, etc.; *ask, ask for,* 43, 45.

Petra, -ae, F., *Petra,* hill near Dyrrachium, 9.

pīlum, -ī, N., *heavy javelin,* 13, 54, 55.

pīlus, -ī, M., *a maniple of the triarii,* 53.

Placentia, -ae, F., *Placentia,* city of Cisalpine Gaul, 34.

plānitia or **plānitiēs,** -ae, acc. -am or -em, F. (plānus, *even*), *flat surface, plain,* 60.

plēnus, -a, -um, adj. [PLE-, *fill*], *full,* 32, 43.

plērīque, -raeque, -raque, adj. [PLE-, *fill*], *the greater part, most,* 17, 32, 48, etc.

plērumque, adv. (acc. N. singular of plērīque, *most*), *for the most part, generally,* 9, 64.

Plotius, -ī, M., *Marcus Plotius,* one of Caesar's followers, 5.

plūrimum, superl. of multum.

plūrimus, -a, -um, superl. of multus.

plūs, comp. of multus; **plūrēs,** -a, *a great number, many,* 18, 29, 42, etc.

poena, -ae, F., *penalty, punishment,* 37.

polliceor, 2, -licitus, *hold forth, offer, promise,* 3, 48.

Pompēiānus, -a, -um, adj. (Pompēius, *Pompey*), *Pompeian, of Pompey,* 21, 29, 32, etc.; M. plu. as noun, *Pompey's men,* 9, 11, 13, etc.

Pompēius, -ī, M., *Cnaeus Pompey,* the Great, 2, 4, 5, etc.

pondus, -eris, N. [PAND-, *pull*], *weight, mass, quantity,* 58, 63.

pōnō, 3, posuī, positus, *put, place, station, pitch,* 4, 7, 8, etc.

populus, -ī, M. [PLE-, *fill*], *people, nation,* 2, 3.

porta, -ae, F. [PER-, *through*], *gate, door,* 2, 3, 20, etc.

portus, -ūs, M. [PER-, *through*], *harbor, port,* 1, 6, 36.

possum, posse, potuī, — (potis, *able* + sum, *be*), *be able, can,* 1, 5, 6, etc.; **plūrimum posse,** *have very great influence,* 31.

post, prep. with acc. [POS-, *behind*], *behind,* 11, 29; *after,* of time, 43; as adv., *later, afterwards,* 28, 29, 30, etc.

posteā, adv. (post ea, *after these things*), *afterwards, later,* 8, 12, 19, etc.

(posterus), -a, -um, adj. (post,

after), *coming after, following,
next,* 5, 8, 40, etc.

postquam, conj. (post, *later* +
quam, *than*), *after, as soon as,
when,* 8, 21, 23.

postrīdiē, adv. (posterī diē, *on the
following day*), *the next day, the
day after,* 1, 8.

Postumus, -ī, M., *Fulvius Postumus,* one of Caesar's followers,
25.

potestās, -ātis, F. (potis, *able*),
power, 36; *opportunity,* 8, 48.

potior, 4, v. dep. n. (potis, *able*), *get
possession of,* 36, 43, 59.

potius, adv. comp. (potis, *able*),
rather, 36.

praebeō, 2, -buī, -bitus (for prae-
hibeō, from prae, *before* + habeō,
hold), *hold forth, present, afford,
furnish,* 30.

praeceps, -cipitis, adj. (prae, *before* + caput, *head*), *headlong,*
13.

praecipiō, 3, -cēpī, -ceptus (prae,
before + capiō, *take*), *anticipate,*
49 ; *advise, direct, order,* 25, 55.

praecipitō, 1 (praeceps, *headlong*), *throw headlong,* 32.

praecipuē, adv. (praecipuus, *es-
pecial*), *chiefly, principally,*
31.

praeclūdō, 3, -clūsī, -clūsus (prae,
before + claudo, *shut*), *shut,
close before,* 3, 43.

prae-currō, 3, -cucurrī (rarely
-currī), —, v. n., *run before,
precede,* 43.

praeda, -ae, F. (prae, *before* +

HED-, *seize*), *booty, plunder,* 9,
22, 45, etc.

prae-dicō, 1 [DIC-, *shew*], *make
known, announce, relate,* 52, 64.

prae-dīcō, 3, -dīxī, -dictus, *say
before ; admonish, command,*
54.

praedō, -ōnis, M. (praedor, *rob*),
robber, pirate, 5, 64.

praefectus, -ī, M. (perf. part. of
praeficiō, *put over*), *director,
commander, prefect,* 23, 64.

prae-ferō, -ferre, -tulī, -lātus, *bear
before, hold forth, display,* 34.

praeficiō, 3, -fēcī, -fectus (prae, *before* + faciō, *make*), *put before,
put over, place in charge of,* 17.

praegredior, 3, -gressus, v. dep. n.
(prae, *before* + gradior, *walk*),
precede, 40.

prae-mittō, 3, -mīsī, -missus,
send ahead, 38, 40, 41.

praemium, -ī, N. (prae, *before* +
EM-, *take*), *reward,* 22, 45.

prae-mūniō, 4, *fortify in front,
secure,* 21.

prae-occupō, 1, *seize beforehand,
preoccupy,* 4, 35 ; *surprise,* 41.

prae-parō, 1, *make ready beforehand, prepare,* 46.

prae-pōnō, 3, -posuī, -positus,
place over, put in command,
51.

prae-saepiō, 4, -saepsī, -saeptus,
fence before, block up, 16.

praescrīptum, -ī, N. (praescrīptus,
perf. part. of praescrībō, *direct*), *previous direction, in-
structions,* 17.

praesēns, -entis, adj. (pres. part. of praesum, *be before*), *in sight, present*, 36.

praesentia, -ae, F. (praesēns, *present*), *presence ;* in praesentiā, *for the time being*, 47.

praesertim, adv., *especially*, 5.

praesidium, -ī, N. (praeses, *one who sits before*), *protection, help*, 6, 13, 17, etc. ; *guard, garrison*, 2, 8, 10, etc. ; *post, redoubt*, 12, 16, 18, etc.

prae-stō, 1, -stitī, -stitus, v. n. [STA-, *stand*], *stand before, surpass*, 11, 14 ; v. active, *fulfil*, 45, 63.

prae-sum, -esse, -fuī, —, v. n., *be before, be in command of, have charge of*, 2, 3, 6, etc.

praeter, prep. with acc. [PRAE-, *before*], *past, before*, of place ; *contrary to*, 24, 33 ; *except*, 16, 27, 44, etc.

praetereā, adv. (praeter ea, *besides these things*), *besides*, 18, 58, 61.

praeteritus, -a, -um, adj. (perf. part. of praetereō, *go past*), *past*, 23.

praeter-vehor, 3, -vectus [VEH-, *carry*], *be borne past, sail past*, 6, 7.

praetor, -ōris, M. (for praeitor, from prae-eō, *go before*), *praetor, a Roman officer next in rank to the consul*, 19 ; *military governor*, 43.

praetōrium, -ī, N. (praetor, *praetor*), *the general's tent*, 45, 56.

praetōrius, -a, -um, adj. (praetor,

praetor), *of a praetor ;* with comitia, *election of praetor*, 45; porta praetōria, *front gate* of a camp, 56 ; M. as noun, *ex-praetor*, 45.

premō, 3, pressī, pressus [PREM-, *press*], *press hard*, 13, 26, 62.

prēndō and **prehendō**, 3, -dī, -sus (prae, *before* + HEND-, *seize*), *snatch, seize*, 32.

prīdiē, II., adv. (prae, *before* + diēs, *day*), *on the day before*, 1.

prīmipīlus, -ī, M. (prīmus, *first* + pīlus, *centurion of the triarii*), *first centurion* of the legion, 19.

prīmō, adv. (abl. N. of prīmus, *first*), *at first*, 8, 30, 46.

prīmum, adv. (acc. N. of prīmus, *first*), *first, in the first place*, 10, 12, 23, etc. ; quam prīmum, *as soon as possible*, 7.

prīmus, -a, -um, adj. superl. [PRI-, *before*], *foremost, first*, 7, 17, 20, etc.; prīmum agmen, *the van*, 8 ; prīmā lūce, *at daybreak*, 26, 60 ; prīmā nocte, *in the early part of the night*, 38, 40.

prīnceps, -cipis, adj. (prīmus, *first* + CAP-, *take*), *foremost, first*, 4 ; as noun, *a company of the heavy-armed soldiers, the second line ;* with prior, *the first centurion of the second line*, 27.

prīncipātus, -ūs, M. (prīnceps, *first*), *first place, supremacy*, 22.

prior, -us, adj. comp., superl. prīmus [PRI-, *before*], *former, first ;* with prīnceps, *first centurion of the principes*, 27.

prīstinus, -a, -um, adj. (for priustinus) [PRI-, *before*], *former, early*, 42, 45.

prius, adv. (prior, *former*), *sooner*, 15; **prius . . . quam**, priusquam, *before*, 30, 43, 48.

prīvātus, -a, -um, adj. (perf. part. of **prīvō**, *deprive*), *private ;* M. as noun, *private citizen*, 63.

prīvō, 1 (**prīvus**, *one's own*) [PRI-, *before*], *deprive, rob*, 52.

prō (**prōd-**, before a vowel), prep. with abl. [PRO-, *before*], *in front of, before*, 20 ; *for, in behalf of*, 6 ; *for, as*, 13 ; *in consideration of*, 63.

prō-cēdō, 3, -cessī, —, v. n., *go forward, advance, step forth*, 4, 39.

procul, adv. (PRO-, *before* + CEL-, *drive*), *in the distance, far*, 8.

prō-currō, 3, -cucurrī and -currī, -cursus, v. n. [CER-, *run*], *run forward, charge*, 53, 55, 56.

prōd-eō, -īre, -iī, -itus, v. n., *go forward, advance*, 5, 48.

prōdō, 3, -didī, -ditus [DA-, *put*], *put forth ; betray*, 58.

prō-dūcō, 3, -dūxī, -ductus, *lead forth*, 20, 34, 44 ; *induce*, 64.

proelior, 1, v. dep. n. (proelium, *battle*), *join battle, fight*, 46.

proelium, -ī, N., *battle, combat*, 10, 12, 14, etc. ; proeliō dēcērtāre, *fight a decisive battle*, 11, 17, 20, etc.

profectiō, -ōnis, F. (proficīscor, *set out*), *departure*, 38, 39, 42, etc.

prō-ferō, -ferre, -tulī, -lātus, *bring forward*, 12, 13.

prōficiō, 3, -fēcī, -fectus (prō, *before* + faciō, *make*), *make headway ; effect, accomplish, be effective*, 21, 38.

proficīscor, 3, -fectus, v. dep. n. (prōficiō, *make headway*), *set out, march*, 1, 2, 3, etc.

profiteor, 2, -fessus (prō, *before* + fateor, *own*), *declare publicly, offer*, 5.

pro-fugiō, 3, -fūgī, —, v. n., *flee, escape*, 3, 65.

pro-fundō, 3, -fūdī, -fūsus [FVD-, *pour*], *pour out ;* sē profundere, *rush forth*, 55.

prōgredior, 3, -gressus, v. dep. n. (prō, *before* + gradior, *walk*), *go forward, advance*, 12, 17, 39, etc.

prohibeō, 2, -hibuī, -hibitus (prō, *before* + habeō, *hold*), *hold back, hinder, stop*, 10, 11, 12, etc.; *forbid*, 7.

prōiciō, 3, -iēcī, -iectus (prō, *before* + iaciō, *throw*), *throw down, give up, yield*, 4, 60.

proinde, adv. (prō, *forth* + inde, *thence*), *in the same manner, just ;* with ac(sī), *just as if*, 23, 35.

prō-nūntiō, 1, *declare publicly, proclaim, announce*, 5, 19, 49, etc.

prope, propius, proximē, adv., *near, nearly, almost*, 1, 12, 17, etc. ; prep. with acc., *near*, 4.

prō-pellō, 3, -pulī, -pulsus, *drive forward, throw down*, 13.

propero, 1, v. n. (properus, *quick*), *make haste, go quickly*, 4, 41.

propinquitās, -ātis, F. (propīnquus, *near*), *nearness*, 39.

propinquus, -a, -um, adj. (prope, *near*), *near, neighboring*, 12, 50; M. as noun, *relative, kinsman*, 63.

propius, comp. of prope.

prō-pōnō, 3, -posuī, -positus, *set before, display, offer*, 16; *publish*, 62; *plan*, 39.

prōpositum, -ī, N. (prōpositus, perf. part. of prōpōnō, *plan*), *plan, design*, 9, 28, 46.

proprius, -a, -um, adj., *own, peculiar; decisive*, 33.

propter, prep. with acc., *near; on account of, because of*, 22, 64, 66.

proptereā, adv. (propter ea, *on account of these things*), *for that cause;* with quod, *because*, 54.

prō-pūgnō, 1, v. n., *rush out to fight, repel an assault, resist*, 12, 30.

prō-ruō, 3, -ruī, -rutus [RV-, *fall*], *cast down, demolish*, 31, 32.

prō-sequor, 3, -secūtus, *follow, pursue*, 17, 53.

prō-tegō, 3, -tēxī, -tēctus, *cover over, protect, shelter*, 9, 20, 58.

prōtinus (-tenus), adv. (prō, *forth* + tenus, *all the way to*), *right on, directly*, 55, 56, 57, etc.

prout, conj. (prō, *in proportion* + ut, *as*), *according as, just as*, 24.

prō-video, 2, -vīdī, -vīsus, *foresee, anticipate*, 9, 39.

prōvincia, -ae, F., *office;* territory governed by a magistrate from Rome, *province*, 36, 42, 62, etc.

proximus or **proxumus**, -a, -um, adj., superl. of comp. propior, *nearer* (prope, *near*), *nearest, next*, 11, 18, 28, etc.

Ptolemaeus, -ī, M., *Ptolemy*, brother of Cleopatra, 63.

Ptolemāis, -idis, F., *Ptolemais*, city in Phoenicia, 65.

Pūblius, -ī, M., *Publius*, a Roman praenomen, 1, 5, 17, etc.

pudor, -ōris, M. [PV-, *cast down*], *shame, sense of shame, disgrace*, 23.

puer, puerī, M. [PV-, *beget*], *boy*, 63.

pūgna, -ae, F. [PVG-, *fix*], *battle, fight*, 47, 52, 54, etc.

pūgnō, 1 (pūgna, *battle*), *fight, contend*, 2, 18, 30, etc.

Pūlio, -ōnis, M., *Titus Pulio*, one of Pompey's officers, 30.

Puteolī, -ōrum, M., *Puteoli*, city of Campania, 34.

puteus, -ī, M. [PV-, *cleanse*], *well*, 16.

putō, 1 (putus, *clean*), *cleanse, clear up; think, consider*, 37.

Pȳrēnaeus, -a, -um, adj., *Pyrenean, of the Pyrenees*, 5.

Q

Q., see Quīntus.

quā, adv. (abl. F. of quī, *who*), *where*, 26.

quadrāgintā, XL., indecl. num. adj. (quattuor, *four*), *forty*, 50.

quadringentī, -ae, -a, CCCC., num. adj. (quattuor, *four* + centum, *hundred*), *four hundred*, 29, 38.

quaerō, 3, quaesīvī, quaesītus [QVAES-, *seek*], *seek, hunt for*, 31.

quaestor, -ōris, M. [QVAES-, *seek*], *quaestor*, a Roman magistrate who had the care of the public money and military stores, 25.

quaestus, -ūs, M. [QVAES-, *seek*], *gain, profit*, 23.

quam, relative and interrogative adv. (quī, *which*), *how?* 35; quam prīmum, *as soon as possible*, 7; quam lātissimus, māximus, etc., *as broad, large*, etc., *as possible*, 11, 12, 13, etc.; *than*, after comp., 6, 15, 35, etc.

quandō, adv. indef.; sī quandō, *if ever, whenever*, 45.

quantus, -a, -um, relative adj., *how great, as great, as much, as*, with tantus, 41; interrogative, *how great? how much?* 43, 52.

quantuscumque,-tacumque,-tum-cumque, indef. relative adj. (quantus, *how great*), *how great soever, however much*, 62.

quartus, -a, -um, IV., num. adj. (quattuor, *four*), *fourth*, 38, 40, 51, etc.

quattuor (quātuor), IV., indecl. num. adj., *four*, 11, 19, 41, etc.

-que, conj. (enclitic), *and*, 1, 2, 3, etc.

quem ad modum, adv., *in what manner? how?* 5.

queror, 3, questus, v. dep. n. [QVES-, *sigh*], *complain*, 22, 58.

quī, quae, quod, pron. interrogative, *which? what?* see quem ad modum; relative, *who, which, that*, 1, 2, 3, etc.; often at the beginning of a sentence to be translated by a demonstrative or personal pron., *he, she*, etc., 3, 5, 6, etc.; indef. with nē, *any, any one*, 11, 60.

quia, conj., *because*, 7.

quīcumque, quaecumque, quod-cumque, indef. relative pron. (quī, *who*), *whoever, whatever*, 1, 4, 14, etc.

quīdam, quaedam, quoddam and quiddam, indef. pron., *a certain, some*, 9, 12, 16, etc.

quidem, adv., *indeed, in fact, moreover*, 20, 29, 37, etc.

quiētē, adv. (quiētus, *quiet*), *quietly*, 13.

quiētus, -a, -um, adj. (perf. part. of quiēscō, *keep quiet*), *quiet, calm*, 1; *inactive, out of the action, resting*, 56.

quīn, conj., after negative expressions, *but that, that, so that not, without*, 12, 14, 56; *who . . . not, but*, 19, 44.

quīndecim, XV., indecl. num. adj. (quīnque, *five* + decem, *ten*), *fifteen,* 11, 20, 26, etc.

quīngentī, -ae, -a, D., num. adj. (quīnque, *five* + centum, *hundred*), *five hundred,* 30.

quīnque, V., indecl. num. adj., *five,* 13, 20, 32.

Quīntus, -ī, M., *Quintus,* a Roman praenomen, 9, 66.

quis, quae, quid, pron. interrogative, *who? what?* 25, 36, 41, etc.; indef. (F. qua), after nē, seu, sī, *any, any one,* 24, 40, 56.

quisnam, quaenam, quidnam, interrogative pron. (quis, *who?*), *who, pray? what, pray?* 46.

quisquam, —, quicquam (quidquam), indef. pron. (quis, *any one*), *any one at all, anything,* 32, 49.

quisque, quaeque, quidque (adj. quodque), indef. pron. (quis, *any one*), *whoever it be, each, every one,* 10, 24, 25, etc.

quisquis,—, quicquid (quidquid), indef. relative pron. (quis, *any one*), *whoever, every one who, whatever,* 45.

quīvīs, quaevīs, quidvīs (adj. quodvīs), indef. pron. (quī, *who* + vīs, *you will*), *whom you please, whoever it be, any one, anything,* 36.

quō, adv. (quī, *who*), used with comparatives, *that, in order that,* 1, 7, 10, etc.; interrogative, *whither? to what place?* 7; relative, *whither, where,* 2, 5, 6, etc.

quod, conj. (acc. N. sing. of quī, *who*), *in that, because,* 1, 4, 8, etc.

quō minus, conj., *that not, from,* after words of hindering, 33.

quoniam, conj., *since, seeing that, because,* 1, 28, 46, etc.

quoque, adv., *also,* 29, 41, 46, etc.

quotiēns, interrogative adv., *how often?* 35.

R

rādīx, -īcis, F. [RAD-, *sprout*], *root,* 15, 21; *base,* 47.

ratiō, -ōnis, F. [RA-, *count*], *reckoning;* ratiōnem habēre, *take account,* 19; *explanation,* 48; *measure, method, plan, resource, kind, way, conduct,* 11, 14, 16, etc.; *regard,* 38, 45; *reason,* 37.

Raucillus, -ī, M., *Raucillus,* a chief of the Allobroges, 22, 42.

re- (red-), inseparable prefix, *again, back, against.*

recēns, -entis, adj., *fresh, young, vigorous,* 56, 58.

receptus, -ūs, M. (recipiō, *withdraw*), *falling back, retreat,* 12, 13, 17, etc.

recipiō, 3, -cēpī, -ceptus (re-, *back* + capiō, *take*), *take back, withdraw, receive, admit, involve,* 2, 3, 17, etc.; sē recipere, *betake* *oneself, withdraw*, 12, 13, 16, etc.; *promise*, 45.

reconditus, -a, -um, adj. (perf. part. of recondō, *hide*), *hidden, concealed, retired*, 65.

recordor, I (re-, *back* + cor, *heart*), *call to mind, remember*, 14, 35, 36.

re-creō, I, *make anew, revive, restore*, 37.

recuperō, I (re-, *back* + CVP-, *wish*), *get back, recover*, 53.

recūsātiō, -ōnis, F.(recūsō, *refuse*), *refusal, protest*, 60.

recūsō, I (re-, *against* + causa, *cause*), *decline, refuse, object*, 6, 12, 14, etc.

red-dō, 3, -didī, -ditus, *give back; render, make*, 42.

red-eō, -īre, -iī, -itus, v. n., *go back, return; turn, take*, 55.

redigō, 3, -ēgī, -āctus (red-, *back* + agō, *drive*), *drive back; reduce, subdue*, 36.

reditus, -ūs, M. (redeō, *return*), *return*, 45.

re-dūcō, 3, -dūxī, -ductus, *lead back*, 8, 13.

re-ferō, -ferre, rettulī, relātus, *bring back, carry back*, 5, 19, 61.

reficiō, 3, -fēcī, -fectus (re-, *again* + faciō, *make*), *make anew; recruit*, 49.

re-fugiō, 3, -fūgī, —, v. n., *run away, escape, flee*, 57, 61.

regiō, -ōnis, F. [REG-, *stretch*], *direction*, 8; *country, region*, 4, 9, 11, etc.

rēgius, -a, -um, adj. (rēx, *king*), *of the king, royal*, 64.

rēgnum, -ī, N. [REG-, *guide*], *kingdom*, 63, 64, 66.

regredior, 3, -gressus, v. dep. n. (re-, *back* + gradior, *walk*), *go back, return*, 12.

rēiciō, 3, -iēcī, -iectus (re-, *back* + iaciō, *throw*), *drive back, repulse*, 13.

religiō, -ōnis, F. (re-, *back* + LIG-, *tie*), *moral obligation, scruple, superstition*, 35.

re-linquō, 3, -līquī, -līctus [LIQV-, *leave*], *leave behind, leave, abandon*, I, 4, 11, etc.

reliquus, -a, -um, adj. (re-, *back* + LIQV-, *leave*), *remaining, the other, the rest of*, 3, 4, 14, etc.; *future*, 23; *following*, 40.

re-maneō, 2, -mānsī, —, v. n., *stay behind, remain*, 49, 59.

remedium, -ī, N. (re-, *against* + MAD-, *measure*), *cure, help*, 16.

remissus, -a, -um, adj. (perf. part. of remittō, *relax*), *relaxed, gentle, mild*, 6.

re-mittō, 3, -mīsī, -missus, *send back*, 59; v. n., *relax, abate, go down*, 6.

re-novō, I [NV-, *now*], *renew*, 55, 62.

re-nūntiō, I, *bring back word, report*, 19, 30.

re-pellō, 3, reppulī, repulsus, *drive back, repulse, defeat*, 17.

repentīnus, -a, -um, adj. (repēns, *sudden*), *sudden*, 35, 43.

reperiō, 4, repperī, repertus (re-,

again + PAR-, *part, breed*), *find, find out*, 16, 19, 47, etc.

re-petō, 3, -petīvī, -petītus, *seek again, fetch*, 39 ; *reckon*, 65.

re-prehendō, 3, -hendī, -hēnsus, *seize ; censure, rebuke*, 17.

reprimō, 3, -pressī, -pressus (re-, *back* + premō, *press*), *hold back, check*, 54, 55.

re-pūgnō, 1, v. n., *fight back, resist, oppose*, 30.

re-quiēscō, 3, -quiēvī, -quiētus, v. n. [CI-, *lie*], *rest, take rest*, 60.

rēs, reī, F. [RA-, *count*], *thing, often best translated by some more definite word suggested by the context*, 1, 2, 4, etc. ; rēs frūmentāria, *grain supply*, 8, 9, 10, etc. ; rēs mīlitāris, *art of war, war*, 24, 27 ; rēs pecūniāria, *money*, 22.

re-servō, 1, *save, reserve*, 23.

re-sistō, 3, -stitī, —, v. n. [STA-, *stand*], *stand back, make a stand, resist*, 26, 32, 55.

respiciō, 3, -spexī, -spectus (re-, *back* + SPEC-, *see*), *look back upon, gaze at*, 53.

re-spondeō, 2, -spondī, -spōnsus, *answer, reply*, 5, 64.

rēs pūblica (rēspūblica), reī pūblicae, F., *the common weal, the state, republic*, 19, 52.

restituō, 3, -stituī, -stitūtus (re-, *back* + statuō, *set up*), *restore*, 23, 27.

retineō, 2, -tinuī, -tentus (re-, *back* + teneō, *hold*), *hold back, detain, keep*, 38, 54, 62.

re-vertor, 3, -vertī, -versus, v. n. (dep. in pres. system only), *turn back, return*, 49, 60.

re-vocō, 1, *call back, call off*, 17.

rēx, rēgis, M. [REG-, *guide*], *king*, 63, 64.

Rhodius, -a, -um, adj. (Rhodus, *Rhodes*), *of Rhodes, Rhodian*, 6, 66.

rīpa, -ae, F. [RIC-, RIP-, *crack*], *river bank, bank*, 5, 34, 38, etc.

rīvus, -ī, M. [RI-, *flow*], *small stream, brook*, 16, 50.

rōbur, -oris, N., *hard wood, oak ; strength, kernel*, 49.

Rōmānus, -a, -um, adj. (Rōma, *Rome*), *Roman*, 2, 3, 34, etc.

rūmor, -ōris, M. [RV-, *sound*], *sound ; report, rumor*, 44.

rūrsum or rūrsus, adv. (for revorsus, *turned back*), *again*, 21, 55, 62.

S

sacerdōs, -ōtis, M. and F. (sacer, *sacred* + DA-, *give*), *priest, priestess*, 65.

sacerdōtium, -ī, N. (sacerdōs, *priest*), *office of priest, priesthood*, 45.

Sacrativir, -virī, M., *Marcus Sacrativir*, a Roman knight on Caesar's side, 34.

saepe, adv., *often*, 35, 48, 58.

sagitta, -ae, F., *arrow*, 11, 16, 19.

sagittārius, -ī, M. (sagitta, *arrow*), *bowman, archer,* 11, 12, 25, etc.

saltus, -ūs, M., *a narrow pass, glen,* 5.

salūs, -ūtis, F. (cf. salvus, *sound*), *soundness, health ; safety,* 5, 6, 32, etc.

salūtō, 1 (salūs, *health*), *wish health, hail, greet,* 34.

sanguis, -guinis, M., *blood,* 52.

sarcina, -ae, F. [SARC-, *bring together*], *package, pack, baggage,* 39.

sarciō, 4, sarsī, sartus [SARC-, *bring together*], *mend, make up for, repair,* 30, 36, 37.

satis, adj., only nom. and acc. sing. [SA-, *sate*], *enough, sufficient,* 54; **satis habēre,** *be satisfied,* 13; as adv., *sufficiently, quite,* 32, 37, 46.

satis-faciō, 3, -fēcī, -factus, v. n., *give satisfaction, make amends,* 23.

satus, see serō.

saucius, -a, -um, adj., *wounded,* 38, 41.

saxum, -ī, N. [SAC-, *split*], *a rough stone, rock, cliff,* 1.

Scaeva, -ae, M., *Scaeva,* one of Caesar's centurions, 19.

scālae, -ārum, F. [SCAND-, *climb*], *ladder, scaling-ladder,* 26, 43.

scapha, -ae, F., *light boat, skiff,* 25.

sciō, 4 [SAC-, *distinguish*], *know, understand,* 48.

Scīpiō, -ōnis, M., *Quintus Caecilius Metellus Pius Scipio,* Pompey's father-in-law, 41,42,43,etc.

scrībō, 3, scrīpsī, scrīptus [SCARP-, *cut, scratch*], *write,* 34, 41.

scūtum, -ī, N. [SCV-, *cover*], *shield, infantry shield,* 19.

sēclūdō, 3, -clūsī, -clūsus (sē-, *apart* + claudō, *shut*), *shut off, cut off,* 32, 59.

sēcrētō, adv. (sēcrētus, *separated*), *privately, secretly,* 23.

secundum, prep. with acc. (secundus, *following*), *following, beside, abreast of, opposite,* 7, 28.

secundus, -a, -um (sequor, *follow*), *following; favorable, auspicious,* 9, 14, 36, etc.

sed, conj., *but on the contrary, but,* 2, 4, 6, etc.

semper, adv., *always,* 47, 58.

senātor, -ōris, M. [SEN-, *old*], *senator,* 34, 65.

senātōrius, -a, -um, adj. (senātor, *senator*), *senatorial, of senator,* 59.

senātus, -ūs, M. [SEN-, *old*], *body of elders, senate,* 22, 50.

sentiō, 4, sēnsī, sēnsus [SENT-, *feel*], *perceive, notice,* 30.

septem, VII., indecl. num. adj., *seven,* 1, 46, 50.

septendecim, XVII., indecl. num. adj., *seventeen,* 26.

Septimius, -ī, M., *Lucius Septimius,* military tribune, one of Pompey's murderers, 64.

sequor, 3, secūtus [SEC-, *follow*], *follow, attend,* 3, 4, 31, etc.; *seek,* 16; *pursue,* 6; *adopt,* 11.

serō, 3, sēvī, satus [SA-, *sow*], *sow, plant,* 11, 21.

sērō, adv. (**sērus**, *late*), *late*, 38.

Servīlius, -ī, M., *Publius Servilius Vatia*, consul with Caesar 48 B.C., 1.

servō, 1 [SER-, *save*], *save, preserve, observe*, 38, 46, 51.

servus, -ī, M., *slave*, 43, 45.

sēscentī, -ae, -a, **DC.**, num. adj. (**sex**, *six* + **centum**, *hundred*), *six hundred*, 26.

sētius (**sēcius**), adv., comp. [SEC-, *follow*], *less*; **nihilō sētius**, *none the less*, 6.

seu, see **sīve**.

sex, **VI.**, indecl. num. adj., *six*, 19, 55, 59.

sexāgintā, **LX.**, indecl. num. adj., *sixty*, 25, 34.

sī, conj., *if*, 6, 12, 17, etc.; *to see if*, 7, 20, 38, etc.

sīc, adv., *in such a way, so*, 20, 43, 51, etc.

Sicilia, -ae, F., *Sicily*, 9.

sīcut, adv. (**sīc**, *so* + **ut**, *as*), *just as, as*, 47.

sīgnifer, -ferī, M. (**sīgnum**, *standard* + FER-, *bear*), *standard-bearer*, 37.

sīgnificātiō, -ōnis, F. (**sīgnificō**, *make signs*), *pointing out; signal, indication*, 28.

sīgnum, -ī, N., *signal*, 13, 39, 47, etc.; *military standard, banner*, 4, 19, 30, etc.

silentium, -ī, N. (**silēns**, *still*), *silence*; **silentiō**, *silently*, 5, 16, 20, etc.

silva, -ae, F., *wood, forest*, 29.

similis, -e, adj. [SIM-, *like*], *like, resembling*, 4, 39.

similiter, adv. (**similis**, *like*), *in a like manner*, 40.

similitūdō, -inis, F. (**similis**, *like*), *likeness, resemblance*, 15.

simul, adv. [SIM-, *like*], *at the same time*, 4, 10, 26, etc.; with **atque**, *as soon as*, 6.

simulācrum, -ī, N. (**simulō**, *make like*), generally used of the gods, *likeness, statue*, 65.

sine, prep. with abl., *without*, 12, 13, 34, etc.

singulāris, -e, adj.(**singulī**, *single*), *singular, unparalleled*, 14, 22, 43, etc.

singulī, -ae, -a, distributive num. adj., *one by one, single, separate*, 51.

sinister, -tra, -trum, adj., *left*, 29, 30, 32, etc.

situs, -ūs, M. [SI-, *sow*], *situation, location*, 29.

sīve or **seu**, conj., *or if*; **seu** . . . **seu**, **sīve** . . . **sīve**, *whether* . . . *or*, 24, 36, 42, etc.

societās, -ātis, F. (**socius**, *associated*), *association, company of publicans* or *revenue collectors*, 63.

socius, -ī, M. (**socius**, *associated*), *companion, ally*, 41, 43.

sōl, **sōlis**, M., *sun*, 17, 43.

soleō, 2, **solitus**, v. n. semideponent, *be accustomed*, 34.

sollicitō (**sōli-**), 1 (**sollicitus**, *disturbed*), *stir up, incite*, 64.

sōlum, adv. (**sōlus**, *alone*), *only*;

nōn sōlum . . . sed etiam, *not only . . . but also*, 22, 36, 55.

solvō, 3, solvī, solūtus (sē, *apart +* luō, *loose*), *loose;* nāvēs solvere, *set sail*, 1, 6.

sonō, 1, sonuī, sonitus, v. n. (sonus, *sound*), *sound, make a noise*, 65.

sonus, -ī, M. [SON-, *sound*], *noise, sound*, 65.

soror, -ōris, F., *sister*, 63.

spatium, -ī, N. [SPA-, *stretch*], *space, extent*, 11, 13, 14, etc.; *distance*, 24, 63; *time*, 26, 37, 38, etc.

speciēs, —, -em, -ē, F. [SPEC-, *see*], *look, appearance*, 30.

spectō, 1 (-speciō, *look at*), *look at, look*, 65; *have in view, plan*, 10, 38, 47.

speculātor, -ōris, M. (speculor, *spy out*), *spy, scout*, 29, 30.

spērō, 1 (spēs, *hope*), *hope, hope for*, 1, 23, 58; *hope, trust*, 6, 8, 30, etc.

spēs, speī, F., *hope*, 15, 16, 17, etc.

spīritus, -ūs, M., *breath; haughtiness, pride*, 35.

spoliō, 1 (spolium, *skin*), *strip; rob, pillage*, 9.

sponte, abl. of (spōns, spontis), F., *free will;* suā sponte, *of their own accord*, 2, 55.

Staberius, -ī, M., *Lucius Staberius*, in command of Pompey's force at Apollonia, 3.

statim, adv. [STA-, *stand*], *on the spot, at once, immediately*, 7, 38, 43.

statiō, -ōnis, F. [STA-, *stand*], *standing place, post, guard*, 56; *anchorage, roadstead*, 1.

statīvus, -a, -um, adj. [STA-, *stand*], *stationary, permanent*, 7.

statua, -ae, F. (status, *fixed*), generally used of men, *statue*, 65.

statuō, 3, statuī, statūtus (status, *station*), *set up, fix, settle upon, decide*, 11, 48.

stīpendium, -ī, N., *money, wages*, 19, 22, 41.

stringō, 3, strinxī, strictus, *draw tight; pluck off*, 21 ; *draw, unsheathe*, 55.

struō, 3, strūxī, strūctus [STRV-, *spread*], *heap up; arrange, make, build*, 58.

studeō, 2, studuī, —, v. n., *be eager for, desire*, 42.

studium, -ī, N. (cf. studeō, *be eager*), *eagerness, zeal*, 24, 37, 41, etc.

stultus, -a, -um, adj. [STOL-, *hard*], *foolish*, 22.

sub, prep. with abl., *under, in*, 4. Assumes the forms su-, suc-, sum-, sup-, and sus- in composition.

sub-eō, -īre, -iī (-īvī), -itus, *go under; undergo, meet, suffer*, 4, 40.

subiciō, 3, -iēcī, -iectus (sub, *under +* iaciō, *throw*), *throw under; bring close, post, expose*, 20, 46, 47.

subiectus, -a, -um, adj. (perf. part. of **subiciō**, *bring close*), *near, bordering on,* 42.

subitō, adv. (subitus, *sudden*), *suddenly, unexpectedly,* 5, 13, 26, etc.

subitus, -a, -um, adj. (perf. part. of subeō, *go under*), *sudden,* 40.

sub-levō, 1, *support; lighten, mitigate,* 36, 43.

sublica, -ae, F. (sub, *under* + LIC-, *crook*), *stake, pile,* 16.

sub-luō, 3, —, -lūtus [LV-, *wash*], *wash at the foot, wash the base of,* 59.

submissus (summ-), -a, -um, adj. (perf. part. of submittō, *let down*), *humble, modest, moderate,* 5.

sub-mittō (summ-), 3, -mīsī, -missus, *let down; send as aid, send as reinforcement,* 25, 27.

sub-moveō (summ-), 2, -mōvī, -mōtus, *send away, drive back,* 55.

subnūbilus, -a, -um, adj. (sub, *a little* + nūbilus, *cloudy*), *somewhat cloudy,* 20.

sub-sequor, 3, -secūtus, *follow after,* 62.

subsidium, -ī, N. (sub, *under* + SED-, *sit*), *line of reserve; aid, assistance, help,* 27, 32, 33, etc.

sub-sum, -esse, -fuī, —, v. n., *be under, be near,* 59.

suc-, see **sub**.

suc-cēdō, 3, -cessī, -cessus, v. n., *go below; take the place of, relieve,* 56; *approach, draw near,* 16.

suc-currō (subc-), 3, -currī, -cursus, v. n. [CER-, *run*], *run to help, aid, be of assistance,* 18, 33, 43.

suī, sibi, sē or sēsē, singular and plu., reflexive pron., *of himself, herself, itself, themselves,* 1, 2, 3, etc.

Sulla, -ae, M., *Publius Sulla,* nephew of the dictator Sulla; one of Caesar's lieutenants, 17, 51, 61.

sum, esse, fuī, —, v. n. [ES-, *be,* FV-, *breed*], *be,* 1, 2, 4, etc.; fut. inf., fore, 8, 39, 48, etc.

summa, -ae, F. (summus, *greatest*), *main thing;* summa rērum, *general welfare,* 17; summa reī, *crisis, issue,* 56; *amount, total,* 51, 65.

summus, -a, -um, adj. (superl. of superus, *upper*), *highest, greatest, utmost,* 14, 16, 17, etc.

sūmō, 3, sūmpsī, sūmptus (sub, *under* + emō, *take*), *take, receive, assume, arrogate,* 3, 17, 63.

sūmptus, -ūs, M. (sūmō, *take*), *expense,* 62.

sup-, see **sub**.

superior, -us, adj. (comp. of superus, *upper*), *upper, higher,* 17, 28, 30, etc.; *preceding, former,* 9, 14, 26, etc.

superō, 1 (superus, *upper*), *surmount; overcome, defeat,* 6, 14, 36.

super-sum, -esse, -fuī, —, v. n., *be over, be left, remain,* 17, 49, 53

suppliciter, adv. (supplex, *suppliant*), *suppliantly, humbly,* 5.

sup-portō, 1, -āvī, — [POR-, *part*], *convey, bring up,* 10, 11, 14, etc.

suprā, adv. (superus, *upper*), *above; previously,* 26, 31, 43, etc.

suscipiō (succ-), 3, -cēpī, -ceptus (sub, *under* + capiō, *take*), *take up; undertake, undergo,* 40.

suspīciō or **suspītiō,** -ōnis, F. (sub, *under* + SPEC-, *see*), *mistrust, suspicion,* 35, 62.

suspicor, 1 (sub, *under* + SPEC-, *see*], *suspect, conjecture,* 8.

sustentō, 1 (sustineō, *hold up*),

hold up, sustain, support, make endurable, 15.

sustineō, 2, -tinuī, -tentus (sub, *under* + teneō, *hold*), *hold up, support; withstand,* 18, 43, 46, etc.

suus, -a, -um, possessive adj. (cf. suī, *of himself*), *his own, her own, their own, its,* 1, 2, 5, etc.; *favorable,* 11, 46; suī, *his (their) men (friends),* 7, 12, 13, etc.

Syria, -ae, F., *Syria,* country in Asia, 63, 65.

Syriacus, -a, -um, adj. (Syria, *Syria*), *Syrian, serving in Syria,* 50.

T

T., see **Titus.**

tabernāculum, -ī, N. (taberna, *hut*), *tent,* 47, 58.

taeter (tēter), taetra, taetrum, adj., *offensive, foul,* 16.

tam, adv., *so much, so,* 49.

tamen, adv., *for all that, notwithstanding, however, yet,* 5, 6, 11, etc.

tametsī, conj. (for tamen etsī), *notwithstanding that, although,* 30, 51.

tantundem (tantumdem), adv. (tantus, *so great*), *just as far, to the same extent,* 26.

tantus, -a, -um, adj., *so great, so much,* 4, 9, 14, etc.; **tantum,** as adv., *so much,* 48, 58; *only,* 5.

tardē, adv. (tardus, *slow*), *slowly,* 45.

tardō, 1 (tardus, *slow*), *make slow, hinder, check,* 33.

tegimentum (tegu-), -ī, N. [TEG-, *cover*], *covering,* 11, 25, 26.

tegō, 3, tēxī, tēctus [TEG-, *cover*], *cover, defend, protect,* 6, 13, 63.

tēlum, -ī, N., *missile, dart, javelin,* 5, 11, 17, etc.

temerē, adv. [TEM-, *stun*], *rashly,* 12, 49.

tempestās, -ātis, F. (tempus, *time*), *season, weather; storm,* 6, 62.

templum, -ī, N. [TEM-, *cut*], *place marked off, temple,* 65.

temptō (tentō) 1 (tendō, *stretch*), *try, attempt, assail,* 18, 23, 46.

tempus, -oris, N. [TEM-, *cut*], *section of time, time,* 2, 5, 6, etc.; *circumstances,* 17; *season,* 16.

tendō, 3, tetendī, tentus or tēnsus [TEN-, *stretch*], *stretch, spread, pitch,* 45.

teneō, 2, tenuī, — [TEN-, *stretch*], *hold, keep, occupy,* 1, 9, 10, etc.; **sē tenēre,** *keep oneself, stay,* 7, 8, 56.

tener, tenera, tenerum, adj. [TEN-, *stretch*], *tender, soft,* 21.

tergum, -ī, N., *back ;* **terga vertere,** *retreat,* 13, 26, 56, etc.; *back, rear,* 11, 48, 55, etc.

terra, -ae, F. [TERS-, *parch*], *dry land, land,* 1, 7 ; *earth, ground,* 16, 60; **orbis terrārum,** *the world,* 10, 35.

terreō, 2, terruī, territus [TERS-, *scare*], *frighten, terrify,* 26, 36, 46, etc.

terror, -ōris, M. [TERS-, *scare*], *fear,* 4, 27, 28, etc.

tertius, -a, -um, III. (ter, *three times*), num. adj., *third,* 8, 20, 50, etc.; **tertiō,** *in the third place,* 10.

testimōnium, -ī, N. (testis, *witness*), *evidence,* 19.

testis, -is, M. and F., *witness,* 52, 65.

Thessalia, -ae, F., *Thessaly,* country in the north of Greece, 42, 43, 44, etc.

Thrācēs, -um, M., *the Thracians,* 57.

Tiburtius, -ī, M., *Lucius Tiburtius,* one of Caesar's followers, 5.

Tillius, -ī, M., *Quintus Tillius,* one of Caesar's followers, 9.

timeō, 2, timuī, — [TIM-, *stun*], v. n., *fear, be afraid,* 4, 13, 32, etc.; v. active, *fear, be afraid of,* 1, 6, 26, etc.

timor, -ōris, M. [TIM-, *stun*], *fear,* 11, 12, 27, etc.

Titus, -ī, M., *Titus,* a Roman praenomen, 5, 30, 65.

tolerō, 1 [TOL-, *lift*], *support, maintain, keep alive,* 16, 21.

tollō, 3, sustulī, sublātus [TOL-, *lift*], *lift ; raise, set up,* 54 ; *take away, carry off,* 63, 65.

tormentum, -ī, N. [TARC-, *twist*], *engine for hurling missiles,* 11, 12 ; *missile,* 17, 20, 26.

Torquātus, -ī, M., *Lucius Manlius Torquatus,* commander of Pompey's forces at Oricum, 2.

tot, indecl. adj., *so many,* 14, 49.

tōtus, -a, -um, adj., *whole, entire,* 3, 8, 11, etc.

trādō (old **trāns-dō**), **3,** -didī, -ditus, *give over, give up,* 34, 50.

trā-dūcō (**trāns-dūcō**), **3,** -dūxī, -ductus, *lead across, lead over,* 39, 50, 63 ; *transfer, promote,* 19.

trāiciō (**trānsiciō**), **3,** -iēcī, -iectus (**trāns,** *across* + iaciō, *throw*), *throw across, shoot across,* 5.

Trallēs, -ium, F., *Tralles,* town in Lydia, 65.

trāns, prep. with acc., *across, on the other side of,* 4.

trānscendō, 3, -scendī, — (**trāns,** *across* + scandō, *climb*), *climb over, cross,* 13, 31.

trāns-eō, -īre, -iī, -itus, *go across,*

cross, 7; v. n., *go across, cross over,* 7, 41; *go over, desert,* 23, 24.

trāns-ferō, -ferre, -tulī, -lātus (trālātus), *bear across ; change, move,* 29.

Trānspadānus, -a, -um, adj. (trans, *across* + Padus, the *Po*), *across the river Po,* in the north-eastern part of Cisalpine Gaul, 49.

trāns-portō, 1 [POR-, *part*], *take across, convey,* 36.

trānsversus (trāv-), -a, -um, adj. (trāns, *across* + versus, *turned*), *turned across, crosswise, at right angles,* 26.

trecentī, -ae, -a, CCC. (trēs, *three* + centum, *hundred*), num. adj., *three hundred,* 29.

trēs, tria, III., num. adj., *three,* 6, 18, 19, etc.

Triārius, -ī, M., *Caius Triarius,* a commander under Pompey, 54.

tribūnus, -ī, M. (tribus, *tribe*), *head of a tribe ; tribune ;* with mīlitum expressed or understood, *military tribune,* colonel; each legion had six; 4, 34, 35, etc.

tribuō, 3, tribuī, tribūtus (tribus, *tribe*), *assign, allot, give,* 1, 4, 22, etc.; *ascribe,* 36.

trichila, -ae, F., *pavilion, bower,* 58.

trīgintā, XXX., indecl. num. adj., *thirty,* 19, 30, 34, etc.

tuba, -ae, F., *trumpet,* a straight trumpet, 13, 52.

tueor, 2, tuitus or tūtus, *look at ; look to, guard,* 56.

Tullus, -ī, M., *Volcatius Tullus,* one of Caesar's officers, 18.

tum, adv., *then, at that time,* 4, 5, 14, etc.; *then again,* 16; **cum . . . tum,** *not only . . . but also, both . . . and,* 9, 14, 16, etc.

tumultus, -ūs, M. [TVM-, *swell*], *uproar, commotion, sudden attack,* 27, 32.

tumulus, -ī, M. [TVM-, *swell*], *rising ground, mound, hill,* 13, 17.

tunc, adv. (tum, *then*), *then, just at that time,* 47, 64.

tunica, -ae, F., *tunic, shirt,* 11.

turmātim, adv. (turma, *troop*), *by troops, in squadrons,* 55.

turris, -is, F., *tower,* 20.

Tuticānus, -ī, M., *Tuticanus Gallus,* one of Caesar's men, 34.

tūtō, adv. (tūtus, *safe*), *safely,* 5.

tūtus, -a, -um, adj. (perf. part. of tueor, *guard*), *safe, secure,* 4, 6, 66.

tympanum, -ī, N., *drum,* 65.

U

ubī, adv., *where,* 30, 65; *when,* 7, 8, 9, etc.

ūllus, -a, -um, adj. (diminutive of ūnus, *one*), *any,* 5, 6, 14, etc.

ultrā, prep. with acc., *beyond,* 6, 29.

ultrō, adv., *beyond ; moreover, besides,* 32 ; *voluntarily, of their own accord,* 36, 43.

umquam or **unquam,** adv., *ever,* 52.

ūnā, adv. (**ūnus,** *one*), *at the same time, together,* 42.

ūndecim, XI., indecl. num. adj. (**ūnus,** *one* + **decem,** *ten*), *eleven,* 1.

undique, adv., *from all sides, everywhere,* 5, 10, 14, etc.

ūniversus, -a, -um, adj. (**ūnus,** *one* + **versus,** *turned*), *all together,* 16, 22, 54, etc.; *all,* 24.

ūnus, -a, -um, I., num. adj., *one,* 1, 5, 7, etc.; *one and the same,* 12; *only,* 26.

urbs, urbis, F., *city,* 41, 43; especially *Rome,* 1.

ūsus, -ūs, M. (cf. **ūtor,** *use*), *use,* *value,* 12, 58, 63; *practice, experience,* 16, 46, 48, etc.; *advantage,* 43; *need,* 46.

ut or **utī,** conj., *when, as,* 1, 5, 8, etc.; *so that, that,* 4, 11, 17, etc.; *in order that, to,* 4, 7, 8, etc.

uterque, utraque, utrumque, pron., *each, either, both,* 7, 12, 26, etc.; plu., *both parties,* 5, 16.

utī, see **ut.**

ūtor, 3, ūsus, *use, profit by, enjoy,* 6, 9, 16, etc.; *adopt, follow,* 9, 44; *find, have,* 10, 22, 65.

utrimque, adv. (**uterque,** *each*), *on each side, on both sides,* 5.

utrum, adv. (**uter,** *which of two?*), *whether,* in direct or indirect questions, 62.

V

vacō, 1, v. n., *be without, be unoccupied, be free,* 15, 39.

vadum, -ī, N. [VA-, *go*], *shallow place, ford,* 7.

valeō, 2, valuī, fut. part. **valitūrus,** v. n. [VAL-, *strong*], *be strong, have power,* 10, 48.

Valerius, -ī, M., *Valerius Flaccus,* one of Pompey's officers, 19.

valētūdō, -inis, F.(**valeō,** *be strong*), *health,* 16, 25, 49.

vallēs or **vallis, -is, F.,** *valley,* 16.

vāllum, -ī, N. (**vāllus,** *stake*), *line of palisades, rampart, wall,* 20, 26, 29, etc.

vāllus, -ī, M., *stake, palisade; rampart,* 26.

valvae, -ārum, F. [VOL-, *roll*], *folding doors,* 65.

varius, -a, -um, adj., *different, varying,* 24.

Varrō, -ōnis, M., *Aulus Varro,* one of Pompey's followers, 5.

Vatīnius, -ī, M., *Publius Vatinius,* one of Caesar's lieutenants, 5, 52.

-ve, conj. (enclitic)[VOL-, *will*], *or if you will, or,* 17, 20.

vectūra, -ae, F. [VEH-, *carry*], *transportation,* 9.

vehementer, adv. (**vehemēns,** *eager*), *eagerly, extremely, very much,* 51.

vel, conj. (old imperative of

volō, *will, choose*), *or if you will, or ;* vel . . . vel, *either . . . or,* 35.

veniō, 4, vēnī, ventus, v. n. [VEN-, *come*] *come,* 1, 2, 5, etc.

ventus, -ī, M., *wind, breeze,* 6, 9, 14.

verbum, -ī, N., *word,* 34.

vereor, 2, veritus [VER-, *guard*], *stand in awe ; fear, be afraid, be afraid of,* 13, 17, 32.

vērō, adv. (vērus, *true*), *in truth, however, but indeed,* 3, 6, 13, etc.; *moreover,* 14.

versor (vorsor), 1, v. dep. n. (vertō, *turn*), *be occupied, be busied, be,* 58.

versus, prep. with acc. (with towns and small islands), *towards,* 59.

vertō, 3, vertī, versus [VERT-, *turn*], *turn ;* sē vertere, *turn, wheel about, change,* 6, 17 ; terga vertere, *retreat,* 13, 26, 56 ; v. n., *turn, change,* 36.

vester (voster), -tra, -trum, possessive adj. (vōs, *you*), *your,* 53.

vestis, -is, F. [VAS-, *cover*], *clothing, garment,* 19.

veterānus, -a, -um, adj. (vetus, *old*), *old, veteran,* 34.

vetō, 1, vetuī, vetitus, *not permit, forbid,* 38.

vetus, -eris, adj. [VET-, *old*], *old, former,* 29, 39.

vēxillum, -ī, N. (vēlum, *sail*), *flag, signal flag,* 51.

vicem, acc. of (vicis), vicis, F., *change ;* see invicem.

victor, -ōris, M. (vincō, *conquer*), *conqueror, victor,* 14, 49.

victōria, -ae, F.(victor, *conqueror*), *victory,* 1, 33, 35, etc.; Victōria, *the goddess of victory, Victory,* 65.

videō, 2, vīdī, vīsus [VID-, *see*], *see,* 5, 6, 7, etc.; pass., videor, *be seen, seem, appear,* 4, 5, 10, etc.; *think,* 46.

vigilia, -ae, F. (vigil, *awake*), *watching ; watch* (a fourth part) *of the night,* 20, 38, 40; plu., *men on watch, guards, sentinels,* 4, 15.

vīgintī, XX., indecl. num. adj., *twenty,* 11, 19, 24, etc.

vīmen, -inis, N. [VI-, *twine*], *pliant twig, osier,* 25.

vīmineus, -a, -um, adj. (vīmen, *osier*), *of osiers, made of osiers,* 26.

vincō, 3, vīcī, victus, v. n. [VIC-, *conquer*], *conquer, be superior,* 11, 30, 35.

vīnea, -ae, F. (vīnum, *vine*), *vine-yard ; arbor-like shed, mantlet,* 20.

violō, 1 (cf. vīs, *violence*), *treat with violence, injure,* 60.

vir, virī, M., *man* (opposed to mulier, *woman*), 24, 53, 61.

virtūs, -ūtis, F. (vir, *man*), *manliness ; valor,* 22, 23, 30, etc.

vīs, —, —, vim, vī ; F., *force, violence,* 6, 12, 55; *onset,* 54 ; plu., vīrēs, -ium, *strength,* 27, 55, 61. (The gen. and dat.

singular are rare and not classical.)

vitium, -ī, N., *fault, imperfection, weakness*, 26, 35.

vītō, 1, *shun, escape*, 5, 11, 42.

vīvō, 3, vīxī, vīctus, v. n. [VIV-, *live*], *be alive, live*, 15.

vīvus, -a, -um, adj. [VIV-, *live*], *alive, living*, 27, 53.

vix, adv., *with difficulty, barely*, 42.

vocō, 1 [VOC-, *call*], *call, summon*, 62.

Volcātius, -ī, M., *Volcatius Tullus*, one of Caesar's officers, 18.

volgō or **vulgō**, adv. (volgus, *crowd*), *among the multitude, commonly, generally*, 15, 24.

volnerō (vuln-), 1 (volnus, *wound*), *wound, injure*, 5, 11, 12, etc.

volnus (vuln-), -eris, N., *wound*, 27, 34, 36, etc.

volō, velle, voluī, — [VOL-, *will*], *wish*, 1, 5, 11, etc.

voluntārius, -a, -um, adj. (voluntās, *will*), *willing, voluntary*; with mīlitēs, *volunteers*, 53.

voluntās, -ātis, F. (vōlens, *wishing*), *wish, will*, 3, 46.

voluptās, -ātis, F. (volup, *agreeably*, which contains VOL-, *will*), *pleasure, delight*, 58.

Volusēnus, -ī, M., *Caius Volusenus*, a commander of Caesar's cavalry, 23.

vōx, vōcis, F. [VOC-, *call*], *voice, tone*, 5; *word*, 15.

Gerund used as noun